高等学校英语专业系列教材

学术翻译实训教程

（轻工篇）

A Practical Coursebook on Academic Translation

(Light Industry)

杨 昊　朱义华　孙志祥　主　编
卞正东　彭方针　谢　瑜　副主编

中国轻工业出版社

图书在版编目（CIP）数据

学术翻译实训教程. 轻工篇/杨昊，朱义华，孙志祥主编；卞正东，彭方针，谢瑜副主编. —北京：中国轻工业出版社，2023.11

ISBN 978-7-5184-4560-8

Ⅰ.①学… Ⅱ.①杨…②朱…③孙…④卞…⑤彭…⑥谢… Ⅲ.①学术—英语—翻译—高等学校—教材 Ⅳ.①H315.9

中国国家版本馆CIP数据核字（2023）第180116号

责任编辑：杜宇芳　　责任终审：李建华
文字编辑：王　若　　责任校对：晋　洁　　封面设计：锋尚设计
策划编辑：杜宇芳　　版式设计：霸　州　　责任监印：张　可

出版发行：中国轻工业出版社（北京鲁谷东街5号，邮编：100040）

印　　刷：三河市万龙印装有限公司

经　　销：各地新华书店

版　　次：2023年11月第1版第1次印刷

开　　本：787×1092　1/16　印张：9.75

字　　数：225千字

书　　号：ISBN 978-7-5184-4560-8　定价：45.00元

邮购电话：010-85119873

发行电话：010-85119832　010-85119912

网　　址：http://www.chlip.com.cn

Email：club@chlip.com.cn

如发现图书残缺请与我社邮购联系调换

211532J1X101ZBW

前　言

为响应国家《新文科建设宣言》有关"打破学科专业壁垒，推动……文科与理工农医交叉融合"的倡议，依据《外国语言文学类教学质量国家标准》（2018）中"各高等学校外语类专业应根据本标准制定适应社会发展需要、体现本校定位和办学特色的培养方案"之要求，我校英语专业人才培养方案提出要依托我校轻工特色，基于国家一流学科食品科学与工程、轻工技术与工程，以及纺织学、设计学等传统优势学科，积极建设具有校本特色与文化内涵的课程及其配套教材，努力培养具备扎实语言功底、广博轻工学科素养和坚定文化自信的语言服务人才，从而体现我校办学特色，实现文理交融。

我们编写的《学术翻译实训教程（轻工篇）》属于学术翻译实训教程系列教材的第一册，旨在全面贯彻新时期高校英语专业人才培养的新要求，在保留词法、句法和语篇翻译技巧解析等传统翻译教材内容的基础上，深度融入了思政和跨学科元素。全书分为5个单元，分别对应"设计学和中华艺术设计（Design Studies and Chinese Art）、食品科学和中华食品文化（Food Science and Chinese Food Culture）、纺织科学和中华服饰文化（Textile Science and Fashion Culture）、生物技术和中华酒文化（Biotechnology and Wine-Liquor Culture）、日用化学和东方美学（Cosmetics and Oriental Aesthetics）"这5个学科方向与文化领域。每个单元精选中英两篇长文［Passage A（英译中）和Passage B（中译英）］作为翻译技巧解析样本、一篇翻译技巧专题短文（Translation Skills）、一个翻译实训工作坊（Translation Workshop），附录含长文完整版翻译、翻译实训工作坊参考答案等，此外文后附有学术词汇表及参考书目。长文选材来源包括学术论文、学术专著、纪录片、科普文献等，我们希望用丰富有趣的文章、鲜活专业的语言和具有一定挑战性的实操训练培养大学生的跨学科意识与翻译能力，树立他们的专业自豪感与文化自信心，加强他们做好对外翻译与传播能力建设的使命感与责任感。

本教材不仅适用于高校英语类专业，尤其是轻工类高校的科技翻译类或学术翻译类课程教学，还可以作为翻译专业本科生、硕士生的专业翻译教材，以及大学英语拓展课程教学的参考教材。原汁原味的语料适合老师在课堂上和学生一起深入挖掘相关专业知识和历史文化，引导学生展开深度学习；高度凝练的翻译技巧主题讲解与丰富多彩的翻译实训配套资源适合学生课后自主学习，并在课堂内外与老师或同伴开展讨论和分析；有的放矢的配套练习适合学生在实训与实践中磨炼技能，在与老师或同伴的互动中提升翻译能力。

本书由江南大学外国语学院的杨昊、朱义华、孙志祥、卞正东、彭方针和谢瑜共同编写。全书由孙志祥负责策划，杨昊和朱义华负责统稿。参与审稿的有江南大学化学与材料工程学院的陈凤凤老师和美国得克萨斯大学达拉斯西南医学中心的彭若诗博士和中南大学外国语学院研究生费洋同学，对于他们所做的大量工作和提出的宝贵意见，编者在此深表感谢。在此，编者还要特别感谢江南大学国家一流专业——英语专业建设经费与江南大学教学改革专项经费的支持，感谢中国轻工业出版社对本教材编写给予的专业建议与大力支持。另外，本教材也是上海外国语大学教材研究院外语教材研究项目"《轻工学术翻译》教材建设研究"（项目编号：2020JS0071-YBK）和 2023 年度江苏省社科应用研究精品工程外语类课题"数字赋能下的外语教育生态研究"（项目编号：23SWC-02），以及江南大学研究生教材建设（项目编号：YJSJC23_009）的阶段性成果。对于本教材所选用案例、期刊、图书等的作者、资源原创者、出版社和项目资助方，编者在此一并致谢。

  本书是编者结合新文科学科交叉的建设背景与我校外语专业校本特色建设需要而编写的第一部学术翻译教材，是"翻译+思政"与"跨学科"双融合的一次大胆尝试，加之编者水平有限，疏漏之处在所难免，敬请专家和读者批评指正。

编者于江南大学
2023 年 8 月 14 日

目　录

Unit 1　Design Studies and Chinese Art ·· 1
　　Passage A　Incremental and Radical Innovation：Design Research vs.
　　　　　　　　Technology and Meaning Change ··· 1
　　Passage B　中国艺术设计的对称性 ·· 6
　　Translation Skills（Ⅰ）　Modulation：Active & Passive（语态转换） ············· 11
　　Translation Workshop ··· 14

Unit 2　Food Science and Chinese Food Culture ··· 17
　　Passage A　Food Culture in China：Diet and Health ·································· 17
　　Passage B　濠江味传 ··· 23
　　Translation Skills（Ⅱ）　Conversion Between the Abstract and
　　　　　　　　　　　　　　Concrete（虚实转换） ··· 28
　　Translation Workshop ··· 32

Unit 3　Textile Science and Fashion Culture ·· 35
　　Passage A　Cotton Growing, Properties and Uses ······································ 35
　　Passage B　时装与世界同步 ·· 40
　　Translation Skills（Ⅲ）　Change of Parts of Speech（词类转换） ················ 46
　　Translation Workshop ··· 49

Unit 4　Biotechnology and Wine-Liquor Culture ··· 51
　　Passage A　The Influence of Raw Materials on Sensory Character ················ 51
　　Passage B　国酒茅台 ··· 56
　　Translation Skills（Ⅳ）　Translation of Long Sentences（长句翻译） ············ 62
　　Translation Workshop ··· 65

Unit 5　Cosmetics and Oriental Aesthetics ·· 67
　　Passage A　Cosmetics：the Chemistry of Charm ····································· 67
　　Passage B　中国彩妆三千年 ·· 75
　　Translation Skills（Ⅴ）　Logical Relationship and Cohesion（逻辑与衔接） ···· 82
　　Translation Workshop ··· 87

Appendix ·· 91
　　Unit 1　Design Studies and Chinese Art ··· 91
　　Unit 2　Food Science and Chinese Food Culture ······································· 98
　　Unit 3　Textile Science and Fashion Culture ··· 106
　　Unit 4　Biotechnology and Wine-Liquor Culture ····································· 113
　　Unit 5　Cosmetics and Oriental Aesthetics ··· 120

Glossary ··· 133
   Unit 1 Design Studies and Chinese Art ······································ 133
   Unit 2 Food Science and Chinese Food Culture ···························· 135
   Unit 3 Textile Science and Fashion Culture ································ 138
   Unit 4 Biotechnology and Wine-Liquor Culture ·························· 140
   Unit 5 Cosmetics and Oriental Aesthetics ·································· 142
References ··· 146

Unit 1　Design Studies and Chinese Art

Passage A　Incremental and Radical Innovation: Design Research vs. Technology and Meaning Change

Warming-up

Work on the following terms and put them into Chinese:

graphic design　　　　　　　　　　　　　_____
incremental innovation　　　　　　　　　_____
radical innovation　　　　　　　　　　　_____
human-centered design　　　　　　　　　_____
affordances　　　　　　　　　　　　　　_____
technological determinism　　　　　　　_____
research into design　　　　　　　　　　_____
research through design　　　　　　　　_____
research for design　　　　　　　　　　　_____
ethnographic research　　　　　　　　　_____

　　The purpose of this paper is to provide a theoretical framework for distinguishing between the procedures of incremental and radical innovation and to address the fundamental activities of innovation. For this purpose, we provide three different ways of treating innovation: as the attempt to find the maxima in a hilly terrain whose topology is unknown and novel, as movements in the product space defined by the two axes of "technology change" and "meaning change", and as a design research quadrangle based on Stokes's two dimensions of "advances in understanding" and "consideration of practicality".

　　We start the paper by suggesting that radical product innovation is driven by either advances in technology or a deliberate change in the meaning of the product, rather than being driven by the human-centered design philosophy widely used in product design. In our examination of both existing products and the literature on innovation, we were unable to find any contrary evidence. Incremental innovation was performed as a result of a deliberate design research strategy or through a series of mutual adaptations by the product developers and the use community to bring the two into better alignment. In contrast, radical product introductions could always be traced to the introduction of a new technology that provided new affordances to the designers or to a new meaning assigned to the product and its uses, allowing for radical changes using existing technologies. Of course, some radical change incorporated both new technologies and meaning changes.

Note that our observations and interpretations are neutral with respect to the ongoing debate between the relative importance of technical or social determinism. One could interpret technology-driven radical innovation as an example of technological determinism; meaning-driven radical innovation as an example of social determinism; and human-centered incremental innovation as either technological or social determinism, depending on the theoretical biases involved. We subscribe to the belief that factors related to both technical and social determinism are always in play.

I. Types of Design Research

The concept of research takes two different forms in design. One perspective sees research as exploration and experimentation that leads to the advancement of knowledge, the development of theories, and the application of theories. This perspective has been the subject of reflections, definitions, and effective classifications by design theorists. For example, Frayling's well-known, three-part classification of design research includes research into design, research through design, and research for design. See also Cross, Friedman, and Feast and Melles. These definitions all share an epistemological base aimed at advancing knowledge.

The other perspective sees research as any activity of collection and analysis of data for a better understanding of a topic (which therefore includes the research a student at an elementary school conducts to write a paper on what tigers eat). This perspective is used by practitioners to indicate their research activities. For example, they might use ethnographic research or observations on people's activities as a means to understand user needs, product research as a means to identify possible solutions, market research as shedding light on the kinds of products people would buy and their price sensitivity, and usability research as indicating the interaction between people and products. In this second perspective, design research focuses on how to improve both products and sales. In this paper we concentrate on this second perspective of design research.

II. Two Types of Innovation: Incremental and Radical

We can identify many kinds of innovation, and classification might vary according to the object of innovation. For example, categories include innovation of socio-cultural systems, of ecosystems, of business models, of products, of services, of processes, of organizations, of institutional arrangements, etc. Classifications might also vary according to the drivers of innovation (technologies, markets, design, users, etc.), or to the intensity of innovation. In this paper we focus on two categories of innovation for products or services:

- Incremental innovation: improvements within a given frame of solutions (i.e., "doing better what we already do");
- Radical innovation: a change of frame (i.e., "doing what we did not do before").

The major difference between the two is whether the innovation is perceived as a continuous modification of previously accepted practices or whether it is new, unique, and discontinu-

ous. Dahlin and Behrens suggest three criteria for identifying an innovation as radical:
- Criterion 1: The invention must be novel: It needs to be dissimilar from prior inventions.
- Criterion 2: The invention must be unique: It needs to be dissimilar from current inventions.
- Criterion 3: The invention must be adopted: It needs to influence the content of future inventions.

The first two criteria define radicalness; the third, success. Although Criteria 1 and 2 can occur at any time, Criterion 3 only occurs if the sociological, market, and cultural forces are in appropriate alignment. Here is where social determinism plays a major role. The correct idea at the wrong time will fail. Examples are Apple's introduction of the QuickTake digital camera and the Newton personal digital assistant in the early 1990s: Despite fulfilling Criteria 1 and 2, both failed in the marketplace, thus failing at Criterion 3. Although the reasons for the failures are complex, Norman, who was an Apple executive at the time, believes these failures would make wonderful case histories for believers in social determinism.

Much of the writing on innovation in the design and management communities focuses on radical innovation. It is often characterized as disruptive or competence destroying, or as breakthrough, with all these labels sharing the same concept that radical innovation implies a discontinuity with the past. Radical innovation has been the center of attention of innovation studies for a number of decades now. It is taught in design and business schools, and has recently been advocated by people discussing innovation and "design thinking". Although radical innovation is what everyone wants given its significant potential to differentiate, successful radical innovation is surprisingly rare, and most attempts at it fail. In fact, Larry Keeley, President of the Doblin Group, estimates the failure rate to be 96%. Successful radical innovation occurs infrequently in any particular area—perhaps once every five to ten years.

Most radical innovations take considerable time to become accepted (i.e., to fulfill Dahlin and Behrens's third criterion). Moreover, a completely novel innovation is impossible: all ideas have predecessors and are always based on previous work—sometimes through refinement, sometimes through a novel combination of several pre-existing ideas. As Apple's introduction of gesture-based cell phones illustrates, ideas do not spring out of thin air. Apple's development of multi-touch interfaces and their associated gestures to control hand-held and desktop systems is one of today's radical innovations. However, Apple did not invent either multi-touch interfaces or gestural control. Multi-touch systems had been in computer and design laboratories for more than 20 years, and gestures also had a long history. Moreover, several other companies had products on the market using multi-touch before Apple did. Although Apple's ideas were not radical to the scientific community, they did come as a major shift in the world of products and how people interact with them and give meaning to them.

Edison's development of the electric light bulb was similar, resulting in a radical, major revolution in home and business. However, Edison did not invent the light bulb; he improved the existing bulbs by extending bulb life and, equally important, he recognized the importance of providing all the necessary infrastructures. Edison brought into view all the system requirements of generation plants, distribution systems, and even indoor wiring and sockets to hold the bulbs. Thus, his efforts revolutionized the product space and the living and working patterns of households and businesses.

Incremental product innovation refers to the small changes in a product that help to improve its performance, lower its costs, and enhance its desirability, or simply result in a new model release. Most successful products undergo continual incremental innovation, intended to lower their costs and enhance effectiveness. This dominant form of innovation is not as exciting as radical innovation, but it is just as important. Radical innovations seldom live up to their potential when they are first introduced. At first, they are often difficult to use, expensive, and limited in capability. Incremental innovations, meanwhile, are necessary to transform the radical idea into a form that is acceptable to the consumers who follow the early adopters. The bottom line is that both forms of innovation are necessary. Radical innovation brings new domains and new paradigms, and it creates a potential for major changes. Incremental innovation is how the value of that potential is captured. Without radical innovation, incremental innovation reaches a limit. Without incremental innovation, the potential enabled by radical change is not captured.

（摘自 *Design Issues* 2014 年第 4 期）

Notes

1.

［原文］ For this purpose, we provide three different ways of treating innovation: as the attempt to find the maxima in a hilly terrain whose topology is unknown and novel, as movements in the product space defined by the two axes of "technology change" and "meaning change", and as a design research quadrangle based on Stokes's two dimensions of "advances in understanding" and "consideration of practicality".

［译文］ 为此，我们提供了关于创新的 3 种不同探讨方式：试图在种类未知的新型丘陵地带找到顶点，在由"技术变革"和"意义变革"两轴所界定的产品空间移动，以及基于斯托克斯（Stokes）的"认识上的进步"和"实用性考虑"两个维度的设计研究四边形。

［解析］ 本句是一个长句，理解的关键在于通过动词搭配把握句子的结构，即"treating innovation: as ... as ... and as ..."。

2.

［原文］ We start the paper by suggesting that radical product innovation is driven by either advances in technology or a deliberate change in the meaning of the product, rather than being driven by the human-centered design philosophy widely used in product design.

［译文］ 本文开门见山地指出，激进性的产品创新是由技术进步或审慎的产品意义变革驱动的，而不是由广泛应用于产品设计的以人为中心的设计理念驱动的。

［解析］ 这里所使用的翻译技巧主要是原文被动语态的翻译，即将"... is driven by ... rather than being driven by ..."翻译成"是由……驱动的，而不是由……驱动的"，用

"是……的"表示被动意义。

3.

［原文］ For example, Frayling's well-known, three-part classification of design research includes research into design, research through design, and research for design.

［译文］ 例如，大家熟知的弗雷灵（Frayling）的设计研究分类由3个部分组成，包括深入设计之研究、通过设计之研究和为了设计之研究。

［解析］ classification一词前面有well-known和three-part两个定语修饰语，如果直译为汉语的两个前置定语，势必会造成"的的不休"的汉语。因此，将原文的three-part前置定语转译为汉语的谓语"由3个部分组成"。当然，诸如research through design这样的新术语存在不同翻译，如"通过设计之研究""基于设计的研究"等。克里斯托弗·弗雷灵（Christopher Frayling）提出了"into, through, and for"（深入设计之研究、通过设计之研究、为了设计之研究）实践模型，布鲁斯·阿切尔（Bruce Archer）提出了"about, for, and through"实践模型（关于设计之研究、为了设计之研究、通过设计之研究），这里的介词翻译非常重要。

4.

［原文］ See also Cross, Friedman, and Feast and Melles.

［译文］ 有关此分类，还可参见克洛斯（Cross）、弗里德曼（Friedman）以及菲斯特（Feast）和梅勒斯（Melles）的论述。

［解析］ 此句是接在上述例句后面的一个短句。如果直译为"还可参见克洛斯（Cross）、弗里德曼（Friedman）以及菲斯特（Feast）和梅勒斯（Melles）"，那么表意不是很清楚，因此采用适当增词的翻译方法——增加"有关此分类"，具有承上的作用；增加"论述"，表明范畴属性。

5.

［原文］ For example, they might use ethnographic research or observations on people's activities as a means to understand user needs, product research as a means to identify possible solutions, market research as shedding light on the kinds of products people would buy and their price sensitivity, and usability research as indicating the interaction between people and products.

［译文］ 例如，他们可能会运用人种学，研究或观察人的活动，从而了解用户需求；以产品研发为手段，找出可能的解决方案；运用市场调研，了解人们具有购买欲望的产品类别以及他们对价格的敏感度；运用可用性研究，说明人与产品之间的交互。

［解析］ 这是一个长句，理解的关键在于把握该句中的省略现象——use ethnographic research or observations on people's activities as…（use）product research as…（use）market research as…and（use）usability research as…汉语译文将这4种情况用分号分隔，层次分明。

6.

［原文］ Although radical innovation is what everyone wants given its significant potential to differentiate, successful radical innovation is surprisingly rare, and most attempts at it fail.

［译文］ 虽然激进性创新具有显著的分化潜力，每个人都希望激进性创新，但令人

惊讶的是，成功的激进性创新非常罕见，大多数尝试都以失败告终。

［解析］ 本句所采用的翻译技巧之一是将原文的副词 surprisingly 另译为汉语的一个分句"但令人惊讶的是"。

7.

［原文］ As Apple's introduction of gesture-based cell phones illustrates, ideas do not spring out of thin air.

［译文］ 苹果公司所推出的基于手势的手机表明，创意并非无中生有。

［解析］ 由于设计研究频繁使用访谈等研究方法，所以论文中往往会出现口头语言和比较形象的描述，这是设计学术语篇的一个显著特征。本句中有"spring out of thin air"，意为"无中生有"。另外，在设计文献中，ideas 多为"创意"的意思。

Passage B　中国艺术设计的对称性

Warming-up

Work on the following terms and put them into English：

对称　　　　　　　　　　_____
儒家　　　　　　　　　　_____
中庸　　　　　　　　　　_____
黄金法则　　　　　　　　_____
道家　　　　　　　　　　_____
四合院　　　　　　　　　_____
牌坊　　　　　　　　　　_____
民间艺术　　　　　　　　_____
自然法则　　　　　　　　_____
良渚文化　　　　　　　　_____

对称性被广泛用于各种情境之中，在中国传统艺术设计当中，对称的概念是最为重要的美学原则之一。对称美源于自然，即道家的自然法则。人体和绝大多数动物都是对称的，彰显出健康与均衡之美，而非对称却留给人以不快的感受。对称也体现了儒家和谐与中庸的中华理念。中国艺术的美学对称原则类似于西方的"黄金法则"，旨在达到均衡。本文目的是探讨中国传统艺术设计中运用的美学对称法则，包括中国古代青铜器、古代建筑和剪纸。

一、中国古代青铜器的对称性

青铜器从功能上基本可分为4类：食器、酒器、水器及乐器。各类器物具有不同的造型和设计，充分显示了古代人民的创造性和技术。尽管如此，对称曾被作为普遍使用的基本美学法则。中国古代青铜器强调形式的均衡和对称，呈现出庄严肃穆之仪。

各种青铜器中，鼎是极为重要的一类。鼎最早用于盛装食物，后来被用于祭祀。许慎在《说文解字》中将鼎描述为有三足两耳。实际上，多数鼎有三足，而有些是四足，如著名的后母戊鼎。在中国历史上的青铜时代，鼎被当作立国之器与国家的象征，代表至高无上的皇权。国家一旦覆灭，鼎必须被搬走。当年商朝消亡周朝鼎盛之时，人们将鼎从亳移至周朝的京都镐京。

鼎所用图式主要是饕餮纹和云纹。饕餮，也称"贪食怪兽"，是一种集自然界各种动物特性的残暴猛兽。饕餮纹一般居中，周围环以云纹。这种残暴的怪兽饕餮从天上俯视凡界，其身体隐藏在云中，所以青铜器上可以看到饕餮的头部而从来看不到身体。自良渚文化时期以来，频现饕餮纹，且各不相同，虽样式繁多，但饕餮纹皆呈对称。一般在图案中以鼻梁为中心，双侧呈对称样式。饕餮纹的整体造型华丽，往往令人倍感肃穆。其图案对称，给人留下凶猛、神秘和可怕的印象。其实，对称为饕餮纹增添了雄伟、威严之象。

二、中国古代建筑的对称性

虽然仅有少部分中国古代建筑遗存下来，但根据考古发现，对称一直被作为中国传统建筑设计的基本原则之一。

中国建筑的基本特点是矩形的空间单位构成整体，北京的四合院就是个例子。我们可以看出四合院的主要结构就是中轴线，二级结构分处两翼形成主要房间和庭院。虽然四合院内容较复杂，包含精雕细琢的屋檐、墙面及门窗，但结构很简单。引领保护老北京遗迹的建筑师刘小石曾说："此处老屋的设计、布局及材料反映了古代人与天之间的和谐理念。"

北京的四合院遵循均衡与对称的原则，体现了中国传统建筑空间的单位组合，紫禁城等处也可以找到类似例证。显然，整座紫禁城是沿中轴线所建的双侧对称结构，中轴线自午门至神武门与北京城的中轴线一致。中轴线上坐落着建筑群最重要的宫殿，包括内外宫院的前三殿和后三宫。某种程度上对称为建筑群平添了庄严与恢宏的气势。更为重要的是，对称有助于将不同宫殿根据其功能和主人分出高低贵贱。

中国古代建筑对于对称的关注不仅体现在整体结构上，也可仅从众多建筑的拱门或门廊中窥见一二。

牌坊是双侧对称的范例，是迄今为止建筑中最常见的对称形式。它是由木料或石材以及镶嵌的琉璃瓦建成的古代的一种拱门，起源于周朝。最初，牌坊作为建筑群、寺庙、公园或城镇的入口标识，后来作为装饰。许多情形下，牌坊也用来纪念某人的功德。对称的牌坊体现了均衡之美，给人以雄健、威严及原始的朴实无华的感觉。

中国古代建筑中除左右对称之外还可看到轴对称。也称为土楼的圆形房屋是大型、封闭、防御式的生土建筑，结构呈环形，有着厚重、夯实的承重土墙，3~5层高，可容纳80家居住，属大型住宅类建筑。圆形房屋轴对称的建筑格局不仅具有宏伟的外观，而且具有精准、有序的内部设计。轴对称设计创造出向心性，突出了巨型天井中心位置的重要性，从而体现了客家宗族集体主义的价值观。

三、中国剪纸的对称性

剪纸是中国的一种民间艺术。对称在中国剪纸当中最初是一种技法，随着复制手段的出现，剪纸效率日益提高，由此造型变得对称起来。然而，中国剪纸中的对称不仅是种技法，它也是美学法则并富有内涵。

中国文化看重偶数，因为偶数传达的是圆满与欢乐。如中国字"红双喜"采用的是反射对称，因此左右图案互为镜像。显然，剪纸通过运用对称原理完满地表现了节庆的主题。

四、结论

正如对中国古代青铜器、中国古代建筑及中国剪纸等中国艺术设计中的各种范例的分析所示，对称因其标志着均衡、中庸、和谐而持久不衰。本文讨论的3个话题展现了对称的种种，它在中国艺术中的重要作用及其丰富的内涵。由此可见，对称作为美学原则与中国文化与哲学的核心价值密切相关，其在中国艺术设计中的重大意义不可忽视。

（摘自2013年出版的《艺术设计专业研究生英语选读》）

Notes

1.

［原文］ 对称性被广泛用于各种情境之中，在中国传统艺术设计当中，对称的概念是最为重要的美学原则之一。

［译文］ Symmetry has been widely used in various contexts. In traditional Chinese art and design, the concept of symmetry is one of the most important aesthetic principles.

［解析］ 原文一个句子被拆译为英文的两个句子。在汉语中，只要各分句之间有意义上的联系，就可以采用逗号连接，分句或多或少，伸缩性是很大的。英语在句法上比较严格，一句话用逗号还是用句号标记，形式上是有限制的，不能随意处理。该句前后讲的是两个相对并列的内容，前面是应用"情境"，后面是"美学原则"，可以采取断句的翻译技巧。

2.

［原文］ 对称也体现了儒家和谐与中庸的中华理念。

［译文］ Symmetry is also the manifestation of Chinese philosophy of harmony and *zhongyong*（the doctrine of the mean）in Confucianism.

［解析］ 汉语原文中的动词"体现"被转译为英语的名词 manifestation。一般认为，汉语是一种动态语言，喜用动词；英语是一种静态语言，喜用名词。此外，从本文的文体来看，它属于学术文体，在这种文体中，较多使用名词。在翻译"中庸"这样的中华文化术语时，可以采用汉语拼音加英文解释的方式，因为它有不少对应的英文翻译，如 doctrine of the mean, golden mean, the mean thought, constant mean, middle way, middle use, unswerving pivot, unwobbling pivot, focusing the familiar，等等。

3.

［原文］ 中国古代青铜器强调形式的均衡和对称，呈现出庄严肃穆之仪。

［译文］ Ancient Chinese bronzes stressed balance and symmetry of form, and communicated solemnity and ceremony.

［解析］ 本句翻译主要强调"呈现"这样的动词在目的语中的正确选词。communicate 一词是设计文献中的常用词汇，如 visual communication 表示"视觉传达"。作为及物

动词，communicate 的最常见含义是"传达，传递，传播"；作为不及物动词，它的最常见含义是"通信，通话，交际，交往，交流思想"。这里顺便提一下，Peter Newmark 提出了 semantic translation 和 communicative translation 两种翻译方法。其中，communicative translation 通常被翻译为"交际翻译"。事实上，所谓 communicative translation 的评价标准就是 accuracy of communication of ST message in TT，也就是说，目的语文本是否准确地传递/传达了源语言文本的信息。因此，把 communicative translation 翻译为"传达翻译"似乎更为贴切。

4.

［原文］ 许慎在《说文解字》中将鼎描述为有三足两耳。

［译文］ Ding was described as a kind of vessel with three legs and two ears in the *Origin of Chinese Characters* (*Shuo Wen Jie Zi*), which is believed to be the first dictionary of Chinese compiled by Xu Shen in 121.

［解析］ 此句翻译采用了文内拓展增词的翻译方法。对于《说文解字》这样的重要文献，我们有必要让目的语读者了解它的重要性和权威性。首先，考虑到《说文解字》可能存在不同的英文译法，如 *Origin of Chinese Characters*，*Explaining and Analyzing Characters*，*The Structure Analysis of Primary Characters and Meaning Explanation of Secondary Characters*，*Explaining Simple and Analyzing Compound Characters* 等，所以在英文翻译 *Origin of Chinese Characters* 后面加注了汉语拼音 *Shuo Wen Jie Zi*；其次，译文中增加了 the first dictionary of Chinese（汉语第一部字典）以及成书时间 in 121（公元 121 年）等文化信息。此外，不能把"三足"字面翻译为 three feet。"鼎"作为中华文化特有的器物，一般采用汉语拼音进行翻译，如"平足鼎"（ding with flat legs），"盘形鼎"（ding with dish-like mouth）。

5.

［原文］ 在中国历史上的青铜时代，鼎被当作立国之器与国家的象征，代表至高无上的皇权。

［译文］ In the Bronze Age of the Chinese history, ding was regarded as the very foundation on which a country was built and a symbol of the nation, representing supreme royal power.

［解析］ 关于本句的翻译，首先要区分句法上的主次关系，即"当作……"和"代表……"之间的内在逻辑关系。将"代表……"翻译成分词短语，就是将它视为次要的补充信息。其次，"立国之器"该如何翻译？我们不妨看看以下译例。

四项基本原则是立国之本。

译：The Four Cardinal Principles are the very foundation on which we build our country.

生命安全和生物安全领域的重大科技成果是国之重器。

译：Major scientific and technological achievements in the fields of life safety and biosecurity are of vital importance to our country.

中国北斗：大国重器

译：China's Beidou Navigation Satellite System: a Pillar of the Great Power

尽管在上下文中，"立国之器"中的"器"是指"鼎"这一具体的"器物"（artifact），但是考虑到它的象征意义，可翻译为"the very foundation on which a country was built"。

6.

［原文］ 国家一旦覆灭，鼎必须被搬走。当年商朝消亡周朝鼎盛之时，人们将鼎从亳移至周朝的京都镐京。

［译文］ Once the country is destroyed, ding will be removed. For example, when *Shang* Dynasty collapsed and *Zhou* Dynasty flourished, dings were moved from Bo to Haojing, the capital of *Zhou*.

［解析］ 英文翻译在两个句子之间增加了 For example 短语，明确两句之间的逻辑关系。另外，原文的第二句使用的是主动态，译文采用了被动态。"人们"这样的泛指主语在英文中通常没有必要说出，用被动态表述非常合适。

7.

［原文］ 这种残暴的怪兽饕餮从天上俯视凡界，其身体隐藏在云中，所以青铜器上可以看到饕餮的头部而从来看不到身体。

［译文］ The mythical ferocious beast taotie is overlooking the mortal world from heaven, with its body hidden in the clouds. Thus only the head of taotie appears on the bronzes.

［解析］ 本句翻译采用了增词和省词翻译技巧，即增加了 mythical 一词，让目的语读者知晓饕餮只是古代中国神话传说中的一种神秘怪物；二是省略不译"从来看不到身体"，因为表意已经非常清楚，没有必要重复。在语义选择上，"天上"和"凡界"相对，分别译作"heaven"和"mortal world"，这里的"天"是指"自然界的主宰或神、佛、仙人及他们的居所"，不宜译为 sky。

8.

［原文］ 自良渚文化时期以来，频现饕餮纹，且各不相同，虽样式繁多，但饕餮纹皆呈对称。

［译文］ The taotie mask patterns have appeared frequently since Liangzhu Culture (3300-2300 BC) and are diverse from one to another. Despite the diversity, the taotie mask patterns are usually symmetric.

［解析］ 由于原文一句话的前后两部分实质上讨论的是两个话题，所以拆译为英文的两句话。另外，"良渚文化"在此作为一个时间概念，目的语读者未必知晓其起止时间（公元前3300—公元前2300年），所以采用增词翻译方法，适度补充相关文化信息，确保目的语读者阅读过程的流畅性。

9.

［原文］ 虽然四合院内容较复杂，包含精雕细琢的屋檐、墙面及门窗，但结构很简单。

［译文］ Although the content of the quadrangle courtyard can be complex — consisting of meticulous design of the eaves and walls as well as windows and doors, the structure is quite simple.

［解析］ 本句翻译巧妙运用了标点符号，破折号明确表明后面的文字为补充说明四合院的内容。

10.

［原文］ 此处老屋的设计、布局及材料反映了古代人与天之间的和谐理念。

［译文］　The design, layout and material of the old houses here reflect the ancient philosophy of harmony between humans and nature.

［解析］　这里翻译的关键是"人与天"。如果字面硬译为 humans and heaven，那么表意是不清楚的。"天"有不同的指称，可能是"天（空）"（sky），"（上）天"（heaven），"自然界"（nature），等等。我们知道，中华文明历来崇尚天人合一，对应的英文表达是：

The Chinese civilization has always valued harmony between humans and nature.

所以，"人与天之间的和谐理念"译为"the ancient philosophy of harmony between humans and nature"。

11.

［原文］　更为重要的是，对称有助于将不同宫殿根据其功能和主人分出高低贵贱。

［译文］　More importantly, symmetry helps to divide the distinct palaces into different status according to their function and the master.

［解析］　本句翻译采用了抽象译法，即将"高低贵贱"这一比较具体的说法，抽象翻译为 different status，而不是 high or low, noble or base。

Translation Skills（Ⅰ）　Modulation：Active & Passive（语态转换）

一般认为，语态转换是一个比较简单的事情。例如在翻译下句时，只要把 by 后面的施事部分变为主语就可以了。

［原文］　Large quantities of fuel are used by modern industry.

［译文］　现代工业耗用大量燃料。

事实上，情况并非如此。在涉及语态转换的情况下，我们翻译时需要注意以下问题。

（一）被动语态翻译中的被动结构形式选择

从结构上来看，英语中的被动过程小句形式比较简单，按照与时、体、情态等特征的复合情况，可以归纳为 9 种形式，如 is designed, was designed, may be designed, has been designed, is being designed, may have been designed, may be being designed, has been being designed, may have been being designed。而且，英语中的被动大多为结构被动，意义被动句要远远少于结构被动句。汉语作为一种无形态变化的语言，被动句有没有形式标志还存在着争议。有学者认为汉语中不但存在被动形式标志，而且除了"被"字之外，还有"教（叫）、让、给、由、遭、受、挨、加以、得到、是……的、的是……、为……所"等 10 多个被动标志。一般认为，由于形式要求具有高度的概括性和规范性，因而汉语中被动句的形式标志只有助词"被"和介词"被""叫""让""给"等标志。此外，"为……所"是介词"为"引入施动者的古汉语遗留下来的被动形式。所以，在翻译的过程中，即便是翻译成被动句，我们也要知道汉语中的被动结构形式多样，需要采用恰当的形式，而不是一味地翻译成"被"字结构。

［原文］　The building of this house is considered to be the turning point in his life, when he left the artistic circles of Munich and moved away from the Jugendstil towards a sober and austere style of design.

[译文]　建造这幢房子被认为是他生命中的一个转折点。当时他离开慕尼黑的艺术圈，抛弃新艺术运动的影响，转向稳重简朴的设计风格。（被动态译为"被"字句）

　　[原文]　In addition, the website is built on the space CMS, our proprietary Content Management System, so Ryan Companies can keep content fresh and relevant.

　　[译文]　此外，网站也是建立在公司所特有的空间"内容管理系统"基础之上的，因此瑞安公司能够持续更新内容，确保内容的相关性。（被动态译为"是……的"）

　　[原文]　The attempt to achieve a visual localization of the rumors circulating and create a chart of these rumors was blocked.

　　[译文]　团队试图对谣言传播进行视觉定位并图示，但遭到阻止。（被动态译为"遭到……"）

　　[原文]　Observers position themselves in relation to these anticipated forms, and the object's behavior is itself conditioned by these moves, fostering something akin to a dance and a constant redefinition of one's own behavior as part of the process.

　　[译文]　观察者将根据这些预期的形式进行自身定位，而物体的行为本身又受到这些动作的制约，从而在此过程中形成一种类似于舞蹈的节奏，并不断地重新定义自己的行为。（被动态译为"受到……"）

　　[原文]　One implication is that spoken or written language alone might not be sufficient; knowledge of practice also must be demonstrated through artifacts and their process of being made.

　　[译文]　这里的启迪之一就是单靠口头或书面语言是不充分的，实践知识还必须通过人工制品及其制造过程加以演示。（被动态译为"加以……"）

　　从所表达的被动意义上来看，汉语的被动句可以分为3种类型：由形式标志的被动句、用词汇手段表达被动意义的被动句、完全靠意合而没有形式标志或使用词汇手段的被动句。汉语中"受事+动词"的格式是汉人自古以来的一种表达习惯。例如，在以下译例中，英文中的被动态被转译为汉语中的主动态，因为交际者凭语感能够认知到它的被动意义。

　　[原文]　The sense of inferiority that he acquired in his youth has never been totally eradicated.

　　[译文]　他在青年时期留下的自卑感，至今还没有完全消除。

　　（二）被动语态的语义色彩及其翻译

　　汉语中的"被"字句除被动意义之外，还多了一层不幸、不如意、不愉快、有所损害的语义色彩，并且这个语义色彩长期存在于汉语实践之中。我们先比较一下以下译例的两种译文。

　　[原文]　But soon this peace and quiet were broken by he First World War.

　　[译文1]　但不久以后，第一次世界大战爆发，打破了这种和平安静的生活。

　　[译文2]　但这种和平与安宁不久就被第一次世界大战打破了。

显然，采用汉语的"被"字被动态翻译原文的被动态，保留了原文"不幸"的语义色彩。以下译例有助于我们进一步理解"被"字所承载的语义色彩。

［原文］ In Rittel and Webber's terms, planners and designers were at the time "forced to expand the boundaries of the systems we deal with."

［译文］ 用里特尔和韦伯的话来说，规划人员和设计人员当时"被迫扩大了我们处理的系统的边界范围"。

［原文］ Planning problems were labeled "wicked", partially because of the confusing fact that social problems relied "upon elusive political judgment for resolution," even while the authors were well aware of the expert's position as a "player in a political game."

［译文］ 规划问题之所以被贴上"诡异"的标签，部分原因在于这一令人困惑的事实：社会问题依赖"难以捉摸的政治判断来解决"，即使作者们也充分意识到专家在"政治游戏中的玩家"身份。

与英语相比，汉语中被动结构的另一个特点是被动态使用的动态性，具体体现在功能负荷量和联想意义等方面。与英语相比，现代汉语较少使用被动态。例如，受西方语言影响较大的老舍在其作品中较多使用被动句，如《骆驼祥子》（人民文学出版社1955年版）全书221页，被动句（显性被动句）使用多达100句，平均0.5句/页，虽然远远少于英语作品（相差8~9倍），但比未受西方语言影响的《红楼梦》中的被动句（<1句/10页）仍然多了不少。可见被动态的功能负荷量不仅随着文体因素而不同，而且与使用者和时代也存在密切的关系。此外，在翻译的过程中，汉语的"把"字句和无主句也能表达原文中的被动结构含义。

［原文］ To explore the use of color, the number of colors was reduced to two to focus on the pattern generated rather than the influence of colors themselves.

［译文］ 为了探索颜色的使用，我们把颜色的数量减少到两种，以便主要关注生成的图案，而不是颜色本身的影响。（被动态译为"把"字句）

［原文］ But that question was wrung from those men again the next night——and got the same retort.

［译文］ 可是，到第二天晚上，这些人又把这个问题搬出来了——同样受到了呵斥。（被动态译为"把"字句）

［原文］ Smokers must be warned that doctors have reached the conclusion that smoking increases the possibility of lung cancer.

［译文］ 需要提醒吸烟者，根据医生的结论，吸烟会增加患肺癌的可能性。（被动态译为无主句）

（三）语态所承载的意识形态等意义潜势及其翻译

英汉语中被动语态过程小句的翻译不仅在结构本身、功能负荷量、联想意义等方面存在差异，同时在参与者的隐现及其意识形态意义方面也存在着差异。

英语中使用被动语态的情况可以归纳为施动者、句法、修辞、文体4个方面：（1）施动者的原因，即不知道或不容易指出施动者，或根据上下文可以清楚地知道施动者，不必说出或不愿说出施动者，或故意避免说出施动者，或在说话人看来受事比施动者更重要；（2）句法的要求，即出于衔接或句法重心的考虑；（3）出于修辞的需要；（4）出于文体的需要，常用于科技文章，避免作者主观臆断，注重事理和客观描述。但是，必须注意的是被动语态的修辞功能。例如，小说 *Jane Eyre* 第五章就通过被动语态使用频率的变化，表示主人翁在准备、出门、别离和去途等不同阶段的心理变化过程，因而在翻译时就不能随意地将被动语态转化为主动语态。

一个句子是否应该从主动语态"转换"为被动语态或者从被动语态"转换"为主动语态，是由它的语篇功能来决定的。因此，我们绝不可以机械地把主动句和被动句等同起来，也不能以为这两类句子在语篇中可以随意地交换使用。

此外，被动语态的使用特别是参与者的隐现往往具有意识形态的动因。省略或隐去被动语态过程参与者除了出于参与者是不言自明的、无关紧要的、无从知晓的以外，还可能出于政治或意识形态的考虑，即采用虚饰化意识形态模式，故意模糊施动者，从而掩饰动因和责任。但是从不出现施动者的被动语态过程小句来看，英语句中约有80%的被动小句不出现施动者。也就是说，在英语中被动小句不出现施动者乃是一种常态。相比之下，对于汉语的被动小句，正常的被动式是必须把主事者说出的。

［原文］ The Philippines and Vietnam allege that Chinese naval vessels have harassed oil-exploration vessels working in what United Nations maritime laws define as these countries' domestic economic zones.

［译文］ 菲律宾和越南均称，它们在其各自专属经济区内工作的石油勘探船一直受到中国海军舰船的骚扰。

原文中的动词 harass 是主动语态，《参考消息》译文编译时把它处理为被动语态。这种特别的处理可能有语言使用习惯方面的原因，但不排除具有意识形态潜势这一点，淡化了中国舰船"主动骚扰"的可能性。相反，在以下译例中，为了强化其中的意识形态潜势，原文中的"被……拘押"结构被处理为英文的"Canada's detention"。这种名物化处理，将它升格为一个"事件"，一种"现象"。

［原文］ 连日来，华为公司首席财务官孟晚舟被加拿大当局拘押一事引发舆论高度关注，受到中方严正交涉、强烈抗议。

［译文］ Canada's detention of Meng Wanzhou, chief financial officer (CFO) of Huawei Technologies Co., Ltd., earlier this month has sparked worldwide attention and drew strong criticism from China.

Translation Workshop

I. Translate the following sentences and pay attention to the modulation of voice

1. Similar arguments can be found on a philosophical level where the material experience, at the center of a new sustainable aesthetic, is argued to influence concrete changes to behavior and ways of living on a societal level.

2. When a user requests a set of resources, it must be determined whether the allocation of these resources will leave the system in safe state.

3. No convincing signs of plant or animal life have been detected by instruments soft landed on Mars.

4. The training in the workshops were preceded by the preliminary course, a trial semester where the personal skills of the students were tested and foundations of craftsmanship and design were taught.

5. While many of the ideas for energy-efficient building design have been around for at least a couple of millennia, they are only now being taken to new heights.

6. 关于具体指控提供给华为的信息非常少，华为并不知晓孟女士有任何不当行为。

7. 今年4月，我在博鳌亚洲论坛年会开幕式上说过，过去40年中国经济发展是在开放条件下取得的，未来中国经济实现高质量发展也必须在更加开放的条件下进行。

8. 设计方案的形成往往来自特定风格的灵感启发，这种风格会引导建筑师和设计师在设计中遵循某种基调。

9. 应始终明确记载所做的修改，这不仅可供参与修复和维护的专业人员日后使用，而且可以为公众提供信息，起到解释作用，这样人们就不会误以为所做的修改是原先设计的一部分。

10. 工业设计兼顾应用艺术和应用科学，它提升产品的审美、设计、人体工程学、功能或使用性，并且可以用于改善产品的适销性甚或生产环节。

II. Translate the following passage into English

中国的园林建筑更富有趣味而非实用，更具寓意尤为重要。这些园林使得城市建筑得以从儒家的束缚中解脱出来。

仅借中文措辞列举一些与园林有关的常见建筑元素就可对此比喻维度窥见一斑。墙面上的洞可以是圆形的"月亮门"，有时又呈现出花形、扇贝形、葫芦形或花瓶状。护拦可以是"冰裂"纹，水上的亭阁即为"船"，而五座亭子相连就变成"帝王五爪龙的爪子"。岩石除非是"弹孔"，否则自然就成为"妖魔和野兽"；柳树"摇曳如舞女的纤纤细腰"；而园林中央的水域是"月亮净化其灵魂"的所在。甚至在建筑平面图中也凸显此种比喻兴致：有些建筑形如梅花或扇面——将拐角处的两个回廊连接在一起的实用造型与清风的蕴意相结合，是一种常见的设计；有时拐角处的两座亭子相连形成一只蝴蝶。现实世界无一不被转换成梦幻诗境。

（摘自2013年出版的《艺术设计专业研究生英语选读》）

III. Translate the following passage into Chinese

Product characteristics specified by industrial designers may include the overall form of the object, the location of details with respect to one another, colors, texture, form, and aspects concerning the use of the product. Additionally, they may specify aspects concerning the production process, choice of materials and the way the product is presented to the consumer at the point of sale. The inclusion of industrial designers in a product development process may lead to added value by improving usability, lowering production costs and developing more appealing products.

Industrial design may also focus on technical concepts, products, and processes. In addition to aesthetics, usability, and ergonomics, it can also encompass engineering, usefulness, market placement, and other concerns — such as psychology, desire, and the emotional attachment of the user. These values and accompanying aspects that form the basis of industrial design can vary — between different schools of thought, and among practicing designers.

Industrial design has also become a major means of building corporate images. At the lowest level, companies have tended to regard the employment of an industrial designer as a kind of status symbol. It is enough to have a designer on the payroll, without going so far as to use him. But large corporations now use designers in a systematic way, as a means of creating personality not merely for one product, but for a whole range of related products, and not just for products alone but a corporate image. If he is descended from the artisan, the architect and the engineer, he can also trace his ancestry to the itinerant vendor of patent medicines.

（摘自 *Design Issues* 2014 年第 4 期）

Unit 2 Food Science and Chinese Food Culture

Passage A Food Culture in China: Diet and Health

Warming-up

Work on the following terms and put them into Chinese:

disharmony within the body   _____
health and longevity   _____
herbal medicine   _____
diet therapy   _____
pre-Qin dynasty   _____
Yellow Emperor   _____
mutton   _____
greens   _____
yin-yang dichotomy   _____
white fungus   _____

Then and now, the Chinese believe that food relates to health and that illness is a disharmony within the body. They believe that maintaining harmony and balance insures health and longevity. When this balance goes awry, they see a need to restore it to make a person's body work more efficiently. This, they say, helps the body heal itself. The Chinese still use traditional and herbal medicinal efforts to restore the body's harmony and balance.

More importantly, the Chinese pay attention to the body long before illness sets in. They use food as preventive medicine and as restorative medicine. To them, food is healing cuisine. The correct foods aid life and health and assure longevity. The science of diet therapy is a respected component of their medical and pharmacological practices.

Confucius (551-479 B. C. E.), a great sage, used and expanded this thinking 25 centuries after the Yellow Emperor in a volume attributed to him called the Book of Songs. He wrote about foods, rules and ethics, and what and how to eat. He explored the principles of balance and gave examples of specific foods with health implications. He expanded upon the interplay of positive and negative, dominant and recessive, better known as the opposing forces of yin and yang. He considered their duality important for order and harmony in the universe and in the human being. He explained they were not rigidly fixed but rather relationships reflecting dynamic interactions, interpretations of everything on earth and in the heavens. He saw the Yellow Emperor as reflection of diet therapy and medical knowledge before the twenty-first century B. C. E. It was pre-Qin Dynasty, and its concepts, he mused, underlie most aspects of Chinese existence, including medicine and health.

Confucius postulated that yin and yang work with the five elements or five phases of wood, fire, earth, metal, and water. He believed that they and the five virtues of benevolence, justice, propriety, sincerity, and wisdom were cosmic forces exerting additional effects on things and more importantly on the eternal cycle of life. Confucius and others saw the five elements as most important because they were the basis of science and cosmology. They were part of everything, including nutrition, health, and medicine.

Why five? The Chinese like to divide things into groups, many having five items. The number five is thought to be lucky because it is uneven and male. Westerners see four points on a compass — north, south, east, and west — but the Chinese see five directions including east, south, center, west, and north. They envision many other groups of five, including five colors of: black, green, red, white, and yellow; and five sacrificial animals to place on their altars — the ox, goat, pig, dog, and fowl. They discuss five body fluids of tears, sweat, saliva, mucus, and urine, and speak of the five emotions of anger, joy/fright, worry, sadness/grief, and fear. Inside a person's body, they believe, are five solid organs of: liver, heart, spleen, lung, and kidney; five hollow organs of: gallbladder, small intestine, stomach, large intestine, and bladder. They also think of five pures that include moon, water, pine tree, bamboo, and plum tree; and even five classics of their literature: *the Book of Documents* or *Shujing*, *the Book of Songs* or *Shijing*, *the Book of Changes* or *Yijing*, *the Book of Rites* or *Liji*, and *Book of Ceremonies* or *Yili*.

There are additional groups of five with special importance for food, diet, nutrition, and health. One is the five aromas of rancid, scorched (or burned), fragrant, rotten, and putrid. Westerners do not limit themselves to five and have at least two others: sweet and floral. Many believe there are even more. The Chinese also have five categories of healing herbs: grass, tree, worm, stone, and cereal. The Chinese word herb includes plants, animals, and minerals. Other items in fives are cereal categories (wheat, glutinous millet, millet, rice, and beans) and meat groups (chicken, mutton, beef, horse, and pork). And there are others.

Not everything is divided into fives. Major causes of disease in Western medicine include germs, mostly bacteria and viruses. In China's ancient medicinal thinking, there are four major causes: external, internal, food, and fatigue. The external causes are sixfold: wind, cold, summer heat, dampness, dryness, and fire. There are seven internal causes: anger, joy, worry, thought, sadness, fear, and shock. There are other groups important to the Chinese, but the most important revolves around and relates to the five elements. Understanding them is the basis of their medicinal thinking.

The five elements are important tenets of feeding and healing. They network and influence each other and are associated with many things, including parts of the body. Each element travels through the body using a particular meridian or pathway as it interacts with the others. Think of a five-pointed star with the element fire as the top point. Next envision lines around the points going from one to the next. This helps understand which element interacts with others. These are unidirectional, going from one exterior point to the next all the way around the star. Other interactions go across the star. Now think of drawing a five-pointed star without lifting the pencil off the paper. These other interactions are following those lines. There is another item of importance because in one of these lines an element generates or creates the other and in the other it subjugates or controls the next. Generating is going around the outside; controlling or subjugating is going across as when drawing the star.

The generating directions are fire to earth to metal to water to wood. The controlling directions are fire to metal to wood to earth to water and back to fire. When generating, think wood burns and generates or creates fire; fire produces ashes that decompose and generate earth; earth creates or generates metal taken from earth; when heated the metal becomes molten; and water helps things grow, generating or creating more wood. Alternately, when thinking controlling, think wood breaks up the earth as it grows; earth controls or subjugates water, keeping it in one place; water subjugates or controls fire, putting it out; fire controls metal by melting it; and metal subjugates wood by cutting it.

Each of these elements is associated with body parts and body pathways. Therefore, together these interrelationships determine not only direction but also actions of food and herbs when consumed. For example, salty herbs relate to the element water and include items such as seaweed. They are cooling foods that act on the kidneys and the bladder. The Chinese consider sweet foods and herbs tonifying and nutritious. They believe that pungent ones mobilize and disperse blood and impact lungs and large intestine. Bitter ones are helpful with coughs and cooling, and they direct things downward to the heart and small intestine. Sour or astringent foods are used for sweating; they act on the liver and gallbladder.

Easier understanding can come when looking at the elements alphabetically, starting with earth. The Chinese say that earth is associated with late summer, the sweet taste, the emotion of worry, and the body parts of stomach, spleen, mouth, and muscle. Fire is associated with summer, bitter taste, joyous emotions, and heart, tongue, blood vessels, and small intestine. Metal's season is fall, its taste pungent, its emotion grief, and the associated body parts of lungs, nose, skin, and the large intestine. Water's season is winter, its taste is salty, emotion is fear; and its related body parts are bladder, bones, ears, hair, and the kidneys. The fifth element is wood. Its season is spring, taste is sour, emotion is anger; and body parts are liver, gallbladder, tendons, and eyes.

It is hard to think of a Chinese dish that is not in some way based upon an ancient sage who designed or wrote about it. Most Chinese people know their history and the important people who influenced it. They know, from thousands of years of traditional practice, how to balance their diet. They discuss the body's energy or qi, but they do not think that food gives energy in the Western sense, but instead in the philosophical sense.

Chinese people know that yang means bright, dry, hot, and male, and that yin means dark, moist, cold, and female. Each of these properties does not appear 100 percent in each food item, but all foods and health conditions, even organs and aromas, have some yin and some yang qualities. There is a predominance of one or the other in larger amounts in each food. They serve some yin or cold foods and some yang or hot foods at every meal. Foods can also be warm or cool, and a few are considered neutral. What is interesting is that Chinese people may not be able to tell which food is which, but they do put a meal together with foods of all of these qualities, and they know what foods not to serve when a person has a particular condition.

Yin or cold food-related items include eating, white foods, bland foods, and boiled foods. Examples of some foods that have mostly yin qualities are bean sprouts, cabbage, carrots, celery, congee, daylily, gingko, and honey. Yang or hot food-related items include drinking, red foods, fried and broiled foods, and spicy foods. Some examples of foods having yang qualities are bamboo, beef, black pepper, chicken, cinnamon, eggs, fatty meats, garlic, dried ginger, and more. Neutral, warm, and cool foods are few in number, but nonetheless important in the yin/yang dichotomy. Neutral foods can include Chinese cabbage, figs, licorice, noodles, peanuts, red dates, shiitake mushrooms, and soft rice. Cool foods include asparagus, bean curd, bean sprouts, citrus peel, eggplant, and tangerines.

Not all diet therapy is based upon yin and yang. Another concept is called bu. All animals are bu to some degree, especially if they are steamed or simmered slowly and herbs added to the pot. Bu foods are easy to digest, rich in protein, and often have many minerals. This category of foods is strengthening and supplementing; it can put the body back into harmony.

Another consideration is foods that look like what they are supposed to strengthen. For example, because they look like a brain, walnuts are thought to increase intelligence. Jujubes, particularly the red ones, are considered to be good for the blood. Ginseng fits into this type of consideration and is the highest class and perhaps the most expensive of medicines. Some believe it looks like a person. It is said to help people, particularly as a yang energy tonic because it is thought to replace lost qi or vital energy. The Italian explorer Marco Polo thought ginseng a wonderful tonic.

There are other rare and exotic items, also costly, that are thought to serve the same or similar purposes. They include sea cucumber, bird's nest, deer antler, shark fin, white fungus, abalone, and other hard to find and expensive items. The Chinese consider them nourishing foods — that is, nourishing in its philosophic sense. All of them can provide the power of suggestion, and Chinese people take them because they believe they work.

Chinese traditional beliefs keep people healthy, diversify food production, and use foods that are available. They are not based upon Western science but rather upon generations of empirical observations, such as when Shennong tried out foods and herbs on himself and recorded his findings. If they were good enough for him, many Chinese people reason, they should work on them.

(摘自 2004 年出版的著作 *Food Culture in China*)

Notes

1.

[原文] Then and now, the Chinese believe that food relates to health and that illness is a disharmony within the body. They believe that maintaining harmony and balance insures health and longevity. When this balance goes awry, they see a need to restore it to make a person's body work more efficiently. This, they say, helps the body heal itself. The Chinese still use traditional and herbal medicinal efforts to restore the body's harmony and balance.

[译文] 一直以来，中国人都相信饮食关系到健康，而疾病则源于体内气血不和。由此他们认为，维系气血调和、阴阳平衡才是健康长寿的关键。平衡一旦被打破，那就有必要通过干预措施进行纠偏，使人体机能恢复正常运转。中国人相信，这一措施有助于身体的自愈。时至今日，中国人依然使用传统疗法和草药来调和气血、平衡阴阳。

[解析] 受限于语言特点和知识深度，西方学者论述中国文化容易浮于表面，缺乏细节描述的同时也无法触及本质，因此我们翻译时在细节上要充实饱满，在原文作者浅尝辄止的核心问题上要补充甚至纠错。原文第一句"disharmony"很显然不能直接翻译成"不和谐"，而须根据中医学的语境翻译成"气血不和"，而这在英文中用一个"disharmony"笼而统之地概括显然无法让西方读者深入理解中医文化。同样，"balance"也不能简单翻译成平衡，可以对应为中医学里面的概念"阴阳平衡"。另外，在翻译中国古典文化类的文章时，可以多使用四字格，使文章读起来简洁凝练。例如"Then and now"可翻译为"一直以来"或者"自古以来"，最后一句中的"still"翻译成"仍然"的同时，我们在句首还补充了"时至今日"，强调中医文化传统的传承。

2.

[原文] More important, the Chinese pay attention to the body long before illness sets in. They use food as preventive medicine and as restorative medicine. To them, food is healing cuisine. The correct foods aid life and health and assure longevity.

[译文] 更重要的是，中国人懂得防患于未然，将食物用于预防疾病和调理身体。中国人还懂得寓医于食，相信合理膳食有助于强身健体和延年益寿。

[解析] 前两句合二为一。把"pay attention to the body long before illness sets in"翻译成俗语"防患于未然"，突出中华医学"不治已病治未病"的理念。接下来，我们用了一系列四字格："food is healing cuisine"翻译成"寓医于食"，而"aid life and health and assure longevity"则很自然地翻译成"强身健体和延年益寿"。

3.

[原文] Confucius (551-479 B.C.E.), a great sage, used and expanded this thinking 25 centuries after the Yellow Emperor in a volume attributed to him called the Book of Songs. He wrote about foods, rules and ethics, and what and how to eat. He explored the principles of balance and gave examples of specific foods with health implications. He expanded upon the interplay of positive and negative, dominant and recessive, better known as the opposing forces of yin and yang.

[译文] 在黄帝诞辰2500年后的春秋时期，圣哲孔子在其编订的《诗经》中运用并

拓展了这些思想。他收编的诗歌涉及了食材原料、饮食礼法、烹饪技法等。诗歌也通过列举有益健康的特定食物搭配探究了膳食平衡的原理。这些诗歌还详述了正向和负向、显性和隐性的相互作用原理，即中医所说的阴阳辨证关系。

［解析］ 这一段译者必须纠正原文中一个明显的错误，即《诗经》并不是孔子本人写的，他仅仅是进行了编订，因此里面所有涉及孔子论述了什么概念的文字都要进行修改。例如，"He wrote about…"应改成"他收编的诗歌涉及了……"，"He explored…"改成了"诗歌也通过列举……探究了……"，"He expanded upon"改成了"诗歌还详述了……"。另外，为使文章读起来更朗朗上口，这里继续尽量使用四字格，例如，"He wrote about foods, rules and ethics, and what and how to eat"翻译成"他收编的诗歌涉及了食材原料、饮食礼法、烹饪技法等"。

4.

［原文］ …and even five classics of their literature: *the Book of Documents* or *Shujing*, *the Book of Songs* or *Shijing*, *the Book of Changes* or *Yijing*, *the Book of Rites* or *Liji*, and *Book of Ceremonies* or *Yili*.

［译文］ ……提到典籍，中国人读"五经"，即《诗经》《尚书》《礼记》《周易》和《春秋》。

［解析］ 根据习惯，我们把五经简称为《诗》《书》《礼》《易》《春秋》，分别对应《诗经》、《书经》（或《尚书》）、《礼记》（或《仪礼》）、《易经》（或《周易》）和《春秋》。原文显然没有遵循这个习惯性序列，重复了《礼》，遗漏了《春秋》（*the Spring and Autumn Annals*）。在翻译时译者一定要修正补缺。

5.

［原文］ The five elements are important tenets of feeding and healing. They network and influence each other and are associated with many things, including parts of the body. Each element travels through the body using a particular meridian or pathway as it interacts with the others. Think of a five-pointed star with the element fire as the top point. Next envision lines around the points going from one to the next. This helps understand which element interacts with others. These are unidirectional, going from one exterior point to the next all the way around the star. Other interactions go across the star. Now think of drawing a five-pointed star without lifting the pencil off the paper. These other interactions are following those lines. There is another item of importance because in one of these lines an element generates or creates the other and in the other it subjugates or controls the next. Generating is going around the outside; controlling or subjugating is going across as when drawing the star.

［译文］ 五行构成了中国传统饮食和疗法的基本原理，它们相互联系，相互影响，与包括人体各部位在内的许多事物相对应。每个元素与其他元素相互作用，经由特定经络或路径贯穿全身。你可以设想有一颗五角星，其 12 点钟方向顶点对应火。接下来设想从这个顶点出发连到下一个顶点的环形路径，这样有助于看清哪个元素在与其他元素发生作用。这条路径是单向的，从一个顶点（一个顶点对应一个元素）通向下一个顶点，直到围绕五角星（的 5 个顶点）形成一个闭环。与其他元素的互动路径横贯这个闭环。再次设想自己一笔勾勒出一个五角星，其五条边对应了每个元素与其他元素（确切来说是另

外两种元素）发生互动的路径。另一个极其重要的概念就是具有不同属性的两套互动路径：第一套路径中，一个元素总是生成另一个元素；而在第二套路径中，一个元素总是克制另一个元素。生成性路径沿圆形闭环运行，而克制性路径则贯穿闭环内部，呈五角星状。

[解析] 这一段是对五行相生相克图的描述，单看文本，读者会觉得源文本的描述过于琐碎和复杂，理不清头绪。在这种情况下，译者需要找到原图，厘清思路，统一措辞，尽量按照原文的描述进行翻译。就本例而言，译者需要明确两点：第一，五行相生相克图中，外围环状路径代表了相生的关系，而贯穿环状内部的直线表示相克的关系；第二，译者要观察到，原文在某些关键概念的所指上措辞不统一，比如作者先是把火的位置称为顶点"fire as the top point"，紧接着又说"going from one exterior point to the next all the way around the star"（5种元素是单向构成环状的，从一个"外侧点"通向下一个"外侧点"，循环往复）。很显然，这个"外侧点"也包含了火。所以，对于五行的位置，应该如何统一措辞呢？事实上，如果火必须出现在"12点钟"位置作为起始点，那么它确实需要一个不同于其他4种元素的名称，但通过简单调研我们会发现，五行只有相对序列，没有"钟表上的"固定位置，因此，我们须使用同一个名称来指代这5个点的位置，通称为"顶点"。

6.

[原文] It is hard to think of a Chinese dish that is not in some way based upon an ancient sage who designed or wrote about it.

[译文] 追根溯源，几乎每一道中国菜的问世或多或少都受到某位先哲的影响，或通过发明创新，或通过著述传播。

[解析] 原文是典型的双重否定表示肯定的句型，翻译成中文须从正面进行阐述。为了表达得更清晰，这里用了增词法，在句子开头添加了"追根溯源"；句尾用了两个四字格，"发明创新"和"著述传播"。

7.

[原文] Chinese traditional beliefs keep people healthy, diversify food production, and use foods that are available.

[译文] 中国传统理念指导人们如何强身健体、丰富膳食，并因地制宜地选用食材。

[解析] 为了表达得更生动，这里没有直译。"keep people healthy"翻译为"指导人们如何强身健体"，后面的"diversify food production, and use foods that are available"通过"丰富膳食"和"因地制宜"两个四字格来表达。

Passage B 濠江味传

Warming-up

Work on the following terms and put them into English:

美食　　　　　　_____

烤乳猪　　　　　_____

舶来品　　　　　_____

本土化
伊比利亚半岛
招牌菜
褐变效应
蛋白质
美食家
乡愁

对于岭南人而言，清明时节还意味着一种美食的香味即将登场。

澳门名厨陈德光又开始了返乡祭祖的旅程。他回归路上的第一件事，就是要选择一只上好的乳猪。乡愁情感之外，是对味道的精进和执着。美味乳猪的背后，居然还有许多有待解读的传说。美食家闫涛和陈德光师傅一样，对乳猪充满兴趣。但是，他关心的是乳猪为什么会有光皮和麻皮之分。美食导演陈晓卿同样对乳猪充满了好奇。但是他的疑问在于，东西方都有乳猪存在，那么我们今天吃到的广式乳猪，究竟是舶来品还是自古有之呢？

陈晓卿："这种烤制的方式肯定是人类最早的烹饪形式，用现代科学的解释就是表皮的美拉德反应，就是一个褐变的过程，在这个褐变的过程中能够（散发）出它的香味，同时在口感上也发生非常重要的改变，就是接近皮的地方是一个酥脆的感觉。"

闫涛："今天我们吃的猪是酥皮，其实里面的肉汁是受到影响的。但是光皮可以把肉汁锁住。"

陈晓卿："实际上光皮和麻皮最大的差异是扎不扎，用钉子扎完了烤，它里边的油脂会更快地散发出来。光皮的可能会把它包得更紧，水分包得更紧，蛋白质和脂肪都包得更紧。"

闫涛："中国的乳猪是酥为上，脆为次，硬为下。也就是说其实在中国古代，最喜欢吃的乳猪口感还是酥皮。但今天真正的广式乳猪其实不是酥皮的。"

今天，许多广式乳猪都喜欢标榜（自己）是正宗的澳门口味。这当中有什么渊源吗？

闫涛："广州是中国开埠最早的城市（之一）。在清朝，只有广州港是一个对外港口[①]。可能有外来文化对它造成一些影响。"

陈晓卿："要回溯最正宗的广式乳猪，可能还是得到澳门去看一看。"

澳门，这个被陈晓卿称为"时间冰箱"的地方，以其独特的文化沉淀能力形成了古今中外文化融合的饮食风貌。澳门的乳猪至今仍然是美食家们慕名向往的味觉地标。舌尖求道，濠江寻味，为什么澳门的乳猪会成为席间翘楚？

闫涛："乳猪到底是我们本土的传统，还是海外的舶来品？广州的很多乳猪要标榜（自己是）正宗澳门乳猪。然后来了澳门，我发现澳门乳猪真不一样。所以说，乳猪到底是本土的还是舶来的？"

陈晓卿："伊比利亚半岛的饮食习惯对广东的烤猪有过影响。真的，这是我吃过的中国乳猪里面最有滋有味的。所谓的有味，就是我们说的香味——美拉德反应，所谓的滋，

[①] 据史料记载，乾隆二十二年（1757年）起只开广州一口通商。

实际上就是它多汁的滋味。"

　　陈晓卿老师所关注的美拉德反应不过是近些年来才被科学界所慢慢论证的一种自然规律。但是智慧的粤菜师傅们早已经熟练地掌握运用了这种原理。乳猪不过是其中的一个代表。在永利轩，这一反应早已被陈德光师傅演绎出一系列精美的菜肴，茶皇鸡等都是脍炙人口的招牌菜。

　　陈晓卿："你看，全是美拉德，都有褐变的。这种褐变的东西，就是糖的转换过程，它实际上让你更容易吸收，更能刺激我们的神经中枢产生快乐的多巴胺。"

　　法国科学家美拉德发现的肉类与糖分的褐变效应，如今被学界称之为美拉德反应。科学家的探索其实是在一次次验证厨师和美食家们共同追寻着的味觉传说。

　　陈德光："这是每个人的心得，经历了无数次的失败，自己慢慢地总结出来的。"

　　米其林粤菜餐厅永利轩厨房的背后，是一间厨艺学院。澳门乳猪等各式美味佳肴和一代代厨师们的手艺在此得以传承和创新。澳门的魅力在于它的包容和积累。在这里，经验被汇聚成智慧。时代洪流里的沧海遗珠，就在澳门被凝聚成璀璨的饮食文化瑰宝。

　　闫涛："限制我们餐饮往前走的一个枷锁就是什么最像老祖宗。其实不是这样的。什么能得到更多人喜爱，什么就是正宗。所以我更喜欢把它说成是全世界，世界美食，这个星球美食的一次不约而同。"

（摘自纪录片《濠江味传》）

Notes

1.

[原文]　对于岭南人而言，清明时节还意味着一种美食的香味即将登场。

[译文]　For Lingnan folks, Qingming Jie（清明节）also serves as a herald of the unique flavor of a culinary delight.

[解析]　岭南是指南岭山脉以南，现指广东、广西和海南3地全境，以及湖南、江西两省部分地区。岭南人可以直译成"Lingnan folks"。Lingnan作为一个地理名词可以留给感兴趣的读者自己查阅，folks一词与下文出现的"返乡"和"乡愁"透出的浓浓家乡情相呼应。为了更好地传播中华文化，在书面文本中，中国传统节日的名称建议直接用拼音表达并用汉字标注，如"Qingming Jie（清明节）""Duanwu Jie（端午节）""Chongyang Jie（重阳节）""Chun Jie（春节）"等。至于这些节日的历史文化内涵，可以适当留白，让感兴趣的外国读者自己去查阅，作为译者我们无须事无巨细。"美味"这里选用了"culinary delight"一词，突出了美味带来的愉悦之情。"即将登场"有"预示着……来临"的意思，因此使用"serve as a herald of"这一表达。

2.

[原文]　澳门名厨陈德光又开始了返乡祭祖的旅程。他回归路上的第一件事，就是要选择一只上好的乳猪。乡愁情感之外，是对味道的精进和执着。

[译文]　Chen Deguang, a renowned chef who works in Macau, began, as usual, a journey home to worship ancestors. His first priority on his way back was to select a premium roast suckling pig. This, apart from a sentiment of nostalgia, represents a spirit of fastidiousness and persistence in pursuing best flavors.

［解析］ 第一句开头用附带定语的同位语表达"澳门名厨"这一身份。第二句，陈德光师傅回乡路上的"第一件事"并非时间先后意义上的第一，而是指重要程度，因此这里应翻译成"first priority"。第三句，"乡愁"不光是"homesickness"意义上的想家，还带有对一去不复返的往昔美好岁月的眷恋，因此用"nostalgia"更为贴切。"精进"和"执着"表面上看意思相近，但联想到名厨对烹饪过程细致入微的要求和对味道的极致追求，前者应该还有对工作或作品精益求精的意味，因此用"fastidiousness"。

3.

［原文］ 但是，他关心的是乳猪为什么会有光皮和麻皮之分。

［译文］ His concern, though, lies in the reason why roast suckling pigs should differentiate into smooth skin and sandy skin at all.

［解析］ 陈德光师傅执着于烤乳猪的味道，而美食家闫涛关心的是烤乳猪是怎么衍生出两种做法的。从上下文来看，原文中的"但是"直接翻译成连词"but"转折的意味并不到位。因此，这里我们把原文中的动词"关心"转换成名词主语"concern"，并在主谓之间插入了副词"though"。另外，"为什么会有光皮和麻皮之分"其实并不是在技术层面上探究这两种做法的原理，而真的是从历史的视角探究衍生出这两种做法的必然逻辑："why…should differentiate into…and…at all"用情态动词"should"和副词"at all"表达这位美食家的疑惑。

4.

［原文］ 美食导演陈晓卿同样对乳猪充满了好奇。但是他的疑问在于，东西方都有乳猪存在，那么我们今天吃到的广式乳猪，究竟是舶来品还是自古有之呢？

［译文］ As a TV culinary producer, Chen Xiaoqing too is fascinated by roast suckling pigs, wondering whether the Guangzhou-style roast suckling pigs as we know them today were homegrown or imported from overseas, given that roast suckling pigs are featured in both Chinese and Western cuisines.

［解析］ 原文中的两句话在译文中通过一个现在分词表伴随的结构"wondering"合二为一。"舶来品"翻译成一个形容词性短语"imported from overseas"，对应土生土长，因此原文中的"自古有之"没有直译，而是用了"homegrown"，因为自古有之自然意味着本土出品。考虑到朗读时的节奏感，两个表达交换了顺序。"东西方都有乳猪的存在"不能简单按字面意思翻译成"There are…"，而须将句子稍稍解读一下，理解为在中西餐里都有烤乳猪这道菜，于是我们想到使用"feature"这个表达，理解为"包括……元素，以……为特色"。"我们今天吃到的广式乳猪"在译文中做了延伸处理，理解为"我们今天所熟知的广式乳猪做法"，使用了英语里的一个固定搭配"…as we know it"。因为前文烤乳猪用了复数表达，所以改为"…as we know them"。类似的表达列举一二：

He planned to end the welfare system as we know it.

译：他计划终止现存的这套福利体系。

The building as we know it is quite different from how it looked when it was first built.

译：我们现在看到的这栋楼和它刚建成时相比已经完全不同了。

5.

［原文］ 中国的乳猪是酥为上，脆为次，硬为下。

［译文］ In Chinese cuisine, the best quality roast pork has soft and crispy skin, the next best in order has crumbly and browned skin, and the most undesirable of all has hard and stiff skin.

［解析］ 带有文言文色彩的汉语晦涩抽象，简短精练，信息含量大。因此译者必须细致理解每个字要表达的意思和其中的逻辑关系。具体到这句话，原句短短九个字，对仗得很工整，意思也不难理解，即对不同品质的烤乳猪进行排序。下一步是措辞：酥有松软而易碎的意思，我们选择"soft and crispy"；单纯的脆，虽然不错，但已经不是最好，联想到前文美拉德反应产生的褐变效应和人们日常的偏好，产生焦皮也属于打了折扣的，综合考量下选择"crumbly and browned"；硬，尤其是僵硬，口感一定是大打折扣了，因此选择了"hard and stiff"。这样，每个层次都用了两个形容词，再加上"为上""为次"、"为下"也尽量选取了对等的表达，因此总体上保持了中文里的对仗性。

6.

［原文］ 澳门，这个被陈晓卿称为"时间冰箱"的地方，以其独特的文化沉淀能力形成了古今中外文化融合的饮食风貌。澳门的乳猪至今仍然是美食家们慕名向往的味觉地标。舌尖求道，濠江寻味，为什么澳门的乳猪会成为席间翘楚？

［译文］ Macau, a city Chen Xiaoqing once called a "time freezer", has created a culinary landscape that brings together cultural elements ranging from traditional to contemporary and from Chinese to Western through its distinctive, all-inclusive cultural values. Its roast suckling pigs have long been a fascinating and much sought-after culinary landmark among gastronomes. But as you plunge yourself into this beautiful port city in seeking out special flavors and stories behind, you might well wonder why on earth do Macau suckling pigs become such an iconic centerpiece of various feasts and banquets?

［解析］ 这段文字中许多文绉绉的表达非常抽象，只可意会，难以言传，翻译时译者要尽量将它们转译成听得懂的语言。比如"独特的文化沉淀能力"，很显然不是自然科学意义上的沉淀，而是指文化吸纳和包容的能力，因此我们可以用"distinctive, all-inclusive cultural values"。翻译"舌尖求道，濠江寻味"时，译者可以想象自己投身于美食之都（濠江是澳门的旧称），尽情寻找美味的同时也聆听着这一切背后的故事，通过画面联想将上下文串联起来："plunge yourself into this beautiful port city in seeking out special flavors and stories behind"。看到"席间翘楚"，译者可以脑补一个画面，就是人们常说的"某某牢牢地占据了C位"，对应"iconic centerpiece"。

7.

［原文］ 科学家的探索其实是在一次次验证厨师和美食家们共同追寻着的味觉传说。

［译文］ What scientists discovered serves only, time and again, as testimonies to the tale of the taste buds chefs and gourmets have long been co-authoring.

［解析］ 虽然原句很通顺，但当译者在头脑里进行预译时会发现，直接转译成英语时短语搭配不是那么恰当。"一次次验证"的只能是理论，不能是传说，但我们可以说"见证传说"。"共同追寻着的传说"其实也无法直译，但我们可以说"共同书写的传说"。

8.

［原文］ 在这里，经验被汇聚成智慧。时代洪流里的沧海遗珠，就在澳门被凝聚成

璀璨的饮食文化瑰宝。

[译文] It is here that experiences collect into wisdom; it is here that the glistening pearls of wisdom (Macau), riding on the wave of the times, are being turned into culinary treasure.

[解析] 像这种带有散文色彩的语句,翻译时一定要在头脑里形成画面,将抽象的表达具象化。

Translation Skills (Ⅱ) Conversion Between the Abstract and Concrete (虚实转换)

由于汉英两种语言的构词特点和表达习惯差异,在翻译过程中,译者时常需要采用虚实转换的策略。所谓虚,就是概念化、抽象泛化的表述;所谓实,就是具象化、形象细致的表达。学术界一种较有代表性的观点认为,汉语的语言思维是一种具体思维,注重感受和提炼综合,擅长用形象的语言表达抽象的事物;而英语的语言思维则是一种抽象思维,注重逻辑和分析解构,擅长用抽象的语言表达具体的事物。然而,无论这一观察在多大程度上反映了客观事实,在翻译实践中,译者绝不应该先入为主地用这一两分法思维指导实践,而是应该秉持实事求是的态度具体问题具体分析。在案例中,我们会遇到抽象化的汉语表达,也会遇到形象化的英语表达,因此,我们应当学会灵活处理源语言和目的语之间的虚实关系,实现目的语语义的通达。

(一) 单词英译汉的虚转实

通常,由形容词或者动词派生出来的抽象名词,由于其一词多义性,翻译成汉语时,需要结合上下文语境考虑是否要添词对抽象概念具体化。这在翻译专业术语时尤为重要。

evaporation	蒸发⇨蒸发作用
oxidation	氧化⇨氧化反应
reduction	还原⇨还原反应
redox	氧化还原⇨氧化还原反应
pasteurization	巴氏杀菌⇨巴氏杀菌法
sterilization	灭菌⇨灭菌处理
catalysis	催化⇨催化作用
eutrophication	富营养化⇨水体富营养过程
hydrolysis	水解⇨水解作用
dehydration	脱水⇨脱水作用
denaturation	变性⇨变性作用
customization	定制化⇨定制化服务
neutralization	中和⇨中和反应;中和作用
polymerization	聚合⇨聚合作用
coagulation	凝固⇨凝固物
spontaneity	自发性⇨自发行为

(二) 语篇翻译的虚转实

汉语,尤其是文言文中,存在着许多模糊性表达。这类表达没有清晰的主谓宾成分,字里行间没有显著的逻辑关系,因此需凭上下文映衬而理解其产生的"意合"效果。当译者产生这种似是而非的模糊感时,不要急于寻找英文中对应的措辞,而是需要通过上下文透彻理解篇章的意思,并在此基础上凝练出主谓宾成分、逻辑关系和所指对象。这一初次加工是把模糊性表达清晰化处理的一个过程,也可以理解为汉语内部发生的一次编码转换。只有完成了这一脱虚向实的转换后,译者才能着手考虑如何将文本转译成英文。

1.

[原文] 凡战法知兵者方知其玄妙,看似单一,其变幻犹如天地行云,无穷无尽,若江河湖海永无枯竭。宫商角徵羽,不过五音,然而五音之重组变化却层出不穷;红黄蓝白黑,不过五色,然五色之幻化交融却令人眼花缭乱;酸甜苦辣咸,不过五味,然五味其浓淡轻重却任由妙手调停。

——电视剧《大秦帝国之崛起》赵括长平之战前的"纸上谈兵"

[译文] Only he who is versed in the art of generalship perceives the subtleties therein. Underlying the seeming simplicity is a vast universe of change as incessant as the ebb and flow of the tides: a mere quintet of five musical notes of gong, shang, jue, zhi, yu is sufficient to compose combinatorial variations that are virtually limitless; a mere quintet of five colors of red, yellow, blue, white and black is capable of painting pictures as dazzling as it is kaleidoscopic; a mere quintet of five tastes of sour, sweet, bitter, spicy and salty leaves ample room for culinary maestros to fine-tune flavors and tastes of food.

[解析] 这段"纸上谈兵"的主题是用兵谋略的千变万化,其中暗含的4个隐喻使行文略显抽象,需要具体化。"天地行云,无穷无尽"实体化为永恒变化的宇宙;"五音之重组变化"具象化为作曲;"五色之幻化交融"具象化为作画;"五味……任由妙手调停"具象化为做菜。

2.

[原文] 古者丈夫不耕,草木之实足食也;妇人不织,禽兽之皮足衣也。不事力而养足,人民少而财有余,故民不争。是以厚赏不行,重罚不用,而民自治。今人有五子不为多,子又有五子,大父未死而有二十五孙。是以人民众而货财寡,事力劳而供养薄,故民争,虽倍赏累罚而不免于乱。

——《五蠹》韩非子

[译文] In the old days, men did not need to farm since supplies of wild fruits and berries were abundant to keep people fed; women did not need to weave since animal skins and hides were sufficient to keep people warm. People did not need to dispute since they lived in plenty without much effort and the size of the population was small while resources copious. Thus even without great rewards and heavy punishments people lived in peace. Today, however, it is not unusual for a man to beget five sons and for his five sons to each produce five sons of theirs, and thus for him to have a total of 25 grandsons while he is still alive. Over time, as the population grows, properties and wealth are increasingly depleted and people stretched themselves thinner and thinner just to be fed and clothed. Thus, people begin to dispute and compete over limited resources, despite even the most generous rewards and harshest punishments, from which chaos and conflicts inevitably ensue.

［解析］ 这段出自于战国时期思想家韩非子的论述生动形象地描述了我们今天所说的社会内卷现象。抓住文章所要表达的这一主旨即可在译文中将隐含的内在逻辑和意思显性化。例如，根据上下文我们可以判断，"丈夫不耕""妇人不织""故民不争"并非丈夫不耕种，妻子不织布，百姓不争斗，而是内含"无须"这层意思。"事力劳而供养薄"，这短短七个字，表达抽象而信息丰富，简言之就是拼尽全力才勉强糊口，因此可以考虑使用 stretch oneself thinner and thinner 和 be fed and clothed 做具象化处理。

3.

［原文］ "限制我们餐饮往前走的一个枷锁就是什么最像老祖宗。其实不是这样的。什么能得到更多人喜爱，什么就是正宗。所以我更喜欢把它说成是全世界，世界美食，这个星球美食的一次不约而同。"

——纪录片《濠江味传》

［译文］ "One of the shackles that hinders us from making progress is the notion of equating the authentic to the traditional. It's not true. As far as I am concerned, the most authentic must be the most popular (among customers). So I would say it's ultimately down to a serendipitous rendezvous among the best foods of this planet."

［解析］ 这是一段口语化的表达。无论是汉语还是英语，口语表达一般都比较随意，有时甚至显得似是而非，语法、逻辑和所指都很难做到书面语那般严谨。因此，译者在翻译时需要根据语境理解说话者要表达的意思，并且，有时需要译者帮说话者把没有表达完整的话以符合逻辑的方式表述出来。例如，这段话最后说道"这个星球美食的一次不约而同"。这句话听着很抽象，而且还没有说完整，留给了观众一定的联想空间。但作为译者，我们必须要顺着说话者的逻辑把话说圆满，这里我们可以将"不约而同"理解为"偶遇"（a serendipitous rendezvous），更有画面感。

4.

［原文］ The force most commonly applied in processing is temperature, whether low (refrigeration), very low (freezing), high (for example, pasteurization or cooking), or very high (canning or sterilization).

［译文］ 食品加工过程中人们通过调节温度来达到保鲜的效果，无论是低温（冷藏）、超低温（冷冻）、高温（例如巴氏杀菌处理或烹煮）或者超高温（罐装或灭菌处理）。

［解析］ 这是一个典型的英译中虚转实案例，将抽象性名词具体化：refrigeration⇨冷藏，pasteurization⇨巴氏杀菌处理，sterilization⇨灭菌处理。

5.

［原文］ Using new advances such as machine learning, a high-resolution library of these biochemicals could enable the systematic study of the full biochemical **spectrum** of our diets, opening new avenues for understanding the composition of what we eat, and how it affects health and disease.

［译文］ 借助机器学习等人工智能技术所构建的涵盖这些物质的高清生化物质档案馆，科学家们可以系统地研究我们饮食中的全套生化物质，为了解我们摄入食物的成分及其对健康和疾病的影响开辟新的途径。

［解析］ "Spectrum"这个词本义为特定物理现象可量化属性的变化范围，可指光谱、声谱、波谱、频谱等，也可广义地理解为谱系，即对特定事物经过系统化分类而形成的大家族，如孤独症谱系障碍（autism spectrum disorder）、政治谱系（political spectrum）等。在这里，biochemical spectrum 如果翻译成"生化谱系"，不但抽象，而且难以理解，这并不是一个得到广泛使用的术语，因此我们将它做具体化处理，根据上下文翻译成"全套生化物质"。

（三）语篇翻译的实转虚

当译者遇到源语言文化中特有的且无法直译成目的语的表达时，应该考虑采用转换的翻译策略。这类情况通常涉及源语言里的俚语、成语或者典故，如果将其直译成目的语会给人生硬突兀、莫名其妙的感觉。在这种情况下，译者有两种选择：第一，采用实转虚策略，对该表达的内涵进行解释；第二，在目的语中寻找具有异曲同工之妙的表达。

1.

［原文］ The new proposals are a halfway house between the original treaty and the revised version.

［译文］ 新提案是原协议和其修订版的折中方案。

［解析］ 原句"a halfway house"从字面看有"半途的房子""中转站"或"中途的旅店"的意思，是一个具体化的表达，但其内涵显然不能这样来解释，而应该根据语境延伸为"折中方案"。

2.

［原文］ All of these factors influence the potential growth of microorganisms. At some levels, their effect might be negligible (for example, a tiny level of sugar will have no meaningful preservative effect), while at others their effect might be undesirable in terms of the food (a level of sugar might be so high that the food is unpalatably sickly sweet). In between, then, is a zone where the level suits the food's flavor and at the same time works effectively to inhibit undesirable microorganisms. In the case of sugar levels, we could term this the sweet spot.

［译文］ 所有这些因素都会潜在影响微生物的生长。当糖含量过低时，它们的效果可能是微不足道的（例如，微量的糖不会起到任何防腐效果），而当糖含量过高时，它们又严重破坏食物的口感（过高的糖分会使食物过于甜腻而难以下咽）。在这两者之间有一个中等区间。当糖含量处于该区间时，食物的口感和风味不仅可以得到有力保障，致病微生物的存活和滋长也可以得到有效遏制。我们可以称这一区间为最优值区间。

［解析］ 原文讲的是糖对食物具有一定的防腐效果，但取决于糖的含量，过高和过低都不会产生理想的效果，因此有一个"sweet spot"。这个表达很应景，很形象，但绝对不能直译成"甜点"，而应该根据上下文解释为"优化点"或"最优值区间"。

3.

［原文］ In theory, the convenience and safety of UHT (Ultra-high temperature processing) milk should be more competitive than pasteurized milk, but the value consumers place on flavor and nutritional quality, both seen to be unacceptably damaged in UHT milk, has kept it alive in the milk market.

［译文］ 按理说，就安全性而言超高温消毒牛奶应该比巴氏消毒牛奶更有市场竞争力，但由于超高温在团灭细菌的同时也彻底破坏了牛奶的口味和营养，能够兼顾安全性、口感和营养的巴氏消毒牛奶自然依旧占据着一席之地。

［解析］ 原文比较了超高温消毒牛奶和巴氏消毒牛奶各自的相对优势，用"kept it alive"来表述巴氏消毒牛奶的市场保有状况。这一表达虽然形象生动，却不能直译成"确保它存活"，而应该解释为"占据着一席之地"。

4.

［原文］ By the time they enter school children command 13,000 words, and then the pace picks up, because new words rain down on them from both speech and print.

［译文］ 通常来说，孩子们进入小学时可以掌握约13000个单词，然后习得频率会加快，因为新单词通过口语交流和书报阅读会源源不断地涌现。

［解析］ 原句主旨是儿童习得词汇的频率，提到进入小学以后，习得频率会突然加快，作者用了"rain down on"这一略带夸张的表达，生动而又形象，颇有"天雨粟"的既视感。但此处我们不能直译成"新词通过……如雨点般袭来"，而需泛化为"源源不断地涌现"。

前文提到，在翻译过程中，实并非一定要转虚。如果可以从目的语中找到神似又意合的表达，译者完全可以采用实转实的策略。例如，短语"cannot hold a candle to something"这一表达源于17世纪欧洲手工作坊里学徒给师傅秉烛照明——如果学徒连这样简单的事情都做不好，那真是一无是处了。字面意思引申为"连给某人点蜡烛照明都不配"，引申意为"远不如某人或某事物"或者"跟某人或某事物没法儿比"。了解了出处，我们发现这个短语是非常生动形象的。如果要实转虚，那么我们可以用"与……无法相提并论"或者"无法与……相媲美"来解释。然而，详加思考后我们会发现，汉语中与这个短语神似而意合的短语有很多，例如带有戏谑意味的口语化表达"连给……提鞋都不配""与……相比就是个小弟""遭遇完败""被吊打""遭完爆"，书面化的表达有"与……不可同日而语""简直是云泥之别（天渊之别）"等。再比如成语"风雨飘摇"，意境与"山雨欲来风满楼"神似，引申为"局势动荡，前途未卜"。翻译成英文我们可以采用实转虚，笼统抽象地理解为"being unstable""being precarious"，或者我们可以借助英文中神似的表达，如"gathering storm""gathering clouds""hang by a thread""a fatal crisis looming large"等。译者应该根据文本性质、上下文、目标读者等实际情况选择最合适的措辞，灵活使用虚实转换策略。

Translation Workshop

Ⅰ. Translate the following sentences and pay attention to abstract & concrete conversion

1. It is in fact remarkable that so much of nature around us turns out to be suitable for, and indeed pleasurable for, human consumption, particularly after it has been subjected to processes

nature never envisaged.

2. As we will see, a large part of the goal of food processing, from the field to the fork, is in controlling the rate at which these changes take place, to maximize the golden period between immaturity and overripeness in which we can best admire nature's fine work.

3. Historically, humans have employed a variety of cooking techniques in order to improve the organoleptic and nutritional quality of food (e.g., increased food digestibility).

4. My argument in a nutshell is this: the more we lift the lid on the genome, the more vulnerable to experience genes appear to be.

5. Across different forms of life, the details of the cell's architecture might vary (and in some cases, like viruses, differ pretty wildly), but most of the reactions those cells engage in on an ongoing basis will be similar.

6. 王安石："善理财者，民不加赋而国用饶。"司马光："天地所生，货财百物，止有此数，不在民间，则在公家。"

7. 这一异乎寻常的化学成分多样性可被视作营养学研究领域的"暗物质"，因为它们中的大部分物质无论对公众还是对流行病学研究而言依然是鲜为人知的。

8. 微生物的繁殖方式多种多样，但最常见的方式是细胞分裂。本质上，一个细胞会生长到它分裂成两个相同的细胞为止。

9. 最初人们认为有4种味蕾，它们相当于味觉范畴的三原色。这4种味蕾分别是咸、甜、酸和苦。然而，现在人们已经认识到，还存在一种品尝"鲜味"的味觉感受器。

10. 癌症、糖尿病及心脏病等所谓的文明病都是由于构成细胞膜的磷脂在某个阶段受到氧化作用而诱发的。

Ⅱ. Translate the following passage into English

每个城市都会通过一个食材产生自己的味觉记忆，这也就是人们常说的"一城一味"。那么方寸之地的澳门，它的"一城一味"是什么呢？谁曾想过，它居然和一个不远万里、风马牛不相及的食材产生了血脉相通的关联。

我第一次来到澳门，看到到处都写着"马介休"，我以为是一个书法家。它是什么？马介休其实是一种来自葡萄牙的咸鱼，就是腌制、干制的鳕鱼。它是经过大量的海盐把它腌制了、变硬的、脱水的一种……其实跟我们中国的咸鱼差不多。但它不是葡萄牙人发明的，是北欧那边的人，他们去葡萄牙度假的时候，把这个鱼带到葡萄牙去，然后葡萄牙人把它带到了澳门，就变成一种澳门特有的吃法。

比老字号更让人尊敬的是华人厨师的老行尊。杨师傅入行超过了60年。每一个来沙利文餐厅的人都知道他烹饪马介休球的功夫十分了得。

杨师傅："其实我们用最简单的食材，很简单的，内容就是薯仔、马介休、鸡蛋，我们加了一些香菜增加它的香味，很简单的。但是你用简单的材料去做一个大多数人都喜欢吃的菜式，我想这个绝对不简单。为什么我们用手做呢，因为我们用手，有触觉，知道它够不够滑。"

像马介休这种外来的食材，经过几代人的融合，终于在某一天无声无息地成为每一个澳门家庭不可分割的一部分。

（摘自纪录片《濠江味传》）

III. Translate the following passage into Chinese

The Dragon Boat Festival is a summer festival that features boat races to honor those who tried to save a beloved scholar-statesman-poet named Qu Yuan. He served in the time of the Warring States (403-221 B. C. E.). The boats used are narrow. Each one has a carved dragon on the bow and one large drum set in the stern. A drummer keeps the two dozen or more oarsmen in one boat rowing together, and the drum's noise is said to frighten away anyone who would harm Qu Yuan. Those watching these races drink protective wines and eat special dumplings.

A story is told that Qu Yuan jumped into a river circa 278 B. C. E., very distressed to learn that he had earned the king's displeasure and was to be exiled. Another tale calls him a statesman who was a victim of palace politics. Whichever is accurate, he did throw himself into a nearby river on the fifth day of the fifth month. Local people used their boats to try to save him. They were unsuccessful. So they made and threw packages of zongzi to divert any predatory sea creature from eating him. These zongzi pitched into the river were made of cooked sticky rice mixed with meat and stuffed into pieces of bamboo to keep them together.

After this, his mourning became an annual festival. Tradition has it that the rice was originally put into bamboo tubes, closed with lily leaves, and tied with colored silk thread to assure that the scaly dragon would not steal them. These days, the dumplings are triangular and wrapped in bamboo leaves. Leaf strips or strings hold them together.

These tribute foods generally have one of three fillings. The first is made of meat, mostly pork, mixed with rice and chestnuts. A second kind is rice and beans with a bit of sapan wood preserved in an alkaline solution such as lye; it is to act as an evil-dispelling agent. The third type is rice powder mixed with pomegranate juice and honey. The last two kinds are said to have medicinal properties that increase as they age. They are recommended for dysentery.

Protective wine was part of the festival. Some of it was dried and painted on foreheads, noses, even ears of children. It was to ward off poisonous creatures. Some was used wet for writing the character wang or guowang, which means king. It was also painted on foreheads for the same purpose. Leaves of calamus and mugwort, two ancient plants, were dipped in wine and put on the gates of homes, also to ward off evil. The calamus looks like swords, and mugwort leaves resemble tigers, both clearly evil items. All the wine-related activities were protectors against one calamity or another.

（摘自2004年出版的著作 *Food Culture in China*）

Unit 3 Textile Science and Fashion Culture

Passage A Cotton Growing, Properties and Uses

Warming-up

Work on the following terms and put them into Chinese:
cotton yarn   _____
staple cotton   _____
cotton gin   _____
staple fiber   _____
the Carolinas   _____
cotton cultivation   _____
seed pod   _____
staple length   _____
foreign matter   _____

Cotton is the world's most widely used fiber. Its popularity stems from both its relative ease of production and its applicability to a wide variety of textile products. The price of cotton yarn, however, is strongly dependent upon the cost of labor, so that in the industrialized nations, where labor is expensive, cotton yarns may be relatively high priced.

Until relatively recent times, however, cotton was not as widely used as wool and linen. This was because it was easier to spin wool or flax into yarn because of their greater length. In addition, cotton fibers have to be separated from the seeds to which they cling. This procedure was very tedious and time-consuming when done by hand. Early machinery could be used on only the longest staple cotton. So labor costs tended to be very high.

The invention of the saw-type cotton gin made possible the exploitation of the short staple fiber, which thrived in the Carolinas and Virginia of the United States. The dramatic increase in productivity, coupled with the low cost of labor in the southern United States, gave cotton a continually expanding portion of the world textile market. Increasing mechanization of fiber and yarn production helped keep the cost of cotton goods low. The development of the textile machinery enlarged the production base.

Cotton cultivation requires warm climates with a high level of moisture or irrigation. The growing season is from six to seven months long. During this period the seeds sprout and grow, producing a white blossom in about 100 days. The blossom produces a seed pod, which matures during the next two months. When the pod bursts, the cotton fibers are ready for picking.

Before yarn manufacture, cotton is graded, sorted, and blended to insure uniform yarn quality. Cotton is graded on the basis of color, staple length, fineness, and freedom from foreign matter. In the United States, cottons are divided into grades according to length of staple, uniformity, strength, color, cleanness and flexibility. These are compared with a standard supplied by the United States Department of Agriculture. The standard provides 6 grades above and 6 grades below the middling grade. The most common grades are:

(1) Strict good middling.

(2) Good middling.

(3) Strict middling.

(4) Middling.

(5) Strict low middling.

(6) Low middling.

(7) Strict good ordinary.

The cotton fiber may be from 0.3 to 5.5 cm long. Under the microscope it appears as a ribbon like structure that is twisted at irregular intervals along its length. The twists, called convolutions, increase the fiber-to-fiber friction necessary to secure a strong spun yarn. The fiber ranges in color from a yellowish to pure white, and may be very lustrous. However, most cotton is dull.

A cross-sectional view reveals that the fiber is kidney-shaped with central hollow core known as the lumen. The lumen provides a channel for nutrients while the plant is growing. The fiber consists of an outer shell, or cuticle, which surrounds the primary wall. The primary wall, in turn, covers the secondary wall surrounding the lumen. The cuticle is a thin, hard shell which protects the fiber from bruising and damage during growth. In use as a textile fiber, the cuticle provides abrasion resistance to cotton.

A relatively high level of moisture absorption and good wicking properties help make cotton one of the more comfortable fibers. Because of the hydroxyl groups in the cellulose, cotton has a high attraction for water. As water enters the fiber, cotton swells and its cross section becomes more rounded. The high affinity for moisture and the ability to swell when wet allow cotton to absorb about one-fourth of its weight in water. This means that in hot weather perspiration from the body will be absorbed in cotton fabrics, transported along the yarns to the outer surface of the cloth and evaporated into the air. Thus, the body will be aided in maintaining its temperature.

Unfortunately, the hydrophilic nature of cotton makes it susceptible to water-borne stains. Water-soluble colorants such as those in coffee or grape juice will penetrate the fiber along with the water; when the water evaporates, the colorant is trapped in the fiber. Perhaps the major disadvantage to cotton goods is their tendency to wrinkle and the difficulty of removing wrinkles. The rigidity of cotton fiber reduces the ability of yarns to resist wrinkling. When the fibers are bent to a new configuration, the hydrogen bonds which hold the cellulose chains together are ruptured and the molecules slide in order to minimize the stress within the fiber. The hydrogen bonds reform in the new positions, so that when the crushing force is removed the fibers stay in the new positions. It is the rupture and reformation of the hydrogen bonds that helps to maintain wrinkles, so that cotton goods must be ironed.

Cotton is a moderately strong fiber with good abrasion resistance and good dimensional stability. It is resistant to the acids, alkalies, and organic solvents normally available to consumers. But since it is a natural material, it is subject to attack by insects, molds and fungi. Most prominent is the tendency for cotton to mildew if allowed to remain damp.

Cotton resists sunlight and heat well, although direct exposure to constant strong sunlight will cause yellowing and eventual degradation of the fiber. Yellowing may also occur when cotton goods are dried in gas dryers. The color change is the result of a chemical reaction between cellulose and oxygen or nitrogen oxides in the hot air in the dryer. Cottons will retain their whiteness longer when line-dried or dried in the electric dryer.

Of major interest is the fact that cotton yarn is stronger when wet than when dry. This property is a consequence of the macro- and micro-structural features of the fiber. As water is absorbed, the fiber swells and its cross section becomes more rounded. Usually the absorption of such a large amount of foreign material would cause a high degree of internal stress and lead to weakening of the fiber. In cotton, however, the absorption of water causes a decrease in the internal stresses. Thus, with less internal stresses to overcome, the swollen fiber becomes stronger. At the same time, the swollen fibers within the yarns press upon each other more strongly. The internal friction strengthens the yarns. In addition, the absorbed water acts as an internal lubricant which imparts a higher level of flexibility to the fibers. This accounts for the fact that cotton garments are more easily ironed when damp. Cotton fabrics are susceptible to shrinkage upon laundering.

Perhaps more than any other fiber, cotton satisfies the requirements of apparel, home furnishing, recreational, and industrial uses. It provides fabrics that are strong, lightweight, pliable, easily dried, and readily laundered. In apparel, cotton provides garments that are comfortable, readily dried in bright, long-lasting colors, and easy to care for. The major drawbacks are a propensity for cotton yarns to shrink and for cotton cloth to wrinkle. Shrinkage may be controlled by the application of shrink-resistant finishes. Durable-press properties may be imparted by chemical treatment or by blending cotton with more wrinkle-resistant fibers, such as polyester.

In home furnishing, cotton serves in durable, general-service fabrics. Although they may lack the formal appearance of materials made from other fibers, cotton goods provide a comfortable, homey environment. Cotton fabrics have been the mainstay of bed linens and towels for decades, because they are comfortable, durable and moisture-absorbent. Polyester/cotton blends provide the modern consumer with no-iron sheets and pillowcases that retain a crisp, fresh feel.

For recreational use, cotton has traditionally been used for tenting and camping gear, boat sails, tennis shoes and sportswear. Cotton is particularly well-suited for tent. A tent fabric must be able to "breathe", so that the occupants are not smothered in their own carbon dioxide. Furthermore, exchange of air with the outside atmosphere reduces the humidity within the tent and keeps it from becoming stuffy. Fabrics woven from cotton can be open enough to provide good air permeability for comfort. Tents should also shed water, when wet by rain, cotton yarns swell, reducing the interstices between the yarns and resisting the penetration of water. Today, however, heavy canvas gear is being supplanted by light-weight nylon in tenting equipment.

Cotton cord, twine and ropes are used in industry to bind, hold, and lash all kinds of things, from bales to boats. Cotton yarns are used to reinforce belts on drive motors and in work clothing.

（摘自《服装英语》）

Notes

1.

［原文］ The price of cotton yarn, however, is strongly dependent upon the cost of labor, so that in the industrialized nations, where labor is expensive, cotton yarns may be relatively high priced.

［译文］ 然而，棉纱的价格在很大程度上依赖于劳动力成本。在工业化国家劳动力昂贵，因此棉纱的价格可能相对较高。

［解析］ 本句翻译的难点在对 so that 的理解上。so that 这个结构既可以表示目的，又可以表示结果，根据此处的上下文，这里应该是表示结果，与本句的前半部分构成因果关系，可以译为"因此"或"所以"。但这个表示因果的词不宜放在"在工业化国家劳动力昂贵"之前，因为后半句的两个小分句之间还存在着另一层因果关系，考虑到全句的连贯性，只需译出后半部分的因果关系，so that 所表示的这层因果关系由汉语的意合特征隐性表达出来。

2.

［原文］ The invention of the saw-type cotton gin made possible the exploitation of the short staple fiber, which thrived in the Carolinas and Virginia of the United States.

［译文］ 锯式轧棉机的发明使短纤维的利用成为了可能，利用短纤维去纺纱在美国的南卡罗来纳州、北卡罗来纳州和弗吉尼亚州盛行了起来。

［解析］ 翻译本句时，要注意 which 所指代的内容。这里的 which 引导一个非限制性定语从句，指代整个前半句所叙述的内容，即由于锯式轧棉机的发明而使得利用短纤维（去纺纱）成为了可能，而不宜把"短纤维"理解为被指代的对象。另要注意，the Carolinas 指的是美国的南卡罗来纳州和北卡罗来纳州。

3.

［原文］ Cotton cultivation requires warm climates with a high level of moisture or irrigation.

［译文］ 棉花种植需要温暖的气候、充足的降雨量或良好的灌溉。

［解析］ 本句需要注意"a high level of"的翻译。如果译成"高水平的"，则与"moisture"（湿度、水分，此处指降雨量）以及"irrigation"（灌溉）的译文构成不当搭配。考虑到汉语的习惯表达，"a high level of moisture or irrigation"翻译为"充足的降雨量或良好的灌溉"。

4.

［原文］ Cotton is graded on the basis of color, staple length, fineness, and freedom from foreign matter.

[译文] 棉花的分等是根据颜色、纤维长度、细度、有无异物等因素而定的。

[解析] 本句中的"on the basis of"应根据汉语的表达习惯译为"根据","freedom from foreign matter"的意思为"无异物",但放到句子中时,考虑到汉语的表达习惯,翻译为"有无异物"方才通顺。

5.

[原文] The twists, called convolutions, increase the fiber-to-fiber friction necessary to secure a strong spun yarn.

[译文] 这种捻度,又称卷绕结构,增加了纤维之间的摩擦,这是确保细纱强度所必需的。

[解析] "spun yarn"指的是"细纱、短纤纱",该术语与"strong"搭配时,不宜翻译为"强壮的",考虑到汉语的搭配习惯,"strong spun yarn"译成"细纱强度"为妥。

6.

[原文] The fiber ranges in color from a yellowish to pure white, and may be very lustrous. However, most cotton is dull.

[译文] 纤维的颜色从淡黄色到纯白色不等,可能非常有光泽。然而,大多数棉花的色泽都是黯淡的。

[解析] 本句要注意"dull"的翻译,这里不是通常意义上的"枯燥乏味"之意。因为上一句出现了"lustrous"(有光泽的)一词,表转折的逻辑关联词"however"表明下一句中的 dull 与 lustrous 构成对比关系,所以应译为"色泽黯淡的"。本句充分说明了"语境决定词义"的道理。

7.

[原文] A cross-sectional view reveals that the fiber is kidney-shaped with central hollow core known as the lumen.

[译文] 横切面显示纤维呈肾脏形状,其中央空心结构称为管腔。

[解析] 本句中的"cross-sectional view"是一个术语,意为"横剖面视图"。而"central hollow core"则是"中央空心结构"的意思。"lumen"是解剖学术语,指"(管状器官内的)内腔",鉴于这里讲的是纤维,所以译为"管腔"。

8.

[原文] It is resistant to the acids, alkalies, and organic solvents normally available to consumers.

[译文] 它对家庭使用的酸、碱和有机溶剂都具有抵抗力。

[解析] 本句中的"normally available to consumers"如果直译为"消费者通常可获取的"也可表达相关意思,但是比较别扭,其实可以意译为"家庭使用的"。

9.

[原文] Cottons will retain their whiteness longer when line-dried or dried in the electric dryer.

[译文] 棉花在自然晾干或用电干机烘干后,其白度会保持得更久。

[解析] 这里的"line-dried"指挂在绳子上自然晾干,"longer"指时间上更长。

10.

[原文] Fabrics woven from cotton can be open enough to provide good air permeability for comfort.

[译文] 棉织物的结构足够稀松，从而能够提供良好的透气性，保证了居住在帐篷里的舒适度。

[解析] 本句中的"open"指织物结构的稀疏；"for comfort"需要进行增补翻译，根据句意扩充译为"保证了帐篷居住的舒适度"。

Passage B 时装与世界同步

Warming-up

Work on the following terms and put them into English：

热衷
小兜肚
柏林国际电影节
松糕鞋
大卖
时装化
《花样年华》
神韵
华服热
中式对襟袄

也正是从20世纪90年代开始，国外的著名时装品牌纷纷瞄准了中国的消费市场，在北京、上海、深圳、广州等大城市开设专卖店，中国本土的时装品牌和时装模特也逐渐引起了人们的兴趣。而随着1988年中国第一本引进国外版权的时装杂志的诞生，越来越多的报纸、杂志、广播、电视、网络等媒体进入到时尚传播领域，世界最新的流行信息可以在最短的时间内传到中国来，来自法国、意大利、英国、日本、韩国的时装、发式、彩妆潮流直接影响着中国的流行风，"时尚"所代表的生活方式和着装风格已被越来越多的中国人所接受和追逐。

在世纪之交的几年间，中国的时装潮流顺应国际趋势，着装风格趋向严谨，特别是白领阶层女性格外注重职业女性风采，力求庄重大方。所谓"原始的野性"，如草帽不镶边、裤脚撕开线等，不再那么受青睐；祖露风开始在一些阶层、一些场合有所收敛，尽管超短裙依然流行，但为了在着装上尽力去表现女性的优雅仪态，很多年轻姑娘穿上了长及足踝的长裙。

与之相映成趣的是，一些时尚青年崇尚西方社会中的反传统意识，故意以荒诞装饰为时髦，如仿效美国电影《最后的莫西干人》的发型，两侧剃光，仅留中间一绺儿，染成彩色；穿"朋克装"——西方社会继嬉皮士以后，又一颓废派青年装，用发胶黏发成兽角状，黑皮夹克绣饰骷髅等；或将衣裤故意撕或烧出洞。于是，在衣服上艺术化"开窗"的做法，在1998年春夏之交时风行开来。这种孔可随意在衣服的任何一个部位挖，孔的边缘处理得非常精致。由于它不同于以半透明质料制成的透明装，因而被大家俗称为"透视装"。进而，整件衣服布满均匀网眼的服装出现了，这与巴黎时装舞台上的"渔网装"显然是同步的。

前几年，中国的大街小巷还流行过"泳装潮"。这里所说的泳装，当然不是商店里出售的用于水中运动的游泳衣，而是指姑娘们青睐的一种出行常服，因为短小性感得接近泳装而得名。想象一下，如果一个女孩上穿一件吊带露脐装，下穿一件仅及大腿根的短裙或短裤，脚蹬一双无后帮凉鞋，如果不是背着挎包，你大概会觉得她是在海边或游泳池旁，而不是在城市的大街上。

21世纪初，成年女性，包括少妇和大学生，仿佛要从服饰上寻回失去的童年似的，一下子热衷上了童装风格。头上娃娃发式，两侧发梢向脸颊勾起，头上还别着蝴蝶形或花卉形的粉红色、柠檬黄色发卡；着装忽而瘦小得可怜，忽而肥大得可爱；很多女孩子足蹬方口偏带娃娃鞋，肩上背着镶有小熊头图案的挎包；还有的大学生索性将奶嘴挂在胸前，一副长不大的样子。

2001年小兜肚一度盛行。柏林国际电影节颁奖仪式上，影星章子怡穿着特制的红兜肚时装，两臂间披了一条长长的红色披帛，看上去像是中国古代的仕女，引起时尚界的关注。此后，她又穿了一件不作任何修饰的菱形兜肚上装出现在MTV颁奖盛典上，于是很快，在各种场合、各类媒体上，一些明星和时尚女性纷纷穿起了各式兜肚。

21世纪初，时尚潮流还有一个体现在鞋上的变化。2002年，原来那种憨憨的松糕鞋已经失宠，出现了鞋头极尖并向上翘起的样式，就像查理·卓别林影片主角的鞋子，而且上面镶缀着亮晶晶的饰物。而一年之后，市面上又在大卖各式仿效芭蕾舞鞋风格的圆头鞋了。

20世纪末，国际时装界青睐起东方风格来，东方的典雅与恬静，东方的纯朴与神秘，开始成为全球性的时尚元素。随着中国在世界地位的提高，穿上华服已经成为海内外华人自豪的象征。中国内地的女性自然而然地穿起了中式袄，很多男人也以一袭中式棉袄为时尚。如今的华服，并不完全是纯正的中式袄褂，很多女式华服已经时装化——上身是一件印花或艳色棉布镶边立领袄，下身配牛仔裤和一双最新流行款式的皮鞋，既现代又复古。

2000年，香港电影《花样年华》在海内外上映，剧中的女主人公在幽暗的灯光下，不断变换着旗袍的颜色和款式（有二十几种之多）时，人们看到了东方美人的古典气质。剧中人穿着旗袍，美丽、优雅而略带忧伤，许多人第一次发现中国传统服装穿起来竟有如此神韵。借着电影的魔力，旗袍热再度升温。

也许没有人会想到，在中国举行的APEC会议——一次颇具影响力的国际性区域合作的经济和政治活动，掀起了新一轮华服热。2001年秋天的上海，当与会各国首脑身穿蓝缎、红缎、绿缎面料的中式罩衫亮相时，全世界都轰动了。国际媒体纷纷登载了元首们着华服的合影，并撰文作有关服装的评论。政治家们为华服做了一次最成功的广告，与其说中式对襟袄迷人，不如说是布什、普京等身着华服所带来的巨大效应，商场里就有顾客对着服装导购人员直言要买一件"普京穿的对襟袄"。而APEC引起华服热，还有一个潜在的基础就是中华民族在国际舞台上发挥着日益重要的影响力。华服热所表现的是中华民族不断增强的自信心和凝聚力。

20世纪业已证明是迄今为止最具时尚意识的世纪,高销售量的服装、配饰、化妆品市场与日益强大的传媒业的发展,使越来越多的人得以走近时装、欣赏时装、以时装为美。时装已构成了大众理解并乐于投资的一种生活方式。

(摘自《中国服饰》)

Notes

1.

[原文] 在世纪之交的几年间,中国的时装潮流顺应国际趋势,着装风格趋向严谨,特别是白领阶层女性格外注重职业女性风采,力求庄重大方。

[译文] In those years at the turn of century, fashion in China kept close pace with the world fashion. Following the international dressing fashion, dressing style tended to be more formal, especially white-collar women who paid particular attention to the charm of being a professional woman. They tried to wear formal and decent dresses.

[解析] 汉语喜欢使用流水句,英译文根据句意进行了断句。从"中国的时装潮流顺应国际趋势"这个小句中拆出两层意思,一是说"中国的时尚紧跟世界时尚的步伐"(fashion in China kept close pace with the world fashion);二是说"追寻国际着装潮流"(Following the international dressing fashion),从而成功断句。另外,"严谨"这个词译得很到位,因为其搭配的对象是"着装风格",所以译为"formal"(正式的)要远胜于汉英词典上常见的"rigorous; strict; precise"等词。"力求庄重大方"这个小句的译文也与前面的流水句断开,独立成一句。"庄重大方"原本是一个很抽象的描述,译文运用了具体化的翻译技巧,译为"They tried to wear formal and decent dresses."(她们倾向于穿正式、体面的女装)。

2.

[原文] 与之相映成趣的是,一些时尚青年崇尚西方社会中的反传统意识,故意以荒诞装饰为时髦,如仿效美国电影《最后的莫西干人》的发型,两侧剃光,仅留中间一绺儿,染成彩色;穿"朋克装"——西方社会继嬉皮士以后,又一颓废派青年装,用发胶黏发成兽角状,黑皮夹克绣饰骷髅等;或将衣裤故意撕或烧出洞。于是,在衣服上艺术化"开窗"的做法,在1998年春夏之交时风行开来。

[译文] Of course, some adolescent young boys and girls who advocated the anti-tradition consciousness of the western society considered the weird as fashionable on purpose, for example, imitating the hairstyle of *The Last of the Mohicans* to shave head on two sides and leave the middle section and dye hair. Some wore "punk dress" — another kind of decadent style youth dress in western society after hippies. They glued the hair into animal horn shape using hair gel and embroidered skeleton pattern on black leather jackets; or intentionally tore or burned holes on the clothes. These were not dominant in China fashion scene. But a very interesting fact was that "opening a window" in an artistic way on clothes became popular at the turn of spring and summer in 1998.

［解析］ 本例中，译者打乱了原文的叙述顺序，根据行文需要进行了句子重构。段首的"与之相映成趣的是"这个小句没有放在段首翻译，而是放在一个大长句之后，用以概括前文，意译为"These were not dominant in China fashion scene. But a very interesting fact was that…"（这些都不是中国时尚界的主流，但一个非常有趣的事实是……），表面上看似乎与原文不符，但仔细一想，之所以能"相映成趣"，不正是说明当时中西时尚主流截然不同吗？

3.

［原文］ 21世纪初，成年女性，包括少妇和大学生，仿佛要从服饰上寻回失去的童年似的，一下子热衷上了童装风格。

［译文］ At the beginning of 21st century, adult women including young ladies and university students fell over themselves for child style clothes and hairstyles as if they wanted to relive their childhood.

［解析］ 流水句是汉语的一个特点。流水句包含若干较短的小句，各小句之间没有关联词连接，如行云流水般，故名。汉译英时，遇到较长的流水句，需要厘清各部分之间的语义关系，拆解后译出，并添加必要的连接词，以体现各部分之间的逻辑关系。断句时，要注意把关系密切的部分安排在一起，可以根据英文习惯调节汉语短句在英文中出现的次序。英文各句的主语尽量一致。如几个小句归并为一句，还要按照各小句意思的重要程度，从高到低，依次用主句、从句、短语、单词来表达。具体到本句中，"成年女性，包括少妇和大学生"两个小句译成英文时，通过"including"一词合并为一个名词性分句作为译文的主语，然后再根据英文习惯，把与主语关系更密切的"一下子热衷上了童装风格"的译文出现的次序提前，最后再用"as if"（仿佛）把剩下的一个小句连接到主句之上。这样就可体现出英语叠床架屋、盘根错节的句法结构。另，"少妇"也可译为"young married women"，"热衷"译为"fall over oneself for"。

4.

［原文］ 柏林国际电影节颁奖仪式上，影星章子怡穿着特制的红兜肚时装，两臂间披了一条长长的红色披帛，看上去像是中国古代的仕女，引起时尚界的关注。

［译文］ In the awarding ceremony of Berlin International Film Festival, the movie star Zhang Ziyi attracted the attention of the fashion circle when she wore a specially made red belly cover, and draped a long piece of red silk around shoulder, which made her look like an ancient Chinese doll.

［解析］ 英语句子开门见山，其主谓结构是全句的"纲"，其余成分是"目"，一般先下结论，后叙事，重心落在句首。本句的主谓结构是"影星章子怡引起时尚界的关注"，这是全句的"纲"，是结论，所以在译文中需要先译出，而把章子怡的着装细节作为叙事部分放在后半部分翻译。另注意"仕女"的翻译，汉英词典上一般译为"traditional Chinese painting of beautiful women"（国画的一种，以美女为题材），而参考译文中用了"doll"一词，通常意为"玩具娃娃"，但根据牛津词典，该词亦有"俊妞；美人儿"的意思。

5.

［原文］ 2002年，原来那种憨憨的松糕鞋已经失宠，出现了鞋头极尖并向上翘起的

样式，就像查理·卓别林影片主角的鞋子，而且上面镶缀着亮晶晶的饰物。

［译文］ In 2002, those cute "sponge cake" shoes were no longer popular while shoes with sharp turning up tips (like Charlie Chaplin style shoes) and decorated with shining adornments appeared.

［解析］ 本句中的"憨憨的"，如果是形容人，则可译为"simple-minded"（头脑简单的），但这里搭配的是"松糕鞋"，所以翻译为"cute"（可爱的）。"查理·卓别林影片主角的鞋子"这个短语中，因为卓别林影片主角就是他本人，所以简译为"Charlie Chaplin style shoes"（查理·卓别林风格的鞋子）。另，松糕鞋是一种新形式的高跟鞋，世界各国非常流行这种新式高跟鞋。爱美的年轻女士们穿上这种鞋底像发糕一样厚的鞋，感觉颇为良好。但是英国和日本的研究机构调查发现，由于松糕鞋鞋底材质的关系，穿这种鞋的女士容易受伤，因此英国和日本把"松糕鞋"和其他高跟鞋一并称作"死亡之鞋"。

6.

［原文］ 而一年之后，市面上又在大卖各式仿效芭蕾舞鞋风格的圆头鞋了。

［译文］ One year after, round tip style shoes that imitated the toe shoes were the rage in the market.

［解析］ 此句应注意"大卖"的翻译，"大卖"实际上是"卖得很好"的意思，换言之，也就是在市场上很受欢迎，所以译文采用了"be the rage"（风靡一时；极为流行之物；风行一时）这一习语。"芭蕾舞鞋"的英文是"toe shoes"（足尖鞋），因为芭蕾舞演员表演时是用足尖走路的，所以其所穿之鞋也被称为"足尖鞋"。

7.

［原文］ 随着中国在世界地位的提高，穿上华服已经成为海内外华人自豪的象征。中国内地的女性自然而然地穿起了中式袄，很多男人也以一袭中式棉袄为时尚。

［译文］ With the rising of China's position in the world, overseas Chinese started to feel proud to wear Chinese costumes, women in China's mainland naturally put on Chinese jackets and many Chinese men consider Chinese cotton jackets as fashionable.

［解析］ 汉语有些句子比较简练，而英语的句子一般容量很大，因此汉译英时，往往有必要将两个或两个以上的汉语句子合译成一个英语句子。含有隐性因果关系的句子往往要合译。本例中"随着中国在世界地位的提高"与后文3个分句构成隐性因果关系，所以合译为宜，以"With the rising of China's position in the world"作为伴随状语，后面跟上3个独立的句子，并以一个"and"连接，表示结果。另外，"中国内地"或"中国大陆"应当译为"the mainland of China" "the Chinese mainland"或"China's mainland"，有时也可简译为"the mainland"，但绝不可翻译成西方媒体所惯用的"mainland China"，因为后者的意思是大陆中国，其言外之意就是还有一个"台湾中国"，从本质上讲，也就是"两个中国"，这是绝对错误的。

8.

［原文］ 如今的华服，并不完全是纯正的中式袄裤，很多女式华服已经时装化——上身是一件印花或艳色棉布镶边立领袄，下身配牛仔裤和一双最新流行款式的皮鞋，既现代又复古。

[译文] Chinese dresses of nowadays are not like those classical traditional Chinese coats or jackets. Many female Chinese costumes adopted the fashionable elements. The costume arrangement looks rather interesting when girls put on print or flamboyant cotton cloth coats with edgings and stand collar, jeans and leather shoes in the latest fashion.

[解析] 汉语是一种"语义型"语言，其句子在很大程度上表现为一种以意合法为主要手段的意念流，断句很不严格。英译时往往要对原文进行断句处理，使译文语义更加清晰。本句中文在英译文中根据语义被断为3句。另要注意"时装化"的翻译，并非所有的"……化"都对译为英文的"-ize/-ization"。有时需要根据具体语境灵活处理，比如此处的"时装化"就意译成了"adopt the fashionable elements"。"既现代又复古"没有机械地译为"both modern and returning to the ancients"，而是用了"interesting"（有趣的）一以概之，这也可算是灵活翻译的一个典型例子。

9.
[原文] 2000年，香港电影《花样年华》在海内外上映，剧中的女主人公在幽暗的灯光下，不断变换着旗袍的颜色和款式（有二十几种之多）时，人们看到了东方美人的古典气质。

[译文] In 2000, Hong Kong movie *In the Mood for Love* was played at home and abroad. The actress in the movie changed cheongsams of different colors and styles (more than 20) under the dark lights. Audiences were amazed by the classical charm of the oriental beauty.

[解析] 本句在译文中根据语义被断为3句。曾被评为21世纪最伟大电影之一的《花样年华》，英文片名 *In the Mood for Love* 出自20世纪30年代的经典英文歌曲 *I am in the mood for love*（我已坠入情网）。这是一首充满着怀旧味道的老歌，不但与电影的情节及调性契合，也完美复刻了男女主人公间的情愫和剧情走向。

10.
[原文] 而APEC引起华服热，还有一个潜在的基础就是中华民族在国际舞台上发挥着日益重要的影响力。华服热所表现的是中华民族不断增强的自信心和凝聚力。

[译文] Another background behind this trend is the more and more important influence that China has on the world stage. The Chinese dress rage also signifies the constantly increasing confidence and cohesion of the Chinese nation.

[解析] 重复是常用的修辞手段之一。英语和汉语都有重复，但重复在汉语中的使用频率远远高于英语，这归因于中西方不同的思维方式：中国人为环形思维方式，而西方人为线性思维方式。汉语喜欢重复，在语言使用中有意运用相同、相似或相对的词语或表达方式，给听话人或读者留下深刻印象；英语中虽然也使用重复，但其指导思想是尽量避免重复，常用替代或省略等表达方法。汉译英时，如果照搬汉语中的重复现象，英语译文就会显得累赘冗长，不合乎英语的表达习惯。因此，汉译英时，应根据具体情况，进行适当变通处理。"华服热"这个词在本例中第一次出现时，为了避免与前文出现的译文"Chinese dress fashion"重复，运用了其上位词"the trend"来指代"华服热"。而第二次出现"华服热"时，则换用了另一个平行表达"the Chinese dress rage"来避免重复。

Translation Skills（Ⅲ） Change of Parts of Speech（词类转换）

由于英语和汉语分属不同语系，两者语法方面差异较大，遣词造句及表达思想的方式也有所差异。英语和汉语在词类方面虽有许多相似之处，但也有不少区别，如英语中有分词、冠词、动词不定式、动名词等，而汉语没有这类词。英语中名词用得比汉语多，许多情况下，英语均用名词表示动作概念，因而译成汉语时必须作相应的转换，这样，译文才能够在"忠实"于原文的同时，也符合汉语的表达习惯。

（一）名词的转换

1. 名词转译成动词
英汉两种语言相比，英语多用名词，而汉语则多用动词。
（1）由动词派生的名词转译成动词，如：
This is a sensual marriage of fabrics and ought to be worn next to the skin.
译：各种面料完美地结合在一起，使得它可以贴身穿着。
They ceased to be merely utilitarian in function, and were exploited, to a striking degree, to indicate class distinction and sex attraction.
译：服装已不仅仅体现为功能上的实用性，而是进一步惊人地用来区别阶层和吸引异性。
（2）具有动作意味的名词转译成动词，如：
This was a short undershirt, about hip length.
译：这是一件短汗衫，长及臀部。
As the fashion-week drew to a close, the models were exhausted.
译：时装周快结束时，模特们彻底累垮了。

2. 名词转译成形容词
（1）形容词派生的名词常常转译成形容词，如：
Ten years ago this dress was considered the last word in elegance.
译：十年前这种连衣裙还算是最高雅的款式呢。
In their own way, the fluted, attenuated lines of her long dresses suggested simplicity.
译：她长裙上有沟槽的细小线条以其独特的方式呈现出一种简约的风格。
（2）有些名词加不定冠词作表语时，如：
The fashion show was a success.
译：这场时装秀很成功。
Hardworking is an absolute necessity to be a fashion designer.
译：想要成为服装设计师，辛勤工作是绝对必需的。
（3）of 加有些名词作表语时，如：
In almost every silhouette, there was a juxtaposition of something grand with something street.
译：几乎每一个服装廓型，既有华丽的元素，也有街头的元素。
Inspiration is of great importance when the designer is working.

译：对于服装设计师而言，灵感是非常重要的。

3. 名词转译成副词

The new mayor earned some appreciation by the courtesy of coming to visit the city poor.

译：新市长有礼貌地前来慰问城市贫民，获得了他们的一些好感。

The designer find difficulty in finding a new fabric to match his fall/winter collection.

译：设计师发现难以找到秋冬发布会上要用的新型面料。

(二) 形容词的转换

1. 形容词转译成动词

英语中表示知觉、欲望等心理状态的形容词在系动词后作表语时，常常转译为动词，此类形容词常见的有：able, angry, afraid, anxious, aware, ashamed, cautious, careful, certain, concerned, confident, doubtful, ignorant, glad, delighted, grateful, thankful 等。例如：

This jacket is reversible, very practical.

译：这件夹克可以两面穿，非常实用。

2. 形容词转译成名词

(1) 英语中有些形容词加上定冠词表示某一类人，汉译时常常转译成名词，如：

the old, the weak, the ill, the disabled, the young 老、弱、病、残、幼

the rich, the poor 富人、穷人

(2) 在英语句子中起表语作用的形容词，有时可转译成名词，如：

The fabric may be fluid, plastic, elastic, ductile or malleable.

译：这种面料具有流动性、可塑性、弹性、延展性或韧性。

Tyra Banks as a supermodel was talented and elegant.

译：超模泰拉·班克斯天资卓越、举止优雅。

3. 形容词转译成副词

(1) 英语名词译成汉语动词时，修饰该名词的形容词往往就相应地转译成汉语的副词。如：

Models took brief, restless naps on cab, struggled to save energy for the next show.

译：模特们不安地在出租车上打了几个小盹儿，为下一场走秀积蓄精力。

(2) 当英语的名词转译为汉语的形容词时，原来修饰名词的英语形容词就相应地转译为汉语的副词，这类常用的形容词有 sheer, clear, right, absolute, close 等，如：

Designer inspired handbags are legitimate handbags that may have a remarkable resemblance to designer handbags but lack branding and in the majority of cases are not true mirror images.

译：仿大牌的包包也是合法的，它们与名牌包外观极为相似，只是没有商标，而且大多并非完全相似。

(三) 副词的转换

1. 副词转译成动词

在英语句子中可以做表语和状语的副词，常常可以转译成动词，如：

The Shipper, Consignee and the Holder of this Bill of Lading hereby expressly accept and agree to all printed, written or stamped provisions, exceptions and conditions of this Bill of Lading, including those on the back hereof.

译：托运人、收货人和本提单的持有人明白地表示接受并同意本提单和它背面所记载的一切印刷、书写或戳印的规定、免责事项和条件。

As the model ran out in a hurry, he forgot to have his shoes on.

译：那个模特匆忙跑出去时，忘记了穿鞋。

2. 副词转译成形容词

（1）英语动词译成汉语名词时，修饰该动词的副词往往转译成形容词，如：

The designer had prepared carefully for his show.

译：设计师为这次时装秀做了细致的准备。

Marc Jacobs's new work impressed the journalists deeply.

译：马克·雅可布新一季的作品给记者们留下了深刻的印象。

（2）副词转译成名词，如：

Yves Saint Laurent in his old age is physically weak but mentally sound.

译：伊夫·圣·洛朗在他年老时身体虽弱，但精神矍铄。

（四）动词的转换

为了使译文更符合汉语的表达习惯，常常将英文句子中的动词转译为名词或副词。

1. 动词转译为名词

英语中很多由名词派生的动词，以及由名词转化而来的动词，在汉语中往往不易找到相应的动词，这时可将其转译成汉语名词。

（1）名词派生的动词，如：

The beautiful Qipao characterized its Chinese traditional motifs.

译：这件漂亮的旗袍有一个特点，就是中国传统图案的运用。

Hippies symbolizes their 1960s, an age of long hair, colorful flowery dresses.

译：嬉皮士成了20世纪60年代的象征，他们留着长发，穿着绚丽多彩的服装。

（2）名词转译而来的动词，如：

This evening suit is designed for Lady Gaga's requirement.

译：此晚礼服的设计，是根据Lady Gaga的要求进行的。

She stood in front of the window with white pajamas, silhouetted against the dawn sky.

译：她穿着雪白的睡衣站在窗前，晨空衬托出她的轮廓。

2. 动词转译为副词

（1）有时英语动词还可转译为汉语的副词，如：

It tends to be difficult to keep a good connection between stencil frames when these vertical stripes are printed by screen printing.

译：用丝网印花来印制这类直条纹样，在接版时往往有困难。

If you go to the beach wearing the black T-shirt, definitely you will get hotter.

译：如果你穿这件黑色T恤去海滩游玩，你必定会越来越热。

（2）在不及物动词前面增加副词。根据英语原文的上下文，有些动词在一定场合可增加适当的副词，才能确切表达意思，如：

The crowds dressed up for the Easter parade melted away.

译：为参加复活节游行精心打扮一番的人群渐渐散开了。

The fashion show has started, but his words poured out.

译：服装秀已经开始了，但是他还滔滔不绝地讲个没完。

（五）介词的转换

1. 介词转译为动词

英语中有许多含有动作意味的介词，如 across，past，toward，over，into 等，汉译时往往可以译成动词，如：

"Coming!" Away she skimmed over the square, up the path, up the steps, and into the fashion house.

译："来啦！"她转身蹦跳着跑了，越过广场，跑上小径，跨上台阶，进了时装店。

This piece does not need to depend on cut for draping.

译：这片布料不需要依赖剪裁来取得悬垂性。

2. 介词转译为连词

英语中有些介词汉译时可转译为汉语的连词。

Embroidery may be damaged beyond repair in a few seconds of carelessness.

译：由于疏忽大意，刺绣可在几秒钟之内被损坏到无法修复的程度。

With all its advantages, the accuracy of the new sewing method can't be blindly trusted.

译：新缝纫方法虽然有种种优点，但是我们不可盲目相信其准确性。

总之，词无定译，在具体的翻译实践中，应从实际出发，根据上下文的需要以及目的语的表达习惯入手进行词类转译，切不可盲目乱译。

Translation Workshop

Ⅰ. **Translate the following sentences and pay attention to transposition**

1. Additives are used to stabilize yarns against ultraviolet radiation.

2. Many times a designer is asked to incorporate parts of a good body into a similarly styled garment or version of the original.

3. Most designer work within the narrow constraints of the category that has been assigned to the manufacturer by the stores to which that firm has successfully sold.

4. The improvement of the luster of cotton fibers is one of the purposes of mercerization.

5. The basis of this report is his 3-year scientific investigation.

6. 只要稍加修理，这台纺机就可再用。

7. 与会代表一致表示坚决支持进一步发展纺织科技。

8. 不过，这种复合材料目前还不能进行商业性生产。

9. 在20年间，我们坐视原料价格下跌。

10. 只有研究这些材料的特性才能更好地利用它们。

Ⅱ. Translate the following passage into English

牛仔装也是从20世纪70年代末传入中国的，穿着者的队伍不断壮大，从时髦青年扩大到各阶层和各年龄段。进入20世纪90年代后，不仅品种逐年发展到短裙、短裤、背心、夹克、帽子、挎包、背包等，颜色也不再限于蓝色，还出现了水洗薄面料等新质料。20世纪80年代初流行蝙蝠衫，这是一种两袖张开时仿佛蝙蝠翅膀的样式。蝙蝠衫领型多样，袖与身为连片，下摆紧瘦，后来演变成蝙蝠式外套、蝙蝠式大衣和夹克等。有趣的是，这种款式在2004年的春夏流行趋势中竟以"复古"的面貌重新出现。

到了20世纪80年代中期，时装的款式越来越多，流行周期越来越短，时装的款式、面料不断推陈出新。上衣有各种T恤衫、拼色夹克、花格衬衣、针织衫，而穿西装、扎领带已开始成为郑重场合的着装，且为大多数"白领阶层"所接受。下装如直筒裤、弹力裤、萝卜裤、裙裤、七分裤、裤裙、百褶裙、八片裙、西服裙、旗袍裙、太阳裙等，也时时变化。20世纪60年代在西方诞生的"迷你裙"在20世纪80年代再度风行时，中国已与世界潮流同步而行了。

（摘自《中国服饰》）

Ⅲ. Translate the following passage into Chinese

No reason exists for feeling that one's body is forbidden topic. What might make it seem so are the associations of fear it has come to carry. After all, it is only in very recent times that the body, after being assiduously concealed for hundreds of years, has been revealed. This process, once begun, seems almost to be escalating. The increasing manifestation of the body has caused a measure of surprise, and the phenomenon is still regarded with deep suspicion.

It must, nevertheless, be acknowledged that we relate many of our concepts of nature to the human body. We refer, for example, to "the foot" of a mountain and "the neck" of a river isthmus, and we say that a tree "stands". Michelangelo extended this parallel when he stated, "The man who cannot master the human body, and particularly its anatomy, will never understand the meaning of architecture."

All our ideas of proportion are related to the body. Our movements arise out of our sight and our instinctive muscular reactions. Whether we are sleeping or walking, our feeling for rhythms is closely connected with our regular heartbeats and the rise and fall of our breathing.

Clothes assume significance only when they are on the body. When they are hung up in a wardrobe, they look pathetically helpless; they seem to be voicelessly denouncing the cruelty of the tailor who forced them into their state of sad dependence. To really understand clothes, it is necessary first to see the reasoning behind them and then to see them, as it were, in action. Clothes are more than just products of a textile factory or exhibits in a museum; they are artefacts, used by people in all activities of daily life—standing, sitting, dancing, working or dying. Their true significance only becomes apparent when we consider how they are related and adapted to the body. So many different human types exist: thin people, fat people, people with large heads, pin-headed people. But human nature being perverse, styles do not always echo the body framework. If the body does not suit a certain style of dress then it is the clothes and not the body which should be modified.

（摘自《服装英语》）

Unit 4　Biotechnology and Wine-Liquor Culture

Passage A　The Influence of Raw Materials on Sensory Character

Warming-up

Work on the following terms and put them into Chinese:

congener　　　　　　　　　　＿＿＿＿＿＿＿＿＿＿
sensory attributes/character　＿＿＿＿＿＿＿＿＿＿
cereal mash　　　　　　　　　＿＿＿＿＿＿＿＿＿＿
gelatinize　　　　　　　　　　＿＿＿＿＿＿＿＿＿＿
kilning stage　　　　　　　　＿＿＿＿＿＿＿＿＿＿
Maillard reaction　　　　　　＿＿＿＿＿＿＿＿＿＿
inorganic constituent　　　　＿＿＿＿＿＿＿＿＿＿
secondary metabolite　　　　＿＿＿＿＿＿＿＿＿＿
yeast strain　　　　　　　　　＿＿＿＿＿＿＿＿＿＿
Saccharomyces cerevisiae　　＿＿＿＿＿＿＿＿＿＿

　　The sensory attributes of whiskies result from compounds that originate from raw materials, which are further modified by the methods used in production. In the whisky industry the compounds responsible for aroma, taste, mouth-feel and appearance are referred to as congeners. Each step in production influences congener levels and hence sensory character. The key stages involved in the production of whisky are outlined in Fig. 1. The starting point in the manufacture of any whisky is the production of a cereal mash. Malt whiskies must be produced using malted barley, though a wide range of different cereals can potentially be used for making other types of whiskies. Despite the choice available, certain cereals are favored by the industry. In addition to barley, these include corn (maize), rye and wheat (Miles and Richards, 2009). Cereals are largely unfermentable in their natural form so they must be converted into a fermentable substrate. This involves breaking down the structural components of the grain to release starch, then enzymatically converting the starch to sugar.

　　There are two ways in which this can be achieved. The first is to malt the cereal, a process of controlled germination

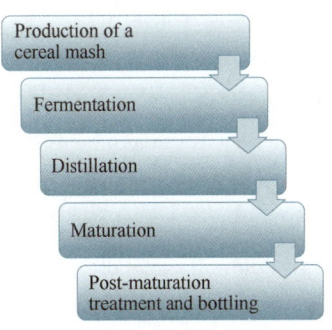

Fig. 1　The key stages in whisky manufacture

and enzyme development. Malting is followed by mashing, where hot water is added to the ground malt, gelatinizing the starch and making it accessible to enzymic degradation. An alternative to malting and mashing is to cook the cereal before adding a small amount of malt or commercial enzymes to provide the required breakdown.

There are a number of variables in the production of the cereal mash that can potentially influence the sensory character of the whisky. The first is the type of cereal. Using maize, for example, will give a spirit with heavy, more oily notes than wheat. Even different varieties of the same type of cereal may result in subtle flavor differences. Regardless of the method used to produce the mash, a heat treatment step will be required. If the cereals are malted, then the main heat input will be during the kilning (drying) stage; while the cooking process requires enough heat input to break down the grain and gelatinize the starch. In both cases the temperatures used are important as a number of flavor-forming reactions are heat-mediated.

One of the most important types of heat-induced reactions are the Maillard reactions, which occur between amino acids and sugars. These reactions can create a wide range of flavors, depending on the types of amino acids and sugars that react, though the main flavors produced tend to be cereal, burnt or toasted notes. High temperatures can denature enzymes and break down sugars resulting in reduced alcohol yields. Hence, a balance must be struck between yield and flavor development, with the former generally being of most interest to the whisky producer at this early stage in production.

The kilning step during malt production offers an opportunity to modify the flavor profile of the whisky. The malt can be smoked by introducing peat smoke into the kiln during the early stage of drying. Flavor-active compounds from the smoke adhere to the surface of the grain. These carry through the production process, giving distinctive smoky, medicinal aromas to the whisky. Peated malts have typically been used in the production of some Scotch and Japanese whiskies, though other countries are now experimenting with the smoking of malt using peat and other materials. Finally, the production of a cereal mash requires the addition of water. Water composition can vary in terms of both organic and inorganic constituents, depending on where the water has been sourced from and the type of supply. Differences in water composition can influence yeast growth and metabolism during fermentation, which has been demonstrated to have a detectable, though subtle, impact on flavor.

The cereal mash is then fermented. Yeast converts the sugars into ethanol giving a "wash" or "beer" with an alcohol content of around 8% to 10% alcohol by volume (abv). During fermentation the yeast also produces a range of secondary metabolites, such as other alcohols, acids, esters, aldehydes, ketones and sulphur-containing compounds. These make an important contribution to sensory character as many of them are highly flavor active. Different yeast strains have slightly different metabolisms. Hence yeast choice can have an impact on flavor, though strain selection is generally based on the ability to give good alcohol yields. Today most whisky producers use commercial cultures of Saccharomyces cerevisiae, though in some cases inocula from previous fermentations or distillery strains mixed with spent brewer's yeast are used. Yeast is supplied in a variety of formats, namely dried, pressed and cream yeast. These different forms can have a subtle influence on the progress of fermentation and hence flavor. In addition, fermentation parameters, such as the capacity of the fermentation vessel, its construction material, the ambient temperature and the fermentation time, can also affect congener formation. Non-yeast microorganisms may also be present during fermentation. At low levels certain microorganisms, such as lactic acid bacteria, can contribute congeners that add to complexity, but high levels of contaminant microorganisms can result in reduced alcohol yields and potential formation of undesirable and atypical flavors.

(摘自 *Whiskies*: *Composition*, *Sensory Properties and Sensory Analysis*)

Notes

1.

[原文] The sensory attributes of whiskies result from compounds that originate from raw materials, which are further modified by the methods used in production.

[译文] 原料所含的化合物赋予了威士忌不同的风味，而酿造工艺会进一步影响其风味特点。

[解析] 本句是典型的英文嵌套句式，通过介词短语和定语从句把句子各部分串联起来。本句要翻得正确，先要理解定语从句修饰的对象；而要翻得达意，需要把"sensory attributes"和"modify"的意思进行灵活处理；要翻得顺畅，还需要调整句子结构。在翻译过程中，词是能独立运用的最小单位，也是思维活动中最活跃的语言单位，选词对英汉互译有重要意义，需要考虑文本特点、语境、情境、语域、文化、交际效果等因素。"sensory attributes"主要是指威士忌在气味、口感、色泽等方面带来的感官体验。此处没有按字面直译为"感官特性"，而是译为"风味"，更符合文本语境表述习惯。"modify"在英中字典或者在线翻译软件中，都倾向于译为"修饰""修改"，但无论是"修改风味"还是"修饰风味"都忽略了译文的可读性，且意义不明朗。在威士忌制作过程中，选料、发酵、蒸馏、烘烤、陈年等过程都会对威士忌最终的风味呈现产生微妙影响，故此处将 modify 译为"影响"，更符合目的语语义与表达习惯。此外考虑到中英文信息重心的不同，英文信息重心偏前，即主句在前，从句在后；汉语倾向于重心偏后，外围信息前置，主句后置。为使译文更通顺，符合汉语的表达习惯，译文还进行了语序调整。

2.

[原文] Malt whiskies must be produced using malted barley, though a wide range of different cereals can potentially be used for making other types of whiskies.

[译文] 尽管在酿造其他种类的威士忌时，可使用的谷物原料品种很多，但麦芽威士忌必须使用发芽大麦作为原料。

[解析] 本句的翻译，使用了词句调整技巧。英语与汉语的语序差异大，翻译时经常需要稍作调整。英语句子的逻辑顺序通常先主后从；结果在先，原因在后；结论在先，条件在后；事实在先，让步在后。汉语正好相反，先偏后正，先因后果，先假设后推论。所以本句在翻译时，将 though 引导的让步从句从英文中的后置语序移到了中文中的前置

位置，这样的译文语序更符合中文"让步在先，事实在后"的语言习惯。再举一例：She persisted in her work when she might take a good rest. 本文也是典型的英文让步从句，如果不改变语序，译成"她还是坚持工作，尽管可以好好休息一下"，有悖汉语常规，所以改成"尽管可以好好休息一下，但她还是坚持工作"。此外，该句中有关词语的翻译及其顺序也没有拘泥于原文，而是根据汉语的行文习惯进行了适当调整。

3.

［原文］ Despite the choice available, certain cereals are favored by the industry. In addition to barley, these include corn (maize), rye and wheat.

［译文］ 生产威士忌的原料颇多，业内喜用的谷物类原料除了大麦之外，还包括玉米、黑麦和小麦。

［解析］ 原文为两个独立的句子，考虑到行文的简洁度与汉语的表达习惯，此处的翻译采用了合译法，将两句合并成一句进行翻译，同时省去了表示转折意义的介词"despite"，避免与前一句表示转折意义的句子出现形式上的重复。

4.

［原文］ Malting is followed by mashing, where hot water is added to the ground malt, gelatinizing the starch and making it accessible to enzymic degradation.

［译文］ 发芽之后进行研磨，将热水注入研磨过的麦芽中使麦芽淀粉糊化，使其易于被酶分解。

［解析］ 本句主要涉及英文被动语态与汉语主动语态的转换问题。英语属形合性语言，讲求形式的完备与逻辑的清晰，主语发挥着开始与统领全句的作用；而汉语属意合性语言，通过词语本身及其语序来传达意义与逻辑，主语的作用不如英语，更加突出谓语的作用，常常出现很多无主语的句子。因此前半句中的两个被动语态形式在翻译后都变成了无主语的主动语态形式。该句中另一个要点是"accessible"一词的翻译，该词根据具体语境可以分别翻译成：可通达的、可接触的、可使用的、可理解的等。在词的处理上，译者需要在理解的同时"抓其意"，在译文产出阶段"译其神"。此处该词并没有刻板地译为"使其可以被酶分解"，而是考虑到前文语境中出现了"研磨过的麦芽"，再结合威士忌制作过程的知识，得知此处的"accessible"强调研磨后的麦芽与酶的接触面积更大了，所以更容易被酶分解，故译为"易于被酶分解"。语言的表达是多样性的，译者需要牢牢把握源语言的意义和目的语的可读性进行处理，切勿对照字典意义生搬硬套。请参考以下例子，进一步理解"accessible"的灵活处理：

Local governments in certain areas are still hard-pressed to make medical services accessible and affordable to the people.

译：医疗方面，特别是群众看病难、看病贵的问题，个别地方政府应对起来还是困难重重。

Mobile payment will be phased in by our overseas missions to make more consular services accessible at fingertips.

译：驻外使领馆逐步开通移动支付，提供更多"指尖上的领事服务"。

5.

［原文］ There are a number of variables in the production of the cereal mash that can potentially influence the sensory character of the whisky.

［译文］ 在制作麦芽汁的过程中，许多因素都可能影响威士忌的风味。

［解析］ 本句简短，处理起来并不难，笔者希望借此总结一下英语中特定句型"there be"句式的处理。"There be"是英文中的常用倒装句型，翻译成汉语时，主要处理成无主语的"有……"或者有主语的"有……"。例如：

There are two kinds of computer: digital and analog.

译：现在有两种计算机：数字计算机和模拟计算机。（无主语）

There are about ninety-two natural elements existing in our nature.

译：自然界有 92 种天然元素。（有主语）

实际上，"there be"结构表现形式多样，翻译形式也多样，还可考虑翻译成汉语的"主题—评论"行文结构。例如：

There is much confusion in current usage between the terms "electricity" and "electronics".

译：目前对于"电学"和"电子学"这两个术语的使用颇为混乱。

原句主题是"electricity"和"electronics"，评论语为"confusion"。译成汉语时，将英文"there be"评论—主题的结构进行了反向处理，从而迎合了汉语的行文习惯。在这一句型中，there 是引导词，根据语义需要，它后面还可跟 exist, happen, occur, appear, come, go, live, stand 等不及物动词作谓语，表示事物的存在、出现、发生或消失等意义，翻译方法类似。

6.

［原文］ The cereal mash is then fermented. Yeast converts the sugars into ethanol giving a "wash" or "beer" with an alcohol content of around 8% to 10% alcohol by volume (abv).

［译文］ 随后对麦芽汁进行发酵。酵母将糖分转化为乙醇，产生酒精含量为 8%~10%的发酵醪液（"wash"或"beer"，威士忌酿造相关术语，指发酵后待蒸馏的发酵酒醪）。

［解析］ 本句对于文中"wash"和"beer"这两个术语概念的翻译使用了"归化翻译+解释"的翻译策略。"wash"和"beer"是威士忌酿造的相关术语，指麦类经发酵后形成的低酒精度发酵酒醪，所以翻译时不能按常规意思去理解，而是要进行一些背景知识的查询后才能正确翻译。同一词在不同的行业领域中可有不同意义，甚至在同一领域的不同门类中意义也不相同。在科技文体中，许多常见词往往转为专业词汇或专业术语概念，翻译时要特别小心这种变化。我们以"work"为例：

在铁道建筑文体中"work occupation time"意思是"封闭线路工作时间"；在物理学文体中，"work"一般翻译为"功"或"做功"。例如：Pushing or pulling, however, does not necessarily mean doing work，意思是"然而，推或拉未必意味着做功"。

在本文这种情况下，"wash"或"beer"这两个词是句中的重点词。通过查询英汉食品词典后，了解这是威士忌专用术语。但是如果仅仅将其归化处理译成酒醪，并不能完全表达出原词的内涵，因为"wash"或"beer"指的是发酵完成即将进行下一阶段蒸馏的醪液，酒精含量有固定范围；而如果将原文直接译成"发酵后待蒸馏的含酒精醪液"，又显得译文略冗长。所以这里在翻译后又增加了对原文的解释，使得译文既保留了形式上的简洁，又实现了意义上的完整。此外，从文化角度出发，将"wash"或"beer"以原文形式写入译文并加以解释，也便于读者更好地了解英文中威士忌酿造的专业用语。

7.

［原文］ Today most whisky producers use commercial cultures of Saccharomyces cerevisiae, though in some cases inocula from previous fermentations or distillery strains mixed with spent brewer's yeast are used.

［译文］ 尽管有时企业会用自己之前发酵用过的酵母，或者混合使用一些废酵母，但现在大多数威士忌企业都是使用商用酵母。

［解析］ 英语属于树状结构型语言，核心词后面往往有较长的后位成分来修饰，如后置状语、后置定语等。英译中时，为了顺应中文的自然语序，时常需要把后置成分提前表述。在本句中，"inocula from previous fermentations" 是介词短语做后置定语，但翻译成汉语时需要处理为前置定语——"之前发酵用过的"，而在 "distillery strains mixed with spent brewer's yeast" 中，后置的过去分词短语 "mixed with spent brewer's yeast" 在翻译成中文时同样可作前置处理，译为"混有废酵母的"，此处结合上下文语境进行了整合，最后译为"混合使用一些废酵母"。"Spent" 在此处的意思是 "used"，结合啤酒酿造工艺可知，酿啤酒时，先要制取酒的原料小麦汁，之后再加入酵母菌及啤酒花等添加物进行低温发酵。发酵之后，酵母菌便功成身退，沉淀于啤酒桶槽中，称为"废弃酵母泥"。不过，此时的酵母泥中含有大量仍具有活性的酵母，可以循环利用。此处的 "spent brewer's yeast（废酵母）" 即表示这种可循环利用的酵母。

Passage B 国酒茅台

Warming-up

Work on the following terms and put them into English：

贵州茅台　　　　　　　　　　_____
酱香型白酒　　　　　　　　　_____
宫廷贡酒　　　　　　　　　　_____
评酒会　　　　　　　　　　　_____
活性微生物　　　　　　　　　_____
制曲　　　　　　　　　　　　_____
固态发酵　　　　　　　　　　_____
勾兑　　　　　　　　　　　　_____
基酒　　　　　　　　　　　　_____
风味物质　　　　　　　　　　_____

一、茅台酒发展历史背景

贵州茅台酒作为我国用粮食酿造的大曲酱香型白酒的鼻祖和典型代表，历史久远而神秘。据传，远古大禹时赤水河沿岸茅台镇的土著居民就已擅长酿酒。

据史料考证，茅台酒起源于公元前135年的西汉时期。当时茅台镇一带就盛产"枸酱酒"，即今天茅台酒的前身。据史料记载，汉武帝饮"枸酱酒"后赞其"甘美之"。从此以后，枸酱酒（茅台酒）就一直为酒中佳酿，成为历代宫廷贡酒。宋元明清时期，茅台酒一直朝贡帝王；1949年之后，更是荣尊国酿。可以说，茅台酒的发展一直与中华民族的发展紧密相连。

1915年，在美国旧金山巴拿马万国博览会上，茅台酒荣获博览会金奖，与苏格兰威士忌、法国科涅克白兰地并列世界三大蒸馏名酒，成为中国民族工商业率先走向世界的代表。

1951年国营茅台酒厂正式成立。酒厂发展迅速，先后十多次在国内外荣获各项大奖，并且相继在各届名酒评酒会上被评为中国老牌四大、八大、十三大、十七大名酒之冠，成为中国酱香型酒典范，被誉为国酒、国礼酒和外交酒。

茅台酒从历史久远的原始小作坊发展到今天的国家特大型企业，与其独特的生产工艺、稳定上乘的质量、独具风格的特点、品牌文化和酿酒生态环境分不开。

二、茅台酒酿造生态环境

茅台酒产于贵州高原西北部的仁怀市茅台镇赤水河东岸的茅台酒厂。厂区群山环峙，依山傍水，气候宜人，海拔450m。该地区气候夏长冬短，空气湿度较大，少见霜雪，年平均气温18℃，最低气温3℃、最高气温40℃，年平均相对湿度78%左右，年平均风速1.2m/s。这种特殊的自然因素形成了酿造茅台酒独特的生态环境。

茅台酒的独特性与茅台镇特殊的气候、水等环境条件密不可分，从而决定了茅台酒是不能易地生产的。茅台镇具有得天独厚的自然条件。一位外交家参观茅台酒厂后说："生产茅台酒比生产原子弹还要困难，因为茅台酒只能在茅台镇这个地方生产，原子弹世界各地都可生产。"

茅台酒的生产集聚了神秘的天、神秘的地、神秘的人。神秘的天是指茅台酒厂的上空活跃着大量活性微生物，茅台酒就是靠这些微生物酿造的；神秘的地是指茅台酒厂所在地有独特的红土地，还包括酿酒用的赤水河河水、当地得天独厚的气候，这些都最适合酿酒；神秘的人是指茅台人在长期酿酒实践中总结归纳，提炼出了非常科学的工艺。所以茅台酒是天、地、人的神秘结合，这种神秘结合酿出了世界上神秘独特的茅台酒。这是其他任何地方无法仿制的，这就是世界白酒行业的奇迹。

三、茅台酒生产原料

茅台酒生产采用茅台本地或周边地区生产的红缨子糯高粱。高粱种植过程中采用纯天然的农家肥，不使用化学肥料和杀虫剂。本地种植的高粱具有皮厚、粒小、胚芽所占比例大、支链淀粉含量高的特点，其吸水量低、耐蒸煮、不易糊化，满足了茅台酒独特生产工艺的原材料要求。淀粉含量大于60%，支链淀粉含量大于88%。

制曲原料采用茅台本地或周边地区生产的小麦。其呈淡黄色、粒端不带褐色，颗粒坚实、饱满、均匀、皮薄、无虫蛀、无霉变、夹杂物甚少，淀粉含量大于60%。

茅台酒采用赤水河水源水作为酿造用水，其水质优良、清洁、无色透明、无沉淀、含杂质少、无异味、水温较低，pH为6.5~7.5。

四、茅台酒生产工艺

茅台酒的生产周期主要包括发酵和蒸馏工艺，约持续 1 年，涉及几个典型的中国白酒酿造工艺，其中堆积发酵、制曲与蒸馏环节都需要比其他中国白酒酿造时更高的温度。例如，生产曲的最高纪录温度可达 67℃。

茅台酒的生产主要由制曲、制酒、勾兑和包装 4 大工艺组成。产品基酒分轮次、典型体、酒精度装入酒缸后放入酒窖进行较长时间的封存储藏，以便后续勾兑。勾兑后储存半年进行装瓶与包装，随后出厂销售。

五、茅台酒中的风味物质

茅台酒在制曲、制酒过程中充分利用了茅台镇独特的生态条件，充分发挥了生态优势。高温制曲、高温堆积发酵、高温厌氧发酵等酿酒环境长期对酿酒微生物进行驯化，各种活性微生物经过遗传、变异、衍化等微生物群落的演替，促成了茅台酒厂区环境中耐高温、耐高酸、耐高酒度等极端微生物的富集。

在茅台酒酿造过程中，各极端微生物代谢产生了多种耐热、耐酸等具有稳定性的酶。这些极端微生物与酶在生产过程产生大量的酒体风味物质。后者随各工艺、工序的进行不断进入茅台基础酒的酒体中，赋予了茅台酒独特的风格和完美的品质。这些都是茅台酒独特的酿造生态环境所赋予茅台酒区别于其他白酒的独特风味特征，这也是茅台酒同其他白酒相比的市场核心竞争力。

（摘自《酿酒科技》2006 年第 10 期刊载文章《剖读茅台酒的微量成分》）

Notes

1.

［原文］ 贵州茅台酒作为我国用粮食酿造的大曲酱香型白酒的鼻祖和典型代表，历史久远而神秘。

［译文］ Kweichow Moutai, the first typical Chinese sauce aroma *baijiu* made from grains and *daqu*（also shortened as *qu*, a leavening agent that forms the starting point for liquor production）, has a long history and a mysterious origin.

［解析］ 原文包含的信息量大，对于不熟悉酿酒专业知识的人来说，"大曲酱香型白酒"的概念颇具挑战性。首先，"茅台酒"的翻译全文是"Kweichow Moutai（贵州茅台）"，简称为"Moutai"，但二者都不是简单地搬用汉语拼音音译为"Maotai"，而是采用威妥玛式拼音（Wade-Giles Romanization）或邮政式拼音（Postal Spelling System）的音译法译为"Moutai"。其次是"白酒"的翻译。"中国白酒"很长时间以来一直缺乏一个官方的、准确的英文名称，如"Chinese spirits（中国白酒）""Chinese distilled spirits（中国蒸馏酒）""Chinese liquor（中国烈酒）"等都称为"中国白酒"。2021 年，新修订的国家标准《白酒工业术语》（*Terminology of Baijiu Industry*）正式出台，对"白酒"的英文名称也同步进行了修订：*Baijiu*。同时，白酒学术界与商业界通过国际期刊和会议，以及白酒展览会、展销会与品酒鉴酒会等载体对此进行广泛宣传，白酒的规范英文译文（Chinese *Baijiu*）逐渐被国内外行业专家及消费者所认知。中国酒业协会于 2020 年 4 月 25

日向海关总署提出申请，建议将海关商品名录中中国白酒的英文名字由原来的"Chinese distilled spirits"更改为"Chinese *Baijiu*"。海关总署在充分听取协会的意见之后，同意在 2021 年的《中华人民共和国进出口税则》中进行修改，新的税则从 2021 年 1 月 1 日起正式执行，从此"中国白酒"就可以直接译为"Chinese *Baijiu*"。接着，是"酱香型白酒"的翻译。酱香型也称茅香型，以茅台酒为代表，属大曲酒类，其酱香突出，幽雅细致，酒体醇厚，回味悠长，清澈透明，色泽微黄。学界与业界一般根据其意义所指译为"sauce aroma *baijiu*"或"sauce aroma type *baijiu*"。而后，是"大曲"的翻译。"大曲"，又名"酒曲"或"曲"，是用来酿酒的一种原料，通常以大麦、小麦、豌豆等为原料，经过粉碎，加水混捏，压成曲醅，形似砖块，大小不等，让自然界各种微生物在上面生长而制成。大曲一般用于蒸馏酒的酿造，用大曲酿造的酒就称之为大曲酒（有时直接简称为大曲）。因此，此处在翻译的时候与前面的内容进行了合译"made from grains and *daqu*"，以表明大曲也是酿造茅台酒的一种原料。而"大曲"本身作为中国酿酒独有的一种原料则直译为"*daqu*"，同时为便于读者了解其属性与功用，减轻认知负荷，增译了部分解释性信息"also shortened as *qu*, a leavening agent that forms the starting point for liquor production"。最后，是汉语中的并列结构"鼻祖和典型代表"的翻译。由于英汉语言在词汇、结构与句法上的差异，翻译时进行了灵活处理，译为"the first typical"之类的修饰结构，而非僵硬地译为"the earliest ancestor and typical representative"之类的表述。

2.

［原文］ 据史料考证，茅台酒起源于公元前 135 年的西汉时期。

［译文］ According to historical sources, Moutai was first developed in 135 BC during the Western Han Dynasty (206 BC-AD 25).

［解析］ 汉语原文中出现了"西汉时期"这样的历史文化概念，而且在原文同一段中还出现了很多类似的文化词汇与概念，如"汉武帝、宋元明清"等，对于不太了解中国历史、中国古代人物的外国人来说可能存在理解上的文化障碍。因此，在翻译时都适当增补了历史时期与历史人物的公元纪年时间信息，分别译为"the Western Han Dynasty (206 BC-AD 25)""Emperor Wu (156-87 BC) of the Han Dynasty (206 BC-AD 220)""the Song (960-1279), Yuan (1206-1368), Ming (1368-1644) and Qing (1616-1911) Dynasties"，让国外受众读到的不是干巴巴的文化历史概念或陌生的人物名字，而是可以具体感受的时间节点或历史人物，同时也从另一个侧面表明了中国酿酒历史的悠久与辉煌，对外宣传了我国灿烂的历史文化。

3.

［原文］ 1915 年，在美国旧金山举办的巴拿马万国博览会上，茅台酒荣获博览会金奖，与苏格兰威士忌、法国科涅克白兰地并列世界三大蒸馏名酒，成为中国民族工商业率先走向世界的代表。

［译文］ At the Panama Pacific International Exposition in 1915 held in San Francisco of America, it won a gold medal, achieving the same international status as the other two distilled liquor brands—Scottish Whisky and French Cognac, making it a pioneer to go international as a representative of Chinese national industry and commerce.

［解析］ 本句翻译主要涉及专有名词的回译问题。比如原文提到的 1915 年的"巴拿

马万国博览会",即首届巴拿马太平洋万国博览会,简称"巴拿马万国博览会",主要是为了庆祝巴拿马运河被开凿通航而举办的一次盛大的庆典活动,会址设在美国旧金山市,也叫"1915 年巴拿马太平洋国际博览会",这就是其英文"the 1915 Panama Pacific International Exposition"的来源,翻译时译者应该了解该博览会的历史,进行准确回译。而原文中的另外两个专有名词,即"苏格兰威士忌"与"法国科涅克白兰地",也应遵循"名随主人"的原则进行准确回译。

4.

[原文] 厂区群山环峙,依山傍水,气候宜人,海拔 450m。该地区气候夏长冬短,空气湿度较大,少见霜雪,年平均气温 18℃,最低气温 3℃、最高气温 40℃,年平均相对湿度 78%左右,年平均风速 1.2m/s。

[译文] The distillery, surrounded by mountains, is situated on the eastern bank of the Red River at an altitude of 450 m. With long summers and short winters, the region enjoys an agreeable climate, high humidity and rare frost or snow weather. Temperatures of the region range from 3 to 40℃ with an annual average of 18℃. The relative humidity there is high, at about 78%, while its wind speed is about 1.2m/s on average through the year.

[解析] 汉语原文结构松散,大量运用主谓谓语句、无主语句,句子内部比较均衡,体现了汉语意合性语言"以意驭形"的典型特征。而英语讲求形式与语法结构的完备,需要通过语法、句法等形式手段来清晰地表达意义,以达到"以形致意"的目的,属于形合性语言。因此在翻译原文时,既需要根据原文逻辑关系进行"同类项"的移位与合并,如将原文前一句"气候宜人"并入后一句有关气候的描述句中进行翻译,又需要根据话题的转换与英语形合的特征进行原文的切分与重组,如原文后一句译成了 3 个英文句子。

5.

[原文] 茅台酒的生产集聚了神秘的天、神秘的地、神秘的人。神秘的天是指……;神秘的地是指……;神秘的人是指……。

[译文] The successful production of Moutai results from a combination of three mysterious factors: firstly, …; secondly, …; and thirdly, …

[解析] 原文采用了总分的描写方式,为了突出茅台酒酿造的独特生态环境,"神秘的"这一形容词重复出现了多次,通过已知信息来引出新信息,既实现了形式上的衔接与主位结构的推进,也实现了语义上的连贯。如果照着字面意义进行直译,多次重复翻译"神秘的"在英语中就会显得十分冗余,因而在翻译时除了总述时使用了"mysterious"来翻译"神秘的",后面分述部分大多采用了承前省略的方式,有效规避对它的重复,而通过"firstly, …; secondly, …; and thirdly, …"与前文"three"的语义共现来间接实现对"神秘的"的翻译,同时也使英文表述在逻辑上更为清晰。

6.

[原文] 茅台酒生产采用茅台本地或周边地区生产的红缨子糯高粱。

[译文] The basic raw materials for making Moutai are *hongyingzi* (meaning "red-tasselled ears") glutinous sorghum.

[解析] 原句中的"红缨子糯高粱"是酿制茅台酒的主要原料,产自茅台镇及其附

近地区。作为该地区特有的物种,在翻译时采用了音译与意译相结合的方式,将其译为"*hongyingzi* glutinous sorghum",而且对音译部分内容还进行了解释,便于读者了解这一特殊物种。

7.

[原文] 本地种植的高粱具有皮厚、粒小、胚芽所占比例大、支链淀粉含量高的特点,其吸水量低、耐蒸煮、不易糊化,满足了茅台酒独特生产工艺的原材料要求。淀粉含量大于60%,支链淀粉含量大于88%。

[译文] The locally-grown sorghum is perfectly suited to the production of Moutai: firstly, it has thick husks and small kernels, with a high proportion of germ and amylopectin starch; secondly, it can stand steaming and boiling, and thanks to its low rate of water absorption, is slow to gelatinize. This low rate of water absorption is another result of its high starch content of more than 60% and specifically, its amylopectin starch content of more than 88%.

[解析] 本小段的翻译采用了移位合并"同类项"与增加逻辑插入成分实施拆分的翻译技巧。首先将"支链淀粉含量高的特点"这一短语下移,与后文具体淀粉含量比例的表述"淀粉含量大于60%,支链淀粉含量大于88%"进行了合并翻译。而后,插入"firstly"与"secondly"将原文描述的高粱特点进行了拆分与分句翻译,使英文表述在结构上更为清晰。

8.

[原文] 茅台酒采用赤水河水源水作为酿造用水,其水质优良、清洁、无色透明、无沉淀、含杂质少、无异味、水温较低,pH为6.5~7.5。

[译文] The water used for distilling Moutai comes from the Red River and it is clean, colorless and transparent. Both its quality and purity level are high, and it is free from deposited solids and flavor taints. Its temperature is on the low side and its pH range fluctuates between 6.5 to 7.5.

[解析] 汉语原句为一长句,包含的内容实际上涉及茅台酒生产用水的水源、水质与特征等多个维度,翻译时可以根据原文对水不同维度的描述进行长句拆分,以便进行翻译,使其内部结构更加分明,逻辑关系更加清晰。因此,原句被翻译成了3个并列句,其中每个并列句又包含两个独立的分句或小句。

9.

[原文] 茅台酒的生产主要由制曲、制酒、勾兑和包装4大工艺组成。

[译文] There are a total of four processes involved in making final products of Moutai: *qu* production, distillate production, blending, filling and packaging.

[解析] 本句翻译重点是要体现术语的准确性,比如"制酒"实际上指生产出蒸馏酒,故而翻译成"distillate production",而不是"liquor production"或"liquor making",因为后两种表述可能包含的是整个茅台酒的制造过程,而不只是其中的一个工艺环节。再如,"包装"是"大包装"的概念,实际上包含了后文提及的"装瓶"与"包装"两个环节,因此将其翻译为"filling and packaging",而不是字面对应的"packaging"概念。

10.

[原文] 高温制曲、高温堆积发酵、高温厌氧发酵等酿酒环境长期对酿酒微生物进

行驯化，各种活性微生物经过遗传、变异、衍化等微生物群落的演替，促成了茅台酒厂区环境中耐高温、耐高酸、耐高酒度等极端微生物的富集。

［译文］ Such processes as *qu* production, stack fermentation and anaerobic fermentation all take place at high temperatures, which constantly promote the domestication of liquor-making microorganisms. Due to the variety of functional microorganisms present in the region and through heredity, mutation and evolution, extreme microbial communities have developed around the Moutai workshops that are resistant to high temperatures, acidity and alcoholicity.

［解析］ 原句体现了汉语善用排比的句式结构与善于使用词语重复来表达意义潜势的特征，如"高温制曲、高温堆积发酵、高温厌氧发酵"与"耐高温、耐高酸、耐高酒度"，但英语语言具有趋于简洁与省略的倾向，因而在翻译时分别采用后置的定语从句"all take place at high temperatures"与前置修辞的形容词"high"来进行表述，避免出现生硬感。

Translation Skills（Ⅳ） Translation of Long Sentences（长句翻译）

（一）句法与长句

翻译的过程就是决策和解决问题的过程。先要确定翻译标准和翻译策略，然后再解决大量的技巧性问题，主要包括词语的翻译、词的搭配、句子结构、句子和句子的连接、如何翻译文化负载词、如何翻译长句和复杂句等。所谓长句，主要是指语法结构复杂、修饰成分较多、内容层次多个叠加的句子。

学者方梦之（2019）提出，在不同的语言中，句子的衔接通常都使用3种手段：句法手段（syntactic devices）、词汇手段（lexical equivalence）和语义手段（semantic connection）。但是不同语言对这3种手段使用的方式和频率很不相同。就句法手段而言，尽管英语和汉语有相似之处，比如可以找到不少含义相匹配的连接词，"if"对"如果"、"although"对"虽然"、"because"对"因为"、"not only… but also…"对"不但……而且……"等，但是以句子为翻译单位时，要考虑句子内部各部分的衔接，在长句和复杂句中特别要考虑各分句间的内在联系。

英语和汉语分别隶属印欧语系和汉藏语系，两者在句法结构上存在着较大差异。英语句法关系重形合（hypotactic），汉语重意合（paratactic）。形合，是指句子内部和句子间的连接常采用句法手段（syntactic devices）和词汇手段（lexical equivalence），连接关系是明显的，有连接词标志；意合，是指句子内部和句子间的连接采用语义手段（semantic connection），句子间的关系往往是内在的、隐含的、模糊的，少用连词。长句翻译时根据中英文表达习惯的不同，需要根据目的语的语言规则采取相应的翻译策略。

（二）英译汉中的长句处理

英语属于形合性的语言，英语句子多属于扩展型。修辞语位置相对灵活，前置后置比较自如,尤其倾向于后置,有利于句子的扩展。而正因如此,英语句子也较容易产生结构复杂、层次变化多样、多种从句(主语、状语、定语、表语从句等)并存的长难句。英语的长句处理关键是正确理解和分析句子内部结构,以及句子间各修饰成分的关系。我们以下面的句子为例,具体分析英文长句的处理步骤:

[原文] Petroleum, consisting of crude oil and natural gas, seems to originate from organic matter in marine sediment.

[解析] "Petroleum"是主语,"consisting of crude oil and natural gas"是后置定语,"seems to originate from"是谓语,"organic matter"是宾语,"in marine sediment"是地点状语。

我们按照以下分解步骤来理解这句话。

① 读句子主干:主语(Petroleum)→谓语(seems to originate from)→宾语(organic matter)。

译:石油看似来自于有机物。

② 读主语的后置分词修饰成分(consisting of crude oil and natural gas)。

译:包含了原油和天然气。

③ 读句子的其他修饰成分,此处是充当形容词功能的介词短语(in marine sediment)。

译:在海洋沉积物中的。

[译文] 包含原油和天然气的石油看似来自于海洋沉积物中的有机物。

再举一例:

[原文] According to the operating conditions of the top condenser, individual components of that mixture will be vented to atmosphere, recycled in the reflux to the top plate of the rectifier, or drawn off in the cold feints for recycling to the top of the analyzer.

[解析]

① 读句子主干:主语(individual components)→并列谓语结构(be vented, recycled, or drawn off)。

译:个别成分被排放、回收和抽出。

② 读主语的后置分词修饰成分(of that mixture)。

译:混合物中的个别成分。

③ 读句子的谓语修饰成分:3个谓语动词的介词短语修饰成分"be vented (to atmosphere)"被排放到大气中;"be recycled (in the reflux) (to the top plate)(of the rectifier)"在回流中被回收到蒸馏塔顶板;以及"be drawn off (in the cold feints) (for recycling) (to the top of the analyzer)"从冷尾酒中抽出到分析器顶部进行循环利用。

④ 读句子的其他修饰成分:"according to the operating conditions of the top condenser"是介词短语作状语,单独拆分处理译为"根据顶部冷凝器的运行状况"。

[译文] 根据顶部冷凝器的运行状况,该混合物的个别成分将被排放到大气中,或在回流中被回收到蒸馏塔顶板,或从冷尾酒中抽出到分析器顶部进行循环利用。

英语的词组与词组、句子与句子之间的结构关系和逻辑比较清楚。英语的关系词包括介词、关系代词、关系副词、连接词等,十分丰富,这些丰富的关系词彼此过渡和连接,在形态上维系了句内和句间的各种关系。因此在翻译英语长句时,我们先要在英语语言呈树状的结构中找出树干,即句子的主谓宾;随后去寻找树干连接的每个枝干,即主语、谓语、宾语对应的修饰成分,而后再看其他剩余成分,最后再进行整合,按照中文的语言习惯将意思表达出来。

(三) 汉译英中的长句处理

基于中英文表达习惯的不同与行文的需要,有时候在中译英的过程中要根据英文的表达需要,对中文原文信息的排列顺序予以调整。汉语是意合的语言,相对于英语复杂的嵌套长句,汉语中出现的长句往往呈现为流水型。汉语流水型句子的特点是一个分句接着一个分句,很多地方可断可连。汉语中句子的概念比较模糊,句号和逗号的使用有较大的随意性,因此如果以句号作为划分句子的标准,汉语长句很多。汉语属于意合语言,句子间的关系往往是内在的、隐含的、模糊的,因此在中译英时,要注意将各个分句之间隐含的关系用显著的句法手段(syntactic devices)和词汇手段(lexical equivalence)进行切分或合并,使译文符合英文的语言习惯。

[原文] 名流酒运用传统工艺结合现代科学技术,配料讲究,工艺独特,金黄透明,味道醇正,富含人体必需的多种氨基酸和微量元素,保持原汁、原色、原味,是不添加任何色素和添加剂的天然养生酒。

[解析] 原文叙述的内容包括工艺技术、配料和产品特点,但各部分内容分布较乱,层次不清,逻辑模糊。仔细分析原文,我们发现从语义的角度主要有四层信息:第一层为总结性信息,传统工艺和现代科学技术结合,工艺独特;第二层信息,配料讲究,无添加;第三层信息,色香味俱全;最后总结,营养丰富。信息分析是中译外译前处理的一种策略,对中文原稿进行一些文字处理,具体处理方法包括分析、编辑、重组、删减、正误、不译、省译等。这些处理方法的目的是充分领会原文精神,尊重并突出原文主要信息,使得外译稿更适合交际需要,符合目的语语言表达与接受习惯,达到译文效果。

[译文] Today, Mingliu Wine is brewed using a combination of traditional techniques and modern technology. The carefully selected ingredients go through a unique process, without additives or colorants, to produce a golden, transparent brew with a pure flavor. The wine is rich in essential amino acids and trace elements, and has a high nutritional value.

美国著名翻译理论家奈达曾提出过翻译的4步模式:分析(analysis)—转换(transfer)—重组(restructuring)—检验(testing)。分析,即从语义和语法的不同层面做文本分析;转换即把分析得到的意义从源语言转移到目的语;重组,即按目的语规则重新组织译文;检验,即对照原文内容与目的语规范检查译文的准确性与流利性。在实际翻译过程中,译者不需要严格按照步骤的先后次序进行翻译。在这4个步骤中,"分析"是最为复杂,也是最关键的。分析的重点在于语义。上述例子使用了语义分析中的层次结构分析法,并且在随后的"转换"步骤中将语义成分进行了重新分布,省略了一些细枝末节,较好地呈现了原文想要表达的意思。

Translation Workshop

I. Translate the following sentences and pay attention to the translation of long sentences

1. Type A congeners, being more volatile at all concentrations of ethanol, migrate to the top of the column.

2. The hot spirit vapor flowing into the base of the rectifier column will be rich in type A and B compounds but contain only a small amount of type C, which will soon be returned to the analyzer.

3. Unless a main supply of drinking water quality is used for all purposes, the water supply for a grain distillery requires careful consideration.

4. There are a number of scientific papers reporting attributes generated by descriptive panels to describe the sensory properties of wine.

5. Descriptive analysis is a term generally used to describe a sensory method by which identification, quantification and description of sensory attributes (the so-called sensory profile) of food by human subjects are obtained.

6. 白酒酿造主要使用的原料是高粱,黄酒酿造的主要原料是稻米,而用于制作酒曲的原料则比较多样化,小麦、大麦等均可制作。

7. 由于中国酒酿造以谷物为主要原料,而谷物的主要成分是淀粉而不是糖,所以中国酒酿造涉及将淀粉分解为可发酵的糖分,然后再将糖分发酵生成乙醇。

8. 由于酒曲这种独特的糖化发酵剂的使用,中国酒的酿造过程采用独特的边糖化边发酵的方式进行,这与西方的发酵方式具有明显的区别。

9. 不同于西方的橡木桶陈酿,中国酒主要采用陶坛进行储存陈酿,这可能与古代中国制陶业的繁荣密切相关。

10. 由于制作工艺的不同,中国白酒的风味千差万别,基于不同的香气特征,中国白酒主要可以分为5种香型:浓香型、清香型、酱香型、蜜香型和其他香型。

II. Translate the following passage into Chinese

During kilning new compounds are formed and others, which exist in the green malt, are destroyed. These chemical changes affect the sensory quality of the final distilled spirit. The types of reaction considered to be of importance during kilning include those based on the enzymic and chemical oxidation of unsaturated fatty acids, the combination of free amino acids and reducing sugars, and the thermal degradation of precursors such as S-methyl methionine, which are synthesized during germination.

The chemistry of the formation of flavor compounds is complex, and becomes increasingly so as kilning temperatures are raised.

The distillation stage is of paramount importance, both as a flavor formation process and as one of separation. Quantitatively, the major flavor-potent compounds (congeners) are produced during fermentation. In sensory terms, many compounds that make significant contributions are often present in only trace amounts. Much work remains to be carried out regarding linking whisky character to chemical composition, and tracing the origin of these components.

(摘自 *Whiskies*: *Composition*, *Sensory Properties and Sensory Analysis*)

Ⅲ. Translate the following passage into English

酒在中国现代经济中占有重要地位。中国是产酒大国,中国酒在中国仍占有主导地位。2014 年中国酒销售收入达到 5418 亿元,利税达到 1251 亿元,其中白酒销售收入有 5259 亿元。中国酒产值占中国食品工业的 5%,其中白酒行业就业人数大约为 43.9 万人,带动农业及相关产业产值达 1100 亿元。

中国酒不是人民生活的必需品,但在中国人的社会生活中酒却扮演着其他食品无法替代的角色。中国古人将酒的作用归纳为 3 类:酒以治病,酒以养老,酒以成礼。

酒以治病,在中国古代酒与治病密切相关。从中国古代"医"字的书写可以发现,酒是医的重要组成部分。关于酒以养老,早在汉代就有书籍总结:酒,百药之长,嘉会之好。酒以成礼,涉及中国人日常生活的许多方面,如古时的宗教、祭祀,现如今的节日、婚嫁等庆祝活动。例如,女儿红的来历就与成礼有关。根据浙江绍兴一带习俗,家中有女儿出生时,家人总要酿制上等黄酒数坛,然后将酒埋入地窖陈酿,一直到女儿出嫁时才将酒取出款待客人。

(摘自《酿酒科技》2006 年第 2 期刊载文章《茅台酒的独特性概述》)

Unit 5 Cosmetics and Oriental Aesthetics

Passage A Cosmetics: the Chemistry of Charm

Warming-up

Work on the following terms and put them into Chinese:

powdered antimony　　　　　　　_____
perfumed hair oil　　　　　　　　_____
cold cream　　　　　　　　　　　_____
lead poisoning　　　　　　　　　_____
foot powder　　　　　　　　　　　_____
soap with grit and flavor　　　　_____
rather unpalatable　　　　　　　_____
do the job quite well　　　　　　_____
tooth enamel　　　　　　　　　　　_____
chemical formula　　　　　　　　_____
rather than　　　　　　　　　　　_____
pure compound　　　　　　　　　　_____
tooth decay　　　　　　　　　　　_____
convert... to...　　　　　　　　_____
sticky dextran　　　　　　　　　_____
brushing and tossing　　　　　　_____
in turn　　　　　　　　　　　　　_____
corneal layer　　　　　　　　　　_____
slough off　　　　　　　　　　　　_____
a moisture content of about 10%　_____
sebaceous gland　　　　　　　　　_____
oily secretion　　　　　　　　　_____
be permeable to　　　　　　　　　_____
exposure to sun and wind　　　　_____
protective film　　　　　　　　　_____
mineral oil　　　　　　　　　　　_____
petroleum jelly　　　　　　　　　_____
a viscous liquid　　　　　　　　_____

a protective coating _____
baby oil _____
fancy cream _____
fatty odor _____
retard rancidity _____
are responsible for _____
metal ions _____
give off _____
pleasant aroma _____
important, but minor, ingredients _____
compound with large molecules _____
in large quantities _____
vary with... _____
concentrated solution _____
be sickeningly sweet _____
odorous compound _____
ethyl alcohol _____
methyl alcohol _____
allergic reaction _____
an adhesive bandage _____
hairy chemistry _____
an anionic type _____
highly basic shampoo _____
strongly acidic shampoo _____
give the hair more body _____
literally _____
given volume _____
advertising gimmick _____
add nothing to _____
the back-to-nature movement _____

Ages ago, primitive people used materials from nature for cleansing, beautifying, and otherwise altering their appearance. Evidence indicates that Egyptians, 7,000 years ago, used powdered antimony (Sb) and the green copper ore malachite as eye shadow. Egyptian pharaohs used perfumed hair oils as far back as 3,500 B.C. Claudius Galen, a Greek physician of the second century A.D., is said to have invented cold cream. Dandy gentlemen of seventeenth-century Europe used cosmetics lavishly, often to cover the fact that they seldom bathed. Ladies of eighteenth-century Europe whitened their faces with lead carbonate ($PbCO_3$), and many died from lead poisoning.

Unit 5 Cosmetics and Oriental Aesthetics

The use of cosmetics has a long and interesting history, but nothing in the past comes close to the amounts and varieties of cosmetics used by people in the modern industrial world. Each year we spend billions of dollars on everything from hair sprays to toe-nail polishes, from mouthwashes to foot powders.

In this chapter, we take a look at a variety of cosmetics. Emphasis is on those that you or a member of your family are most likely to use.

I. Toothpaste: Soap with Grit and Flavor

After soap (which doesn't count, because the law says it isn't a cosmetic), toothpaste is the most important cosmetic product. The only essential components of toothpaste are a detergent and an abrasive. Soap and sodium bicarbonate would do the job quite well but would be rather unpalatable. The ideal abrasive should be hard enough to clean the teeth but not hard enough to damage the tooth enamel. Some abrasives frequently used in toothpaste have been criticized as being too harsh.

Any pharmaceutical grade of soap or detergent probably would work satisfactorily. Most toothpastes today are full of minty flavors, colors, aromas, and sweet tastes. Ingredients include sweeteners such as sorbitol, glycerol, and saccharin; flavors such as peppermint oil and mint; thickeners such as cellulose gum and polyethylene glycols (PEGs); and preservatives such as sodium benzoate.

A variety of formulas for toothpaste are available. The formula for a cosmetic is not a chemical formula, because cosmetics are mixtures rather than pure compounds. Instead, it is more properly called a recipe, that is, a list of materials and directions for preparing a product.

Tooth decay is caused primarily by bacteria that convert sugars to sticky dextrans or plaque and to acids such as lactic acid ($CH_3CHOHCOOH$). Acids dissolve tooth enamel. Brushing and tossing remove plaque and thus prevent decay.

Many modern toothpastes contain stannous fluoride (SnF_2). A compound shown to be effective in reducing the incidence of tooth decay.

II. Skin Chemistry: Creams and Lotions

Skin is a complex organ that encloses our bodies. The outer layer of skin is called the epidermis. The epidermis, in turn, is divided into two parts: dead cells on the outside (the corneal layer), and living cells beneath the corneal layer that continually replace corneal cells that are sloughed off. Cosmetics are applied to the dead cells of the corneal layer.

The corneal layer is composed mainly of a tough, fibrous protein called keratin. Keratin has a moisture content of about 10%. Below 10% moisture, the skin is dry and flaky. Above 10%, conditions are ideal for the growth of harmful microorganisms. Skin is protected from loss of moisture by sebum, an oily secretion of the sebaceous glands. One interesting property of skin is that it is insoluble in water (otherwise we would dissolve in the shower). It is, however, slightly permeable to water and light.

Exposure to sun and wind may leave the skin dry and scaly. Washing too often also removes natural skin oils. A variety of creams and lotions are available to treat dry skin. An essential ingredient of each is a fatty or oily substance that forms a protective film over the skin. Typical ingredients are mineral oil and petroleum jelly; sometimes both are used in the same preparation. These are mixtures of alkanes obtained from petroleum. Petroleum jelly is a higher-boiling fraction than mineral oil. The former is a semisolid; the latter, a viscous liquid. Other ingredients include natural fats and oils, perfumes, waxes, water, and emulsifiers (compounds that keep the oily portions from separating from the water). Natural materials used on the skin include lanolin, a fat obtained from sheep's wool, and olive oil. Often, beeswax is added to harden the product.

Some creams have been formulated with hormones, queen bee jelly, and other strange ingredients. None of these has been found to confer any particular benefit. Creams and lotions protect the skin by providing a protective coating and by softening it, much as plasticizers soften plastics. Such skin softeners are called emollients. You could just as well use petroleum jelly (one trade name is Vaseline) or a good grade of white mineral oil (sometimes called baby oil) as the fancy creams.

Skin moisturizers? The term is undefined. Components called moisturizers are usually petroleum jelly, a mineral oil, or a similar substance. They may serve to keep the skin softer, in part, by physically preventing the loss of moisture through the protective film.

Ⅲ. Lipsticks: Caster Oil and Color

Lipstick is quite similar to skin creams in composition. It is made of an oil and a wax. To keep the lipstick firm, a higher proportion of wax is used than in creams. Dyes and pigments provide color. The oil is frequently castor oil. Waxes often employed are beeswax, carnauba, and candelilla. Perfumes are added to cover up the unpleasant fatty odor of the oil. Antioxidants are also employed to retard rancidity. Bromo acid dyes such as tetrabromofluorescein, a bluish red compound, are responsible for the color of most modern lipsticks. These compounds often are adhered to metal ions to form colored complexes called lakes.

Because it has little in the way of protective oils, the skin of the lips is easily dried out, leading to chapped lips. With or without coloring, lipsticks do protect the lips from drying.

Ⅳ. Perfumes, Colognes, and Aftershaves

No one wants to smell bad. Many people like to give off the pleasant aroma of a fruit or a flower, perhaps moderated a bit to avoid overwhelming a neighbor's nose. Perfumes are among the most ancient and the most widely used of the cosmetics. Their chemistry, however, is exceedingly complex.

Originally, perfumes were extracted from natural sources. Nowadays, chemists have identified many of the components and synthesized them in the laboratory. The best perfumes, perhaps, are still made from natural materials, because chemists have so far been unable to identify all the many important, but minor, ingredients.

A good perfume may have a hundred or more constituents. Often the components are divided into three categories, called notes, based on differences in volatility. The most volatile fraction (that which vaporizes most readily) is called the top note. This fraction, made up of relatively small molecules, is responsible for the odor when a perfume is first applied. The middle note is intermediate in volatility. It is responsible for the lingering aroma after most of the top-note compounds have vaporized. The end-note fraction has low volatility and is made up of compounds with large molecules.

Several compounds with flowery or fruity odors are synthesized in large quantities for use in perfumes. Odors vary with dilution. A concentrated solution (lots of compound in a small amount of water or other solvent) may be unpleasant, yet a dilute solution (a small amount in lots of solvent) of the same compound may have a pleasant aroma.

Many flowery or fruity odors are sickeningly sweet, even in dilute solutions. Compounds such as the musks often are added to moderate the odor. Musks and similar compounds have extremely disagreeable odors when concentrated, but often are pleasant at extreme dilution.

A perfume usually consists of 10% to 25% odorous compounds and fixatives. The remainder is ethyl alcohol, which serves as a solvent. Colognes are diluted perfumes. They often contain only 1% or 2% perfume essence. Thus, colognes are about 10% as strong as perfumes. Dilution can be made with ethyl alcohol alone or with alcohol-water mixtures. Just use your favorite perfume and mix thoroughly. (Do not use ethyl alcohol that has been denatured by methyl alcohol or other toxic ingredients.)

Aftershave lotions are similar to colognes. Often, menthol is added for a cooling effect on the skin.

Perfumes are used to impart a pleasant odor to many products. Some people have allergic reactions to one or more components of perfumes. Before using any cosmetic, you should test your skin for sensitivity. Place a drop of the cosmetic on the inside of your elbow. Cover the spot overnight with an adhesive bandage. If there is no reaction (reddened skin or itching), the product should be reasonably safe for you to use. Stop using any cosmetic when any sort of problem develops.

V. Hairy Chemistry: Hair Care and Conditioning

Like skin, hair is composed of the fibrous protein keratin. When hair is washed, the keratin absorbs water and is softened and made more stretchable.

Modern shampoos use a synthetic detergent as a cleansing agent. In shampoos for adults, the detergent is usually an anionic type, such as sodium dodecyl sulfate. For shampoos used on babies and children, the detergent is often an amphoteric type that is less irritating to the eyes.

The only essential ingredient in shampoo is a detergent of some sort. What, then, is all the advertising about? You can buy shampoos that are fruit and herb flavored, protein enriched, pH balanced, and made for oily and dry hair. Let's have a look at some of the gimmicks.

Hair is protein with acidic and basic groups on the protein chain. It stands to reason that the acidity or basicity of a shampoo would affect hair. Hair and skin are slightly acidic. Highly basic (high-pH) or strongly acidic (low-pH) shampoos would damage the hair. More important, such products would irritate the skin and eyes. Most shampoos, however, have pH values between 5 and 8, a difference too slight to affect the hair or scalp in any significant way. Shampoos that irritate the eyes usually do so because of other ingredients, not because of a too-high or a too-low pH.

Because hair is protein, protein in shampoos does give the hair more body—or so the advertisements claim. Some white glues are protein, too. Protein in shampoos literally glues split ends together and coats the hair, making it thicker. If that is what you want, then protein shampoo is for you.

Shampoos for oily or dry hair differ in the relative amounts of detergent in given volumes. Those for oily hair presumably are more concentrated. There seems to be little standardization in formulations from one brand to another, however. Shampoos for oily or dry hair seem to be mainly an advertising gimmick.

How about all those flavors and fragrances? Ample evidence indicates that such "natural" ingredients as milk, honey, strawberries, herbs, cucumbers, and lemons add nothing to the usefulness of shampoos or other cosmetics. Why are they there? Smells sell, and there is an appeal to those taken by the back-to-nature movement. There is one hazard to the use of such fragrances: bees, mosquitoes, and other insects like fruit and flower odors, too. Using such products before going on a picnic or a hike could lead to a bee in your bonnet.

VI. Cosmetics: Economics and Advertising

Most cosmetics are formulated from inexpensive ingredients. Many highly advertised cosmetics are sold at high prices. Are they worth it? That's a judgment that lies outside of the realm of chemistry. If a product makes you look better or feel better, what value can be placed on it? Only you can decide.

No attempt has been made here to tell you everything there is to know about cosmetics. Many volumes that discuss these interesting chemicals in much more detail are available in libraries. We hope, however, that the knowledge you gained here, coupled with that required on cosmetic labels, will make you a better-informed consumer. You don't have to pay a lot for extra ingredients that contribute little or nothing to the function of a cosmetic.

(摘自 *Cosmeceaticals and Cosmetic Practice*)

Notes

1.

［原文］ Ages ago, primitive people used materials from nature for cleansing, beautifying, and otherwise altering their appearance.

［译文］ 很久以前，原始人类使用天然材料进行清洁、美化和其他行为方式来改变容貌。

［解析］ 翻译该句的难点在于对 otherwise 的准确理解，此处 otherwise 连接副词，修饰 altering，并与 cleansing 和 beautifying 关联，意思是"以其他方式"或"用别的方法"，

为了说明改变容貌的行为方式有多种，因此译成"其他行为方式"。

2.
[原文] The only essential components of toothpaste are a detergent and an abrasive.
[译文] 牙膏的主要组分只不过是清洁剂和研磨剂。
[解析] 翻译该句的难点在于对 only 的准确理解。Only 是英语中常用词汇之一，有多种意义和用法，如：（表示比较而言唯一真实、恰当或必要的情况）只，只有，仅；（引出发生的必要条件）只有……（才）；（表示不再有趣、重要或困难等，尤其用于想要纠正错误观点时）只不过，仅……而已；（强调数量少或时间短）才，仅仅；（强调并非全部，只是一小部分）只，仅仅；（用于 can 或 could 之后，强调除此以外别无可为）只（能）；刚才；刚刚；（强调行动或行为恰当）完全，真正；（用于动词前，表示结果令人遗憾、不尽如人意）愈加，只会；在很大程度上；非常；极其。本文的主题是让读者了解常用化妆品的基本知识，不要屈花冤枉钱。因此 only 被译成"只不过"。如果译成"唯一的"，与 components 的复数形式相矛盾。

3.
[原文] Tooth decay is caused primarily by bacteria that convert sugars to sticky dextrans or plaque and to acids such as lactic acid ($CH_3CHOHCOOH$).
[译文] 蛀牙主要是由细菌引起的。细菌将糖转化为黏性葡聚糖，形成牙菌斑，并产生乳酸（$CH_3CHOHCOOH$）等。
[解析] 这是一个复合句。本句的译法注意两点：一是主句是被动句"Tooth decay is caused primarily by bacteria that..."，使用"由"字把原句转化成汉语句式；二是使用断句法将定语从句"...that convert sugars to sticky dextrans or plaque and to acids such as lactic acid （$CH_3CHOHCOOH$）"与主句断开，翻译时重复先行词 bacteria（细菌）。

4.
[原文] The epidermis, in turn, is divided into two parts: dead cells on the outside (the corneal layer), and living cells beneath the corneal layer that continually replace corneal cells that are sloughed off.
[译文] 表皮又分为两部分：外部是死细胞层（角质层），角质层下面是活细胞层。角质细胞脱落，活细胞不断进行替换。
[解析] 长句的译法有顺译法、倒译法和分译法。本句采用顺译法。

5.
[原文] One interesting property of skin is that it is insoluble in water...
[译文] 皮肤有一个有趣的特性，即它不溶于水……
[解析] 该句的翻译要点：一是将名词短语 One interesting property of skin 译成小句"皮肤有一个有趣的特性"，二是将形容词 insoluble 译成动词，词性转换是英汉翻译中常用的翻译技巧。

6.
[原文] Typical ingredients are mineral oil and petroleum jelly; sometimes both are used in the same preparation. These are mixtures of alkanes obtained from petroleum. Petroleum jelly is a higher-boiling fraction than mineral oil. The former is a semisolid; the latter, a viscous liquid.

［译文］　凡士林和矿物油是两种具有代表性的原料成分，这两种成分有时在同一配方中使用。凡士林和矿物油是从石油中获得的烷烃混合物。凡士林是一种沸点高于矿物油的分馏物，呈半固体状态；而矿物油是一种黏稠的液体。

［解析］　原文是由4个句子组成的句群。翻译句群需考虑句子间的衔接与连贯。翻译时注意把握 mineral oil 和 petroleum jelly 出现的顺序。第4个句子中的 The former 指的是 petroleum jelly，the latter 指的是 mineral oil，而第一句中的 mineral oil and petroleum jelly 与第4句中的叙述顺序相反，翻译时我们将 mineral oil 和 petroleum jelly 的顺序颠倒过来，译成"凡士林和矿物油"，使译文衔接得更加连贯。

7.

［原文］　Often the components are divided into three categories, called notes, based on differences in volatility. The most volatile fraction (that which vaporizes most readily) is called the top note. This fraction, made up of relatively small molecules, is responsible for the odor when a perfume is first applied. The middle note is intermediate in volatility. It is responsible for the lingering aroma after most of the top-note compounds have vaporized. The end-note fraction has low volatility and is made up of compounds with large molecules.

［译文］　通常，这些成分根据挥发性的差异被分为三类，即三种香调（notes）：前调（top note）、中调（middle note）和基调（end note）。最易挥发的部分被称为前调，由相对的小分子化合物组成。当香水刚涂抹时，前调成分负责产生气味。中调成分的挥发性居中。当大部分前调成分挥发后，中调成分负责产生持久的香气。基调成分的挥发性较低，它由大分子化合物组成。

［解析］　该句群的翻译技巧体现了汉语的"总说—分说"特征。译文先列举3种"香调"，再依次叙述各香调的特征和作用。

8.

［原文］　a pleasant aroma

［译文］　香气宜人

［解析］　试比较"宜人的香气"。前者更符合汉语表达习惯。英语中的"定语+中心语"和汉语的"主语+谓语"可以互译，这种词序调整是常见的翻译方法，它是由英汉定语语序差异所致。

9.

［原文］　Many flowery or fruity odors are sickeningly sweet, even in dilute solutions.

［译文］　许多花香或水果香气即使在稀释溶液中也会过于甜腻，让人作呕。

［解析］　该句中的副词 sickeningly 修饰形容词 sweet，实际上是说"甜"的后果，因此译成"过于甜腻，让人作呕"。

10.

［原文］　Compounds such as the musks often are added to moderate the odor.

［译文］　为了调和这种气味，通常会添加麝香类物质。

［解析］　compound 有"化合物""复合物"的意思，而麝香不是"化合物"。从本句内容和上下文来看，此处的 compounds such as the musks 可译成"麝香类物质"。

11.

［原文］　Stop using any cosmetic when any sort of problem develops.

Unit 5　Cosmetics and Oriental Aesthetics

［译文］　如有任何反应，请勿使用。
［解析］　本句采用"正说反译"的翻译技巧，将 Stop using 译成"请勿使用"。

12.
［原文］　It stands to reason that the acidity or basicity of a shampoo would affect hair.
［译文］　很显然，洗发水的酸碱度会影响头发。
［解析］　"It stands to reason that…"这个句式可以表达三层意思：1) 指 that-clause 所述是"显而易见""不言而喻"的，相当于"It is obvious/clear/apparent that…"；2) 指 that-clause 所述是"毫无疑问""不容置疑"的，相当于"There is no doubt that…"；3) 指 that-clause 所述是 reasonable or logical，即"合乎情理""理所当然"的。此处是第一个意思。

13.
［原文］　Hair and skin are slightly acidic. Highly basic (high-pH) or strongly acidic (low-pH) shampoos would damage the hair.
［译文］　头发和皮肤呈弱酸性。强碱（高 pH）或强酸（低 pH）的洗发水会损伤头发。
［解析］　注意专业词汇的表达。be slightly acidic 译成"呈弱酸性"，highly basic (high-pH) or strongly acidic (low-pH) shampoos 译成"强碱（高 pH）或强酸（低 pH）的洗发水"。

14.
［原文］　Protein in shampoos literally glues split ends together and coats the hair, making it thicker.
［译文］　洗发水中的蛋白质可以将分叉的发梢黏合在一起，并包覆在发丝上，使发丝变得更粗。
［解析］　the hair 译为"发丝"。如果译成"头发"，则不准确。

15.
［原文］　You don't have to pay a lot for extra ingredients that contribute little or nothing to the function of a cosmetic.
［译文］　你不必为化妆品中的一些额外成分支付过多的费用，因为这些成分对化妆品的功效几乎不起作用。
［解析］　原句中的定语从句 that contribute little or nothing to the function of a cosmetic 在逻辑上与主句 You don't have to pay a lot for extra ingredients 具有因果关系，翻译时注意逻辑分析与调整。

Passage B　中国彩妆三千年

Warming-up

Work on the following terms and put them into English：
山寨欧美化妆品

东方审美	_____
迎合	_____
原始人类	_____
化妆	_____
大量甲骨文、金文、竹简的记载	_____
脂、泽、粉、黛	_____
铜镜	_____
《诗经》	_____
汉代陶俑	_____
彩妆配方	_____
享有盛名	_____
缓步慢行的阶段	_____
追溯到	_____
红山文化女神像	_____
红色的朱砂	_____
《新唐书·百官志》	_____
文化碰撞	_____
口红"达人"	_____
神灵的用品	_____
回归王座	_____
厚积薄发	_____
一见倾心	_____
《新唐书》	_____
彰显美德	_____
使用简便又便于携带	_____
一妆多用	_____
代称呼	_____
西域	_____
想方设法	_____
抛砖引玉	_____
在浩如烟海的传统文化中立足	_____

随着传统文化的崛起，国内化妆品从山寨欧美化妆品，即标榜原料、包装、功效等与国外大牌处于同一水平的同质低价战略，转而向内求，根据传统文化与东方审美定位品牌、包装、原料等，并由此涌现出一些深受年轻消费群体欢迎的品牌。

不论是彩妆还是化妆工具等，在我国古已有之，且已成体系。中国彩妆该如何把自己完美嫁接到传统文化中，打造出受消费者喜爱的品牌，迎合审美的回归？唯有真正了解彩妆的历史。

中华民族有着悠久的历史、深厚的文化底蕴，也是世界上最早使用和制作化妆品的民族之一。彩妆起源于原始社会，原始人类将不同的颜料涂抹在皮肤上，一是为了生存，二是为了繁衍后代。进入奴隶社会后，彩妆迎来了新纪元。在夏、商、周时期，人们多忙于生存，很少有时间和精力化妆。但在祭祀的时候，为了沟通神明，祭司会给自己化妆。从大量甲骨文、金文、竹简的记载中可以看到，当时的人们已在使用脂、泽、粉、黛了。

在有文字记载的历史中，化妆品与不同时代的美女一起出现，文人骚客的诗词中也多见对不同妆容的描写。

夏商时期，化妆的群体主要集中在上层社会。殷商时期发明了铜镜，这极大地满足了人们化妆时观看容颜的需要，促进了化妆品的发展。《诗经》记载有这样的故事：丈夫出征，妻子便蓬头散发，原因不是没有"膏沐"，而是不知道打扮给谁看。可见周朝时已经有了成熟的化妆品；商朝末期，已经有了彩妆"燕支"，亦作"胭脂"。

随着社会经济的发展，人们的审美意识发生了转变。秦朝到两汉时期，化妆越来越大众化，在贵族与平民中，女性都很重视自己的妆容。从出土的汉代陶俑可以看到，其面部有明显的妆容。相关史料记载，汉代女性喜欢在脸颊上涂抹朱粉。到了魏晋南北朝，化妆品的品类越来越多，妆面也变得丰富多彩。

在大唐盛世，彩妆更是盛行，女性大多使用各色彩妆来装扮自己，妆容主要集中在额头、面颊、眉毛、眼等几个部位。盛唐时，"红妆"是此时最为流行的妆面；中唐以后，曾流行过一种"白妆"，即在脸部、颈部、胸部擦白粉，起到美化的装饰作用；除此之外，还有一种妆面"赭面"，即把脸部、颈部等部位涂成红褐色。

在两宋时期，随着社会经济的发展，彩妆也发展到了新的高度，历史文献中甚至出现了完整的彩妆配方。南宋时期，杭州粉在民间已享有盛名。

在明清时期，随着妆面更加简约、清淡，彩妆的发展进入了缓步慢行的阶段。民国时期，受欧美文化以及好莱坞影星的影响，人们的审美开始西化，使用的彩妆也是国外产品，或是国内化妆品企业仿制欧美彩妆生产的产品，传统彩妆的发展被按了暂停键。

一、花钿

花钿又被称为花子、面花、贴花，是贴在眉间和脸上的一种小装饰。古代做花钿的材料十分丰富，金箔、纸、鱼鳞、蜻蜓翅膀等都能用来做花钿。

花钿的颜色有红、绿、黄等。花钿的形状除梅花状外，还有各式小鸟、小鱼、小鸭等，十分美妙新颖。

二、彩妆王者口红

在古代，口红被称为口脂、唇脂，自古以来就受到女性的喜爱。在我国，口红可以追溯到红山文化女神像。这座神像诞生于5000多年前，人们从神像的嘴唇上发现了红色的朱砂，这就是最早的"口红"。

当下，口红是所有女性必备的彩妆产品。在古代，口红却是一种奢侈的彩妆。纵览从秦朝到清朝的历史资料，对口红记载最多的是唐朝。《新唐书·百官志》有关于口脂的记载，"腊日，献口脂"。

除此之外，唐朝出现了各种以口脂为主的妆容，多见于文人的诗词。受吐蕃服饰、妆面的影响，唐朝出现了"啼妆""泪妆"。这类妆面是文化碰撞后的结果，但因其没有美感，很快就消失了。

到了近现代，口脂发展成了口红。张爱玲就是民国时期的口红"达人"。张爱玲喜欢化妆，从她的文字中可以找到一些她对化妆品的描写。

在历史上，朝代越强盛，口红的颜色与妆容越多，从唐朝时的文学作品中可见一斑。口红经历了数千年的发展，从神灵的用品变成了现在的日用彩妆，其原料、形状、色彩、包装等，随着审美与使用者的变化，从简单纯朴变得越来越丰富。时至今日，在品牌化过程中，口红的定位也越来越多元化，东方与西方、现代与古代、奢侈品与实用品等，交织成了让消费者一见倾心的产品。

在新冠疫情的影响下，口红的市场表现一直比较低迷，但随着疫情的有效控制，将来口红也一定会回归王座。在此之前，应该是口红厚积薄发的重要时期。

三、男女通用粉底

粉是用来涂抹脸部、脖子、手臂等部位的白色粉末，在古代多是天然的米粉、糊状的铅粉（又名铅华）、檀红色的铅粉（又名檀粉），以及珍珠粉等。与现在一样，粉是古人常用的基础彩妆。

铅粉质地细腻，色泽润白，并且易于保存，所以深受古人喜爱，逐渐取代了米粉的地位。铅粉的制作过程复杂得多，最初的铅粉没有经过脱水处理，多呈糊状。汉代以后，铅粉多被吸干水分制成粉末或固体形状。

除了单纯的米粉、铅粉以外，后来出现了采用不同原料制作而成的"紫粉""迎蝶粉""玉女桃花粉""玉簪粉""珠粉"等，还有以产地出名的"杭州粉""范阳粉""定粉""桂粉"等。最有特色的是南宋妆粉，其被制作成不同形状的粉块，如圆形、方形、四边形、八角形、葵瓣形等，还印有不同的花纹，如梅花、兰花、荷花等。

我国从古至今皆以白为美，古代女性与男性在有条件时会搽粉。据《新唐书》记载，杨贵妃的三位姐姐应召入宫，其脂粉费最多的时候达百万钱。

男子化妆自古有之，读三国、魏晋、隋唐等时期的历史与文学作品，会看到很多当时的名人会簪花傅粉施朱。古人化妆，一是修饰容颜，二是彰显美德。

四、消失在历史中的额黄

额黄，又叫鸦黄，是在额间涂上黄色，起源于南北朝，在唐朝盛行。《中国历代妇女妆饰》记载：这种妆饰的产生，与佛教的流行有一定关系。南北朝时，佛教在中国进入盛期，一些妇女从涂金的佛像上受到启发，将额头涂成黄色，之后这一做法逐渐流行起来。

至宋代时额黄还在流行，诗人彭汝砺诗曰："有女夭夭称细娘，真珠络髻面涂黄"。这反映出古代女性对额黄的喜爱。

五、画眉墨黛

黛是古代的眉笔，是一种黑色矿物，也被称为石黛。描画前必须先将石黛放在石砚上磨碾，使之成为粉末，然后加水调和。磨石黛的石砚在汉墓里多有发现，说明这种化妆品在汉代就已经在使用了。

有史料记载，除了石黛，还有螺子黛与青雀头黛等。螺子黛常见于各种影视剧，是隋唐时的眉笔。它产于波斯国，是经过加工的各种形状的黛块，是我国进口的最早的彩妆之一。螺子黛的制作过程和外形与墨锭相似，但使用方法比墨锭简单，不需要研磨，蘸水即可画眉。青雀头黛也是一种进口彩妆，南北朝时由西域传入中原，是一种深灰色的画眉材料。

到了 20 世纪 20 年代初，随着西洋文化的东渐，我国妇女的化妆品也发生了一系列的变化。画眉材料，尤其是杆状的眉笔和经过化学调制的黑色油脂，由于使用简便又便于携带，一直沿用到今天。

六、一妆多用胭脂

胭脂是一种红色的颜料，是古代口红与腮红等彩妆的总称，可以一妆多用。在历史文献中，关于胭脂的写法有很多，如"焉支""烟支""鲜支""燕支""燕脂""阏氏"等。

关于胭脂的来源，有很多传说。一种传说是胭脂来源于"阏氏"，这个名称是匈奴贵族正妻的称呼，因为她们常用"阏氏"妆饰脸面，所以"阏氏"成了她们的代称呼。另一种传说是，"胭脂"实际上是一种名叫"红蓝"的花朵，它的花瓣中含有红、黄两种色素，花开之后被整朵摘下，然后放在石钵中反复杵槌，淘去黄汁后即成鲜艳的红色颜料，张骞出使西域时带回中原。

在早期，胭脂有两种，一种是以丝绵蘸红蓝花汁而成，被称为"绵燕支"；另一种是加工成小而薄的花片，被称为"金花燕支"。这两种胭脂都可经过阴干处理，使用时只要蘸少量清水即可涂抹。

到了南北朝时期，人们在这种红色颜料中又加入了牛髓、猪胰等物，使其成为一种稠密润滑的脂膏，质地更为细腻，使用后兼具滋润皮肤的效果，燕支也被写成"胭脂"。

直到民国时期，胭脂仍是我国女性使用的主要彩妆之一。

七、美甲蔻丹

蔻丹是一种花，俗名千层红，又名指甲草。在我国古代，很多人家都会养一些指甲草，采集好花瓣，加上明矾捣烂，敷在指甲上几个小时或隔夜，可以把指甲染成粉色和红色。

在诸多古代彩妆中，蔻丹是最天然无害的彩妆之一。用蔻丹染指甲，在我国唐朝时期就已经成为了流行的风尚。到了明代，皇室女性会用阿拉伯胶、凤仙花、明矾、蛋白、明胶与蜂蜡等成分制成漆，把指甲涂成红色或黑色。

除了对指甲进行染色外，古人还想方设法对自己的指甲进行保护，由此产生了护指套。吉林榆树大坡老河深汉墓出土的金护指，就是保护指甲所用。这不仅是美丽的标志，也彰显了尊贵的地位。

八、结语

从口脂到蔻丹，这些传统彩妆从出现到发展经历了上千年，也由此出现了很多相关的传说、典故与诗词。对于民族彩妆来说，这些都是祖先流传下来的宝藏。我国历史与文学作品中对于彩妆的记载多如繁星，本篇文章呈现的不足其中一二。汇总这些内容，旨在抛砖引玉，引发民族化妆品产业对传统文化的兴趣与思考。至于化妆品品牌如何在浩如烟海的传统文化中立足，又如何引起消费者的兴趣，则需要在实践中进行摸索。

（摘自《中国化妆品》2020 年第 7 期文章《从春秋到民国——浅谈中国彩妆三千年》）

Notes

1.

［原文］ 随着传统文化的崛起，国内化妆品从山寨欧美化妆品，即标榜原料、包装、

功效等与国外大牌处于同一水平的同质低价战略，转而向内求，根据传统文化与东方审美定位品牌、包装、原料等，并由此涌现出一些深受年轻消费群体欢迎的品牌。

［译文］ With the rise of traditional Chinese culture, domestic cosmetics, which once counterfeited European and American cosmetics, claiming the raw materials, packaging, and efficacy of their products were of the same quality as those of foreign brands but with lower prices, have turned to seek development of Chinese own products. With brands, packaging and raw materials positioned anew in line with traditional culture and oriental aesthetics, some of the domestic brands have become very popular among young consumers.

［解析］ 原文是一个复合句，句子较长，翻译时先确定语义中心，理清句子各部分之间的逻辑关系，按语义层次断句，造出符合英语句法特点的句子。该句的语义中心是"国内化妆品……转而向内求"，翻译成英语句子的主干"domestic cosmetics... have turned to seek development of Chinese own products..."；"山寨欧美化妆品，即标榜原料、包装、功效等与国外大牌处于同一水平的同质低价战略"，是说明国内化妆品"转向内求"的背景情况，译成定语从句"which once counterfeited European and American cosmetics, claiming the raw materials, packaging, and efficacy of their products were of the same quality as those of foreign brands but with lower prices"，整个句子呈现出英语句式的树状结构特征。"根据传统文化与东方审美定位品牌、包装、原料等"是"转向内求"的标准和要求，按照这一标准和要求，"涌现出一些深受年轻消费群体欢迎的品牌"，两者具有条件或因果关系，使用"with…positioned anew…"结构，将两者合并，译成"with brands, packaging and raw materials positioned anew in line with traditional culture and oriental aesthetics, some of the domestic brands have become very popular among young consumers"，根据语义层次，独立成句。

2.
［原文］ 进入奴隶社会后，彩妆迎来了新纪元。
［译文］ Slave society saw a new era of makeup.
［解析］ 该句译文使用英语特有的句型，在此句型中 see 使用无生命的名词作主语，是一种拟人的用法，意为"经历、见证、目睹"，语言简洁生动。

3.
［原文］ 商朝末期，已经有了彩妆"燕支"，亦作"胭脂"。
［译文］ In the late Shang Dynasty, there was a makeup called *yanzhi*（燕支），also called *yanzhi*（胭脂 rouge）.
［解析］ 本文有很多中国化妆品名称的词汇，这些词汇具有特定的文化色彩，翻译时尽量保持原语文化，有助于中国文化的对外传播。因此该句中的"燕支""胭脂"的翻译采用音译法，译成 *yanzhi*，又因"燕支"与"胭脂"同音，所以在 *yanzhi* 后分别注上汉字"燕支"和"胭脂"，以示 *yanzhi* 在汉语中有不同的写法。

现列举本文中出现的其他中国化妆品名称及其翻译方法：
［原文］ 花钿又被称为花子、面花、贴花，是贴在眉间和脸上的一种小装饰。
［译文］ *Huadian* is also called *huazi*, *mianhua*, and *tiehua*. It is a kind of small flower ornament pasted on women's foreheads and faces.（音译法）

［原文］ 在古代，口红被称为口脂、唇脂，自古以来就受到女性的喜爱。

［译文］ In ancient times, lipstick was called *kouzhi* or *chunzhi* (fat used for lip make-up), and it has been loved by women since ancient times. （音译+注释）

［原文］ 在古代多是天然的米粉、糊状的铅粉（又名铅华）、檀红色的铅粉（又名檀粉），以及珍珠粉等。

［译文］ In China ancient times, the most common powders included rice powder (powder made by grinding natural rice), paste-like lead powder [*qianfen*, also known as *qianhua* (white lead)], lead powder with sandalwood red [also known as *tanfen* (sandalwood powder)] and pearl powder and so on. （音译+注释）

［原文］ 消失在历史中的额黄

［译文］ *E'huang* (yellow foreheads) lost in the history （音译+注释）

［原文］ 画眉墨黛

［译文］ *Dai* (a black pigment used by women in ancient times to paint their eyebrows) （音译+注释）

［原文］ 有史料记载，除了石黛，还有螺子黛与青雀头黛等。

［译文］ Besides *shidai*, there are historical records of *luozidai* (livid eyebrow paint) and *qingquetoudai* (dark gray eyebrow paint). （音译+注释）

［原文］ 在历史文献中，关于胭脂的写法有很多，如"焉支""烟支""鲜支""燕支""燕脂""阏氏"等。

［译文］ In historical documents, there are many spellings of rouge, such as *yanzhi* (焉支), *yanzhi* (烟支), *xianzhi* (鲜支), *yanzhi* (燕支), *yanzhi* (燕脂), *yanzhi* (阏氏) and so on. （音译+原文）

［原文］ 美甲蔻丹

［译文］ *Koudan* (nail enamel/nail polish)（音译+对等注释）

［原文］ 蔻丹是一种花，俗名千层红，又名指甲草。

［译文］ *Koudan* (impatiens flower) is a kind of flower, with its popular names as *qiancenghong* (thousand-tier-red flower) or fingernail grass. （音译+注释）

4.

［原文］ 民国时期，受欧美文化以及好莱坞影星的影响，人们的审美开始西化，使用的彩妆也是国外产品，或是国内化妆品企业仿制欧美彩妆生产的产品，传统彩妆的发展被按了暂停键。

［译文］ During the period of the Republic of China, the aesthetics of people began to be westernized under the influence of European and American cultures and the Hollywood movie stars. As a result, they chose to use foreign makeup products or their imitations that domestic cosmetics companies produced. And thus, the development of traditional makeup was paused.

［解析］ 原文句子较长，先理清句子各组成部分间的因果逻辑关系，进行断句。翻译时使用了表示因果关系的关联词 as a result 和 and thus，将原句译成3个句子。

5.

［原文］ "腊日，献口脂"。

［译文］ *kouzhi* was offered to the dinitaries on the Laba Festival, one of the Chinese Traditional Festivals.

［解析］ 译文中对"腊日"做了注释，即"…the Laba Festival, one of the Chinese Traditional Festivals"，让读者了解文化背景。

相同的译法本文还有：

［原文］ 受吐蕃服饰、妆面的影响，唐朝出现了"啼妆""泪妆"。

［译文］ Under the influence of *Tubo* (Tibetan regime in ancient China) costumes and makeup, "weeping makeup" and "tears makeup" appeared at that time.

［原文］ 据《新唐书》记载，杨贵妃的3位姐姐应召入宫，其脂粉费最多的时候达百万钱。

［译文］ According to *the New Book of Tang*, when three sisters of Yang Guifei (Yang Yuhuan, Emperor Xuanzong's favorite concubine during his later years) were once called into the palace, they were vouchsafed as many as hundreds of thousands of silver coins for cosmetics.

［原文］ 张骞出使西域时带回中原。

［译文］ Zhang Qian (an outstanding diplomat in the Han Dynasty) brought the kind of flower back to the Central Plains during his diplomatic mission to the Western Regions.

6.

［原文］ 张爱玲就是民国时期的口红"达人"。

［译文］ Eileen Chang, a modern Chinese writer, was a lipstick "master" of the Republic of China.

［解析］ 关于人名的翻译，我们遵从"名从主人"的原则。张爱玲英文名为 Eileen Chang，而不是 Zhang Ailing。

7.

［原文］ 在我国古代，很多人家都会养一些指甲草，采集好花瓣，加上明矾捣烂，敷在指甲上几个小时或隔夜，可以把指甲染成粉色和红色。

［译文］ In ancient China, many people would plant *koudan* in their home, collect its petals, and mash and apply on nails. A few hours later or overnight, the nails were dyed pink and red.

［解析］ 本句翻译采用顺译法，即译文基本上保留原文的逻辑顺序。英语和汉语在描述行为过程时，逻辑思维顺序基本相同，语义排列也基本相同，翻译时可使用此法。在主语转换的地方，可以断句。

Translation Skills (V) Logical Relationship and Cohesion（逻辑与衔接）

(一) **Hypotaxis and Parataxis**（形合和意合）

所谓形合（hypotaxis），指的是句中的词语或分句之间用语言形式（如关联词）连接起来，表达语法意义和逻辑关系。*The American Heritage Dictionary* 给形合定义为："The dependent or subordinate construction or relationship of clauses with connectives, for example, I shall despair *if* you don't come."形合采用词汇手段（lexical devices）或句法手段（syntactic devices）实现内部的连接或句子间的连接。英语中起连接作用的词语包括连词（如 and, or, but, if, when 等）、副词（如 therefore, hence, consequently 等）、形容词（如 nex, final 等）、代词（如 other, still another, this, that 等）、各种短语（介词短语如 in a word, in short, at least, for example, in addition, by contrast 等；形容词短语如 more than, rather than 等；动词短语如 to sum up, to put it another way, to be more exact 等），以至短句（如 that is to say）。英语句子的特点是注重形式和功能，英语的句法特征是形合（hypotaxis），强调显性连接，因而英语造句主要采用形合法。

所谓意合，指的是词语或分句之间不由语言形式连接，句中的语法意义和逻辑关系通过词语或分句的意义表达。*The World Book Dictionary* 给意合定义为："The arranging of clauses one after the other without connectives showing the relation between them. Example: The rain fell; the river flooded; the house washed away."汉语中也有相关的连接词语，如"因此""以免""然后""否则"等，但是使用频率偏低；还有句法手段，如"语序排列""反复""对比""紧缩"等，但是这些句法往往简明紧凑，互文见义，一般不需要关联词，语义明确。汉语句子的特点是"以意统形"，句法特征是意合，强调意义/隐性关联而不在意词语之间和句际之间的形式连接，因而汉语造句主要采用意合法（parataxis）。

英语的形合特征要求在理解英语时，可以通过逻辑关系词或连接词弄清语句的逻辑关系；汉语的意合特征要求在理解汉语时可以通过意义的把握，理清词、句之间暗含的逻辑关系。在语义呈现阶段，英译汉时要根据对英语句子的结构、形式分析，确定汉语的功能、意义，组词造句，简约隐含；汉译英时，要根据对汉语句子的功能、意义分析，确定英语句子的结构、形式，连词成句，严谨外显。英汉互译往往是英语语法型语句与汉语语义型语句之间的转换，充分实现目的语语境中的"形合"和"意合"。

英语重形合并不表明它就没有意合句，汉语重意合也不表明它没有形合句。一般地说，英语形合句多，汉语意合句多。但其多少与文体密切相关。英语中文学、科技等各种文体形合句均占优势，而汉语中现代科技、论述等庄重文体与文学文体相比也多采用形合句，以表达清晰的逻辑关系和复杂的思想内容。轻工学术翻译属科技翻译大类，英语、汉语表达上形合句均占优势，但在英汉互译过程中，要根据实际情况把握两种语言形合、意合的具体语境，通过修改和调整，做到"形合"和"意合"兼备，避免过于重视形合而忽视意合或过于重视意合而忽视形合。请看下例：

[原文] At present, China has become the second largest cosmetics consumer market in the world, second only to the United States, and its growth rate is faster than the global average. It is estimated that, by 2025, the scale of China's cosmetics market will reach 500 billion yuan, and that online consumption scale will reach 50% then, with more diversified consumption functions, and more abundant product types and structures. China's huge population will give impetus to the sustainable development of cosmetics in the future. Global cosmetics giants will penetrate into the domestic market with the help of online shopping platforms, while local Chinese enterprises need to improve their market competitiveness through technological innovation of products, marketing promotion adapted to the new mode of effectiveness, differentiation and transformation of product structures.

[译文] 目前，中国已成为世界第二大化妆品消费市场，仅次于美国，增长速度高于全球平均水平。据估计，到2025年，中国化妆品市场规模将达到5000亿元，网上消费比例将达到50%，消费功能更加多样化，产品种类和结构更加丰富。中国庞大的人口将推动未来化妆品的可持续发展。全球化妆品巨头将借助网上购物平台进入国内市场，而中国本土企业则需要通过产品的技术创新、适应新的有效模式的营销推广、产品结构的差异化和转型来提高自身的市场竞争力。

[解析] 原文属于论述文体，起连接作用的词法和句法有13处，译文共有6处，明显少于原文，体现了英语重形合、汉语重意合的特征。但是译文中的形合法运用得当，结构严谨，语义关系明确。

（二）Cohesion and Coherence（衔接与连贯）

衔接（cohesion）和连贯（coherence）是语篇的两大基本特征，合格的语篇都必须衔接合理，符合逻辑，语义连贯。

衔接是指语篇内各部分之间有语法和/或词汇方面的联系。语篇中的语句通过照应（reference）、替代（substitution）、省略（ellipsis）、联结（conjunction）等语法衔接（grammatical cohesion）形式和原词复现（reiteration）、同义（synonymy）、下义（hyponymy）、搭配（collocation）等词汇衔接（lexical cohesion）形式形成表层结构的一致。

连贯是指语篇内不同组成部分之间在意义和/或功能上的联系。连贯使得语篇中的语句在主题思想、语义结构、逻辑关系、组篇功能等各方面形成一个深层意义上的有机整体。连贯是衡量语篇完整性及语篇整体质量的准则，没有连贯就没有语篇。

语篇表层的衔接关系是建立在深层的连贯关系基础上的，语篇深层的连贯性是通过各种衔接手段的应用以及语言结构与叙述顺序的合理安排来实现的。恰当地使用一定的衔接方式实现语篇连贯是语篇生成的目的。

在语篇翻译中，要充分认识到衔接与连贯的重要性。以语篇为基础的翻译活动，翻译的直接对象和最终产品都是语篇，翻译的过程实际上就是语篇连贯的识别与重构过程，因此，在理解原文时，要认真领会、把握其中外在的衔接手段和内在的逻辑连贯关系，在进行译文表达时，要能创造性地运用衔接手段再现原文的连贯性。

英汉语篇互译时，原文语篇是连贯的，译文语篇也必须是连贯的，但是不同的语言表达方式反映了思维模式的不同，其衔接手段和连贯机制也有所不同。英语重形合，汉语重意合，这就意味着英语造句谋篇注重结构形式，常常借助各种显性连接手段，汉语造句谋篇则注重功能意义，少用或不用连接手段。因此，在英汉语篇互译时，为了产生连贯的译文语篇，语篇的衔接方式有可能保留，也有可能改变和有所增减。

[原文] In terms of the part of the body, traditional cosmetics can fall into the following categories: the head and face, the oral lip, the hair and mustache, body cleaning and perfuming, the hand and foot, and so on. They have basically covered all parts of the body. In terms of purpose, they can fall into the following categories: whitening the skin and beautifying the face, removing spots and black spots, moistening the skin and removing wrinkles, adding good odor to the mouth, protecting the teeth and beautifying the lips, blackening and nourishing the hair, removing scars and warts, preventing and curing acne and cracked skin on hand and foot, etc. In variety, there are the face rouge, hand cream, mouth rouge, face drug, paste rouge, face brightener, jade polishing powder, hair moisturizer, face powder, beauty treatment powder, bathing bean, facial cleanser, face ornaments, eyebrow blackener, bathing dew, fragrant dew, etc. In usage, there are the spreading method, friction method, bathing method, infusion method, grinding method, etc.

[译文] 传统化妆品，按照身体适用部位可以分为头部、面部化妆品，口唇用化妆品，头发、胡须用化妆品，身体清洁、调香化妆品，手部、脚部用化妆品等类别。这些化妆品基本覆盖了身体所有部位。按照用途可分为美白美容、祛斑祛黑、润肤祛皱、口腔增香、护齿美唇、乌发养发、祛疤祛疣、防治痤疮和手足皮肤皲裂等类别。按照品种划分，有腮红、护手霜、口红、面药、胭脂膏、高光、玉石抛光粉、润发产品、散粉、美容护肤粉、沐浴豆、洗面奶、面饰、眉黑剂、沐浴露、香露等类别。按照使用方法划分，有涂抹、摩擦、沐浴、注射、研磨等类别。

[解析] 原文段落共 5 句，分别从身体适用部位、用途、品种和用法对传统化妆品进行分类。前两句根据身体使用部位进行分类，第一句中的 body 与 head, face, lip, hair, mustache, hand, foot 构成上下义关系；第二句和第三句的主语代词 they 代替第一句中的 traditional cosmetics，实现了替代衔接；第一、三、四、五句使用了介词短语 in terms of the part of the body, in terms of purpose, in variety 和 in usage，不仅清楚地表明段落的结构层次，而且 purpose, variety, usage 与第一句中的 body 一样与其主句的内容分别构成上下义关系。该段落的主题是描述传统化妆品的类别，从不同的角度展开具体分类，层次清楚，语义连贯。

译文基本上保持了原文的结构，对应地译成 5 句。译文中第二句的主语"化妆品"代替原文中的 they，符合汉语中重复名词实现替代衔接的表达习惯。译文中第一、三、四、五句使用了 4 个"按照"和 4 个"类别"，其中第四句和第五句中"类别"是增补上去的概括词，段落内部衔接得当，语义逻辑上连贯流畅。

（三）Adjustment of Logical Connection in Translation（译文逻辑连接的调整）

逻辑指的是思维的规律。逻辑思维（logical thinking）是指符合某种人为制定的思维规则和思维形式的思维方式，我们所说的逻辑思维主要是指遵循传统形式逻辑规则的思维方式。思维方式是指人们看待事物的角度、方式和方法。思维方式与语言密切相关，是语言生成和发展的深层机制，一个民族的语言集中体现了该民族的思维方式。

中西方不同的思维方式影响着汉英语言不同的表达形式。西方倡导严密的科学态度和逻辑分析，通过逻辑分析实现对事物的认识和了解，强调严密的语言体系，把语言作为逻辑思维的外在表现。语法从属于逻辑，句子成分可与逻辑范畴等同。英语造句谋篇重形合，音节构成词，由词构成句子，句子构成文，都有严格的形态规定，比较注重结构形式和逻辑的合理性，呈现为显性的逻辑关系。而中国只求整体把握和领悟，汉语表现为含蓄和模糊，注重辩证逻辑而不注重形式逻辑，其逻辑关系往往通过语言环境和语言内在的联系来表现和解读，呈现为隐性的逻辑关系。英汉互译时，我们要充分挖掘原文的逻辑关系，按照目的语的行文习惯，充分考虑译文读者的逻辑思维模式，来重建原文的逻辑关系，让译文读者对原文中的意思能够了解透彻。具体来讲，由于思维模式的差异，英汉语言在原因、条件、目的、结果、转折、让步、肯定否定等逻辑关系表达时有所不同，我们在翻译过程中，要注意逻辑关系的调整，对原文信息进行切分，理顺原文的逻辑关系，确立逻辑层次，按照目的语的特点调整语句结构、合理安排语序、增减关联词、正确选择时态语态的表现形式，采取适当的表现法，构建译文，保证译文逻辑明晰流畅。

[原文] What is a cosmetic? The U.S. *Food, Drug, and Cosmetic Act* of 1938 defines cosmetics as "articles intended to be rubbed, poured, sprinkled or sprayed on, introduced into, or otherwise applied to the human body or any part thereof, for cleansing, beautifying, promoting attractiveness or altering the appearance...." Soap, although obviously used for cleansing, is specifically excluded from coverage by the law. Also excluded are substances that affect the body's structure or functions. Antiperspirants, products that reduce perspiration, are legally classified as drugs. So are antidandruff shampoos. The main difference between drugs and cosmetics is that drugs must be proven "safe and effective" before they are marketed; cosmetics generally do not have to be tested before they're marketed. Most brands of a given type of cosmetic contain the same (or quite similar) active ingredients. Thus, advertising is usually geared to selling sex, smell, and status rather than the actual components.

[译文] 什么是化妆品？美国1938年颁布的《食品、药品和化妆品法案》将化妆品定义为"为了达到清洁、美化身体，增加魅力，改变容貌等目的，而以涂抹、洒泼、洒喷或雾喷、导入或其他类似方法用于人体的任何部位的物品"。尽管肥皂是常见的用于清洁的物品，但是法律明确规定肥皂不属于化妆品类。还有些物品因其影响人体的结构或功能，也不属于化妆品类，如止汗剂和去屑洗发剂。止汗剂因其具有减少人体排汗的功能，法律规定其属于药品类；去屑洗发剂（因其具有抑制皮脂分泌等作用）也属于药品类。药品和化妆品的主要区别在于：药品需要证明"安全有效"才能在市场上销售，而化妆品通常不需要证明就可销售。特定类型的化妆品，虽然品牌多样，但其活性成分相同（或相近），因此，化妆品广告通常不提及其组成成分，而是以其能够提高性别魅力、修正人体气味、让人保持良好状态为卖点进行宣传。

[解析] 原文段落由9个句子组成，从不同的侧面呈现了"化妆品的范畴"这一段落主题。行文逻辑如下：第一句提出话题"什么是化妆品"，第二句给出"化妆品的定义"，第三、第四、第五、第六句列举不属于化妆品但易于误解的常用物品并说明理据，第七句指出药品和化妆品的区别，第八和第九句说明化妆品的成分及其对化妆品广告的影响。段落内部使用了一些逻辑连接词，如for, or, although, also, so, before, thus, rather than等。原文逻辑层次清楚，句子内部、句子与句子之间在语言结构上衔接得当，段落层面上语义逻辑连贯流畅。

译文由7个句子组成，按照原文的逻辑层次顺序从前往后翻译形成段落，也使用了一些逻辑连接词，如而、但是、还有、也、如、因、但、因此等，在段落或语篇层面上常常采用这种翻译方法，尤其是科技类型的段落或语篇翻译，译文的逻辑层次和原文基本保持顺序上的一致。在句子和词汇层面上，原文第二句中的"articles intended to be rubbed, poured, sprinkled or sprayed on, introduced into, or otherwise applied to the human body or any part thereof, for cleansing, beautifying, promoting attractiveness or altering the appearance ...."表达词序和习惯都和汉语相差很大,我们就从后面开始翻译,即"为了达到清洁、美化身体,增加魅力,改变容貌等目的,而以涂抹、洒泼、洒喷或雾喷、导入或其他类似方法用于人体或部分人体的物品"。这种倒叙法是英汉互译中经常使用的翻译方法。例如:在英语句子里面,一般是先主再从,而汉语是先从后主;英语里的时间状语一般放在后面,而汉语放在前面;等等。在翻译时,一般要进行语序的调整,以符合目的语的表达习惯。为了表达顺畅,译文常常进行肯定与否定表达方式转换,如原文第三句和第四句中的 excluded 译为"不属于"。原文第四、第五、第六句属于一个语义层次,其中第五、第六句是举例说明第四句的"有些物质因影响人体的结构或功能,不能称为化妆品",因此翻译时第五、第六句的部分内容与第四句进行合并,增加了逻辑连接词"如",即"还有些物品因其影响人体的结构或功能,也不属于化妆品类,如止汗剂和去屑洗发剂"。然后译文再分别叙述"止汗剂"和"去屑洗发剂"。这种合译法是根据原文语句的句义及其中的主次、逻辑、修饰关系,将几个短句糅合在一起,组成一个简单译句使得译文言简意赅,语义流畅。原文第四句和第五句中的两个以 that 引导的定语从句,在逻辑上与句子其他部分具有因果关系,因此分别译成"因其影响人体的结构或功能"和"因其具有减少人体排汗的功能"。为了达到逻辑意义上的完整,第六句译文增补了"因其具有抑制皮脂分泌等作用"。原文第七句中两个分句中被动语态在译文中转换成主动语态,before 译成"......才......",实现了英语到汉语思维模式的转换。原文第八句中 Most brands of a given type of cosmetic 逻辑上与后半句具有转折对比关系,因此译成"特定类型的化妆品,虽然品牌多样,但其活性成分相同(或相近)"。原文第九句中的 rather than the actual components,其译文"通常不提及其组成成分"进行了前置处理;对 selling sex, smell, and status 进行了语义增补,译成"提高性别魅力、修正人体气味、让人保持良好状态",译文读来通顺达意、符合汉语表达习惯。原文第八、第九句在段落结构上属于一个语义层次,连接紧密,因此合译成一个并列复合句,使用逻辑关联词"虽然、但、因此、而"等,逻辑关系清楚,语义连贯。

通过以上分析,我们可以看出英汉翻译时逻辑关系调整的重要性。这种逻辑关系调整主要体现在词语、句子和篇章三个层面。因此,在理解原文时,要弄清这三个层面各自内部及相互之间内在的逻辑关系,然后找出英汉两种语言在逻辑上的对应关系,选择适当的转换方法——语序调整法、分合译法、正反译法、增减译法等,和适当的逻辑关系表达手段,译成符合目的语逻辑的译文。

Translation Workshop

I. **Translate the following sentences and pay attention to hypotaxis and parataxis**

1. Both inorganic and organic pigments and metallic lakes are used to give intensity and variation of color.

2. A good lipstick is easy to apply, giving a film on the lips that is neither excessively greasy nor too dry, that is reasonably permanent but capable of deliberate removal, and which has a stable color.

3. Even the healthy and normal skin may vary from time to time and need particular care to correct any departure from normality.

4. Skin care, which has the maintenance of a soft, supple and clean skin and the prevention of effects due to external causes such as excessive exposure to cold, heat, sun, wind, etc.

5. Colorless foundation is available to consumers that reacts and creates a perfect match with any skin tone once it is applied to the face.

6. 随着中式审美的觉醒及文化自信的回归，更多化妆品品牌将中国传统文化提炼创新，应用于国产化妆品包装设计，使国产化妆品有了更大的发展空间。

7. 纯植物与中草药是国产化妆品的代名词之一，其品牌优势就在于中华传统草药及其天然植物提取物健康、温和的吸引力，这与如今消费者追求健康安全的心理是相符的。

8. 维生素C，又称抗坏血酸，自20世纪50年代起就广泛应用于美白祛斑类化妆品中，是目前应用最广的一种美白成分添加剂。

9. 近几年中国本土化妆品品牌崛起趋势明显，这些品牌普遍使用的中式风格的包装设计，强调国产品牌的身份，引导消费者去发现品牌底蕴和文化内涵，成功打造了东方美学代表品牌的形象。

10. 随着材料的改进，高功能化妆品已经开发出来，可以隐藏瑕疵，遮掩雀斑，缓解皮肤粗糙，不因皮脂或其他原因而脱落。

Ⅱ. Translate the following passage into Chinese

Today, consumers are looking for science-driven skin care that can improve and prevent skin aging, protect skin from environmental damage and provide therapeutic options for a myriad of skin problems. They want products that are natural, non-irritating, preservative-free, green and fully tested. This is a tall order for manufacturers who have to balance product safety, stability, consistency and efficacy while at the same time meeting consumer demands. The future of cosmeceuticals depends on innovation. Identifying product niches, new actives and more effective delivery systems will no doubt give way to a plethora of cosmeceutical products with broader clinical applications.

In spite of industry's best efforts, consumers remain skeptical about cosmeceuticals. They are confused about ingredients and distrust product claims leaving them to wonder if these products are really worth the money. When shopping for cosmeceuticals, consumers are confused by ambiguous package labeling that lacks specific information including the concentration of key active ingredients. Many of these concerns could be addressed if stricter regulations were in place for cosmeceutical products. There are also significant challenges that must be met in order for cosmeceuticals to be legitimized in the eyes of physicians. Many dermatologists state that they do not believe in the validity of cosmeceuticals since they lack the scientific rigor that is applied to pharmaceuticals. This is a valid complaint that can only be addressed if manufacturers test products in an objective manner in order to substantiate claims. It is encouraging that some of the newer cosmeceuticals have been tested in double-blind vehicle-controlled studies designed to confirm their efficacy. In order to assist physician members in gathering credible information about cosmeceuticals, the American Academy of Dermatology (AAD) has convened the Work Group on Complementary and Alternative Medicine. This group includes dermatologists and members of the governing bodies that regulate cosmetics. Through this group we hope to provide AAD members with easy access to safety and efficacy data on cosmeceutical products and other alternative treatments.

(摘自 *Cosmeceaticals and Cosmetic Practice*)

III. Translate the following passage into English

在化妆品的领域里，中国化妆品品牌总是难望境外品牌之项背。国内中高档商场被洋品牌盘踞，本土品牌难见踪影，基本退出一二级主流渠道，品牌能见度几乎为零，消费影响力近乎为"0"。

谁来演绎世界上人数最多的中国女人的美？制造中国女人美的梦工厂到底在哪里？

也许是经济基础决定了心理走向，也许是文化渗透改变了东方人的认知。直到金融危机席卷全球，中国经济经受住了考验，中国化妆品品牌的未来才呈现出那么一丝曙光！

欧莱雅、资生堂、宝洁、联合利华等得益于中国市场贡献其市场利润的同时也撩开了它们高贵的面纱。对于消费者而言，顶礼膜拜的心态渐渐消退，进而转变为对品牌的多元化选择。这种消费心理的转变带给了中国化妆品品牌巨大的市场空间。霸王、丸美、名门闺秀、美肤宝、迪彩、婷美等一大批优秀品牌的市场趋势印证了这一点。

伴随着中国女性的成长，以及代表着东方性格的化妆理念、美容理念、养护理念等系统观念的诞生和传播，新东方式化妆品将以全新的产品形态出现，这为中国化妆品品牌提供了巨大的市场机遇。

有空间，有机遇！中国化妆品市场山雨欲来风满楼！即将到来的是中国化妆品品牌崛起的大时代！

面对一个即将发生变革的世界，中国化妆品品牌应该做好哪些准备呢？

首先，中国的化妆品企业要在品牌战略上做好与强者竞争的准备。

其次，中国化妆品品牌要做好"切割市场"的准备。中国女性消费者的化妆品消费特征已经从"跟风式潮流"转化为"丰富的个性化需求"。这种需求的显著变化使得化妆品企业有更多的角度去进行定位。每一次成功的差异化定位都可能成就一个伟大的品牌。

传统的金字塔型品牌格局势必被打破，中国化妆品品牌不能永远居于第三阵营（第一阵营为欧美品牌，第二阵营为日韩品牌，第三阵营为本土品牌）。中国的化妆品品牌只要拿出第一的气势，勇于抢占品牌新高度，在有力的营销支持下，一定会被很大一批消费者所认同，进而与外资化妆品品牌分庭抗礼。

再次，中国化妆品品牌必须做好"东方型"产品研发的准备。所谓东方型产品是指建立在东方文化基础之上与消费者沟通的产品。这种产品可以采取新的产品形态，也可以采取新的产品概念。吉利能够收购沃尔沃在某种程度上说明了外资品牌并不是不可挑战的神话。只要在战略上，"抢占高度，与强者并行"；在策略上，"挖掘角度，清晰化定位"；在产品上，"大胆求新，敢于创意"，中国化妆品品牌将完全有能力迎接新市场机遇下的挑战。

有信心的女人最美丽！有信心的品牌最耀眼！

正所谓"天与不取，反受其咎"，当时代给予中国化妆品登上世界化妆品品牌之巅的机会时，中国的化妆品品牌不应胆怯，更不应拒绝！

坦然地迎接挑战，拿出全球志！打造中国势！

（摘自《营销界·化妆品观察》2010年第7期文章《谁来拯救中国的美》）

Appendix

Unit 1　Design Studies and Chinese Art

Warming-up（Passage A）

graphic design　　　　　　平面设计
incremental innovation　　　渐进性创新
radical innovation　　　　　突破性创新
human-centered design　　　以人为中心的设计
affordances　　　　　　　　功能可供性
technological determinism　　技术决定论
research into design　　　　深入设计之研究
research through design　　　通过设计之研究
research for design　　　　　为了设计之研究
ethnographic research　　　　人种学

Translation（Passage A）

渐进性创新与激进性创新：设计研究与技术及意义变革

本文旨在提供区分渐进性创新和激进性创新过程的理论框架，并讨论创新的基本活动。为此，我们提供了关于创新的3种不同探讨方式：试图在种类未知的新型丘陵地带找到顶点，在由"技术变革"和"意义变革"两轴所界定的产品空间移动，以及基于斯托克斯（Stokes）的"认识上的进步"和"实用性考虑"两个维度的设计研究四边形。

本文开门见山地指出，激进性的产品创新是由技术进步或审慎的产品意义变革驱动的，而不是由广泛应用于产品设计的以人为中心的设计理念驱动的。在我们对现有的产品和创新文献的考察中，我们无法找到任何反证。渐进性创新是审慎的设计研究战略的结果，或通过产品开发者和使用群体的一系列相互调适，使两者更加趋向一致的结果。与此相反，激进的产品推出总是可以追溯到新技术的引入，该技术可以给设计师或给产品及其用途的新的意义提供新的功能可供性，以至使用现有的技术也能带来激进性变革。当然，某些激进性变革既包括新技术也包括意义变革。

请注意，相对于时下技术和社会决定论的相对重要性之间的争论，我们的观察和诠释都是中立的。我们可以把技术驱动的激进性创新解释为技术决定论的例子，把意义驱动的激进性创新解释为社会决定论的例子，把以人为中心的渐进性创新解释为技术或者社会决定论，这都取决于所涉及的理论偏向。我们相信，与技术和社会决定论相关的因素始终都在发挥作用。

一、设计研究分类

在设计研究中，研究的概念有两种不同的形式。一种观点认为，研究是带来知识进步、理论发展和理论应用的探索和实验。这种观点一直是设计理论家反思、定义、有效分类的对象。例如，大家熟知的弗雷灵（Frayling）的设计研究分类由3个部分组成，包括深入设计之研究、通过设计之研究和为了设计之研究。有关此分类，还可参见克洛斯（Cross）、弗里德曼（Friedman）以及菲斯特（Feast）和梅勒斯（Melles）的论述。这些定义都以认识论为基础，旨在推动知识的进步。

另一种观点认为，研究是为了更好地理解某个主题而进行的数据采集和分析活动（因此这包括一名小学生为了写一篇有关老虎饮食的文章而进行的研究）。从业者一般使用这种观点标示他们的研究活动。例如，他们可能会运用人种学研究或观察人的活动，从而了解用户需求；以产品研发为手段，找出可能的解决方案；运用市场调研，了解人们具有购买欲望的产品类别以及他们对价格的敏感度；运用可用性研究，说明人与产品之间的交互。在这第二种观点中，设计研究主要关注如何改进产品以及如何提高销售量。我们在本文中集中讨论第二种设计研究观点。

二、两种类型的创新：渐进性创新与激进性创新

我们可以发现很多种创新，分类也可能因创新对象而有所不同。例如，创新类别包括社会文化制度创新、生态系统创新、商业模式创新、产品创新、服务创新、流程创新、组织创新、制度安排创新等。分类也可能因创新的驱动因素（技术、市场、设计、用户等）而有所不同，或因创新的力度而有所不同。我们在本文中重点关注产品及服务的两类创新：

- 渐进性创新：给定解决方案框架内的提高（即"把我们已经做的做得更好"）；
- 激进性创新：框架的变化（即"做我们之前没有做过的"）。

两类创新之间的主要区别在于，是把创新视为对以前认可的做法的不断改进，还是认为创新就是新的、独特的、非连续的。达林（Dahlin）和贝伦斯（Behrens）提出了激进性创新的3个识别标准：

- 标准1：发明必须具有新颖性：它应不同于以往的发明；
- 标准2：发明必须具有唯一性：它应不同于当前的发明；
- 标准3：发明必须得到采用：它应影响到未来发明的内容。

前两个标准界定了激进性，第3个标准界定了成功。虽然标准1和标准2在任何时候都可以达到，但是只有当社会、市场和文化力量基本处于同一水平时，才会达到标准3。这是社会决定论发挥重要作用的地方。正确的想法在错误的时间也会失败。例如，苹果公司在20世纪90年代推出了QuickTake数码相机和牛顿个人数字助理，尽管满足标准1和标准2，但两个产品在市场上都失败了，因为失败在标准3上面。虽然失败的原因很复杂，但是诺曼作为当时苹果公司的高管认为，这些失败将成为社会决定论信徒的绝佳案例。

设计和管理界有关创新的很多论述都聚焦在激进性创新上。激进性创新常常被定性为颠覆性的或能力摧毁型的，或者是一项突破。所有这些标签都有一个相同的概念，即激进性创新意味着与过去的不连续性。数十年来，激进性创新一直是创新研究关注的焦点。设

计和商学院都开设激进性创新课程，讨论创新与"设计思维"的人最近也很推崇激进性创新。虽然激进性创新具有显著的分化潜力，每个人都希望激进性创新，但令人惊讶的是，成功的激进性创新非常罕见，大多数尝试都以失败告终。事实上，据德布林（Doblin）集团总裁拉里·基利（Larry Keeley）估算，失败率高达96%。成功的激进性创新在所有领域都不常见——也许每隔5~10年才会发生。

大多数激进性创新都花了相当长的时间才为人们所接受（即满足达林和贝伦斯的标准3）。此外，完全新颖的创新是不可能的：所有的创意都有前人的影子，总是基于以前的工作——有时是细化，有时是若干既有创意的新颖组合。苹果公司所推出的基于手势的手机表明，创意并非无中生有。苹果公司开发了多点触控界面及相关手势来控制手持式和桌面系统，这是当今激进性创新之一。然而，苹果公司既没有发明多点触控界面也没有发明手势控制。多点触控系统在计算机和设计实验室已经存在20多年了，手势也有很长的历史。此外，其他几家公司也在苹果公司之前在市场上推出了使用多点触控的产品。虽然苹果的创意对于科学界来说并非激进性的，但是它们确实在产品世界以及人们与产品的交互方式方面实现了重大转变，并赋予产品意义。

爱迪生开发的电灯泡也有类似之处，这项发明在家庭和企业掀起了一场大革命。但是，爱迪生并没有发明灯泡，他只是通过延长灯泡寿命，改进了现有的灯泡。他认识到提供所有必要的基础设施的重要性，这一点也一样重要。爱迪生考虑到了发电厂、配送系统，甚至是室内布线、安灯泡的插座等所有系统要求。因此，他的努力彻底改变了产品空间，以及家庭和企业的生活和运行模式。

渐进性产品创新是指产品的细小变化，这些变化有助于提高产品的性能，降低产品成本，并增强产品的合意性，或者直接导致新型号的发布。大多数成功的产品都经历了不断的渐进性创新，意在降低成本，提高效能。这种创新的主导形式并没有激进性创新那样激动人心，但也同样重要。激进性创新最初推出时很少能够实现它们的潜能。它们往往难以使用，价格昂贵，性能有限。与此同时，渐进性创新需要把激进的创意转化为消费者可以接受的形式，因为消费者往往都是跟着尝鲜的。这里的本质内容就是两种形式的创新都是必要的。激进性创新带来了新的领域和新的范式，为重大变革创造了潜能。渐进性创新就是如何抓住这种潜能的价值。没有激进性创新，渐进性创新就达到了极限。没有渐进性创新，产品就无法抓住激进性变革所带来的潜能。

Warming-up（Passage B）

对称	symmetry
儒家	Confucianism
中庸	*zhongyong*（doctrine of the mean）
黄金法则	golden rule
道家	Taoism
四合院	quadrangle courtyard
牌坊	*paifang*
民间艺术	folk art
自然法则	law of nature

良渚文化　　　　　　　　*Liangzhu* Culture

Translation（Passage B）

Symmetry in Chinese Art and Design

Symmetry has been widely used in various contexts. In traditional Chinese art and design, the concept of symmetry is one of the most important aesthetic principles. Symmetrical beauty is derived from nature, i. e. , law of nature in Taoism. The human body and almost all animals are symmetric, which shows a beauty of health and balance. Rather, asymmetry leaves people an impression of displeasure. Symmetry is also the manifestation of Chinese philosophy of harmony and *zhongyong* (the doctrine of the mean) in Confucianism. The aesthetic principle of symmetry in Chinese art is similar to the "Golden Rule" in the West, the aim of which is to achieve balance. This essay aims to discuss the aesthetic principle of symmetry used in traditional Chinese art and design, including ancient Chinese bronze artwork, ancient Chinese architecture and Chinese paper cutting.

Ⅰ. Symmetry in Ancient Chinese Bronze Artwork

Basically, bronzes can be classified into four types in terms of function: food vessels, wine vessels, water vessels and musical instruments. Various shapes and designs can be found in each type, fully demonstrating the creativity and skills of the ancient people. Despite this, symmetry was used as a universal basic aesthetic principle. Ancient Chinese bronzes stressed balance and symmetry of form, and communicated solemnity and ceremony.

Among the various kinds of bronze vessels, *ding* is a significant category. Originally, *ding* was used as food vessels and later evaluated to sacrificial vessels. *Ding* was described as a kind of vessel with three legs and two ears in the *Origin of Chinese Characters* (*Shuo Wen Jie Zi*), the first dictionary of Chinese compiled by Xu Shen in 121. Actually, most of the *dings* have three legs while some have four, like the famous *Hou Mu Wu Ding*. In the Bronze Age of the Chinese history, *ding* was regarded as the very foundation on which a country was built and a symbol of the nation, representing supreme royal power. Once the country is destroyed, *ding* will be removed. For example, when *Shang* Dynasty collapsed and *Zhou* Dynasty flourished, *dings* were moved from Bo to Haojing, the capital of *Zhou*.

The pattern applied on *ding* basically consists of taotie and clouds. Taotie, also known as "beast of gluttony", is a ferocious creature combining all sorts of animal characteristics in the natural world. Taotie is usually at the center of the *ding*, surrounded by clouds. The mythical ferocious beast taotie is overlooking the mortal world from heaven, with its body hidden in the clouds. Thus only the head of taotie appears on the bronzes. The taotie mask patterns have appeared frequently since Liangzhu Culture (3300-2300 BC) and are diverse from one to another. Despite their diversity, the taotie mask patterns are usually symmetric. Generally, the patterns mark the bridge of nose as the central line and both sides are situated in a symmetrical fashion. The integral shape of taotie pattern usually appears to be gorgeous and gives people a feeling of solemnity. The taotie pattern is symmetric and leaves people an impression of being ferocious, mysterious and terrible. As a matter of fact, symmetry adds to the majesty and prestige of the taotie pattern.

II. Symmetry in Ancient Chinese Architecture

Although only a small portion of Chinese architecture survived from antiquity, archaeological evidence shows that symmetry has been adopted as one of the basic principles of traditional Chinese architecture design.

The basic feature of Chinese architecture is rectangular-shaped units of space joined together into a whole. The quadrangle courtyard, or *siheyuan*, in Beijing is a typical example. It can be seen that the main structure of the quadrangle courtyard features a central axis, and the secondary structures are positioned as two wings on either side to form the main rooms and yard. Although the content of the quadrangle courtyard can be complex — consisting of meticulous design of the eaves and walls as well as windows and doors, the structure is quite simple. Liu Xiaoshi, a leading architect active in the preservation of old Beijing, once said "The design, layout and material of the old houses here reflect the ancient philosophy of harmony between humans and nature."

Quadrangle courtyards in Beijing demonstrate the combination of units of space in traditional Chinese architecture abiding by the principles of balance and symmetry. Similarities can be found in other examples like the Forbidden City. It is apparent that the whole Forbidden City is bilaterally symmetrical along the central axis. It runs from the Meridian Gate to the Shenwu Gate, and is coincident with the central axis of the city of Beijing. Situated along the central axis are the most significant palaces of the architectural complex, consisting of the three front halls and three back halls of both outer and inner courts. Symmetry, to some degree, adds to the stateliness and magnificence of the architectural complex. More importantly, symmetry helps to divide the distinct palaces into different status according to their function and master.

The concern with symmetry in ancient Chinese architecture can not only be seen from the integral structure, but also from the archways or doorways of many buildings.

Paifang, or archway, is an example of bilateral symmetry which is by far the most common form of symmetry in architecture. It is an ancient arch made of wood or stone and inlaid with glazed tiles. Its origin dates back to the Zhou Dynasty. Originally, paifang served as a marker for the entrance of building complexes, temples, parks, or towns. Later it was built for decoration. In many situations, paifang is also made in memory of someone for his merits and virtues. Paifang is symmetric, which shows the beauty of balance and leaves people an impression of virility, stateliness and simplicity.

Apart from bilateral symmetry, rotational symmetry can also be seen in ancient Chinese architecture. The round houses, also known as *Tulou*, is a large, enclosed and fortified earth building, circular in configuration, with very thick load-bearing rammed earth walls between three and five stories high, housing up to 80 families. It is a category of large-scale residential buildings. The architectural composition of rotational symmetry of round houses not only appears to be majestic from the outside, but also involves precise and ordered design of the interior. The rotational symmetry design fulfilled the creation of centripetalism, emphasizing the significance of the central position of the huge patio, and demonstrating the Hakka's value of clan collectivism.

III. Symmetry in Chinese Paper Cutting

Paper Cutting is a kind of folk art in China. Symmetry is adopted in Chinese paper cutting primarily as a skill. With the advent of replicating, paper cutting becomes more efficient and the image thus becomes symmetric. However, symmetry in Chinese paper cutting is more than a skill; it also serves as an aesthetic principle and has rich connotations.

Chinese culture values even number since it conveys the meaning of completeness and jollity. Paper cutting involves the red Chinese character 囍, meaning "Double Happiness". It adopts reflection symmetry and thus the bilateral sides of the pattern are mirror symmetrical to each other. It is apparent that paper cutting successfully expresses the theme of feast by adopting the symmetry principle.

IV. Conclusion

As shown through the analysis of various examples in Chinese art and design, including ancient Chinese bronze artwork, ancient Chinese architecture and Chinese paper cutting, symmetry perpetuates itself for its mark of balance, *zhongyong* and harmony. The three topics discussed in the essay demonstrated the variety of symmetry, the significant role it plays in Chinese art as well as its rich connotations. Hence it can be seen that symmetry, as an aesthetic principle, is closely bounded up with the core value of Chinese culture and philosophy and that the significance of symmetry in Chinese art and design cannot be ignored.

Translation Workshop

I. Translate the following sentences and pay attention to the modulation of voice

1. 在哲学层面上，我们可以找到类似的论点。一般认为，在这一层面上，处于新的可持续美学中心的物质体验影响着社会层面所发生的行为和生活方式变化。

2. 当用户需求一组资源时，必须确定这些资源是否会让系统处于安全状态。

3. 在火星上软着陆的仪器目前尚未探测到任何令人信服的动植物生命迹象。

4. 先进行工作坊训练，然后才开始测试学期的基础课程，检测学生的个人技能，讲授手工艺及设计基础。

5. 虽然节能建筑设计的许多创意至少已有几千年的时间了，但是直到目前才被提到新的高度。

6. The Huawei has been provided very little information regarding the charges and is unaware of any wrongdoing committed by Meng.

7. As I explained at the Boao Forum for Asia in April, China's economic growth over the past four decades has been achieved with a commitment to opening-up. In the same vein, high-quality development of China's economy in the future can only be guaranteed with greater openness.

8. Projects are often inspired by a particular style, which provides a theme for architects and designers to follow.

9. Modifications should always be clearly recorded, not only for future use by professionals involved in restoration and upkeep, but also as interpretative information available to the public, so that changes are not passed off as part of the original design.

10. Industrial design is the use of both applied art and applied science to improve the aesthetics, design, ergonomics, functionality, usability of a product, and it may also be used to improve the product's marketability and even production.

Ⅱ. **Translate the following passage into English**

A Chinese garden architecture is more playful than useful and, above all, more metaphorical. Gardens allowed the normal city architecture to be liberated from Confucian rectitude.

To list some common architectural elements in a garden with those Chinese phrases that have been associated with them will cast some light on this metaphorical dimension. Holes through a wall can be circular "moon gates", while sometimes they are in the shape of flowers, shells, gourds or vases. Balustrades can take on the pattern of "cracked ice"; pavilions over the water are "boats"; and five pavilions set together become "the claws of the five-toed imperial dragon". Rocks, of course, are "goblins and savage beasts", unless they are "bullet-holes"; a willow tree "sways like the slender waist of a dancing girl"; and the heart of the garden, the water, is where "the moon washes its soul". This delight in metaphor is noticeable even in the plans of buildings: some are in the shape of plum blossoms, or fans — a popular design since they combine the idea of cool breezes with a useful form for linking two galleries round a corner. Sometimes two pavilions are joined together at the corners to form a butterfly; reality everywhere is transformed into a poetic conceit.

Ⅲ. **Translate the following passage into Chinese**

工业设计师明确说明的产品特性可能包括产品的整体形态、细节部位、色彩、纹理、形状，以及有关产品使用的方方面面。此外，他们还可以对生产流程、材料选择以及产品在卖场向消费者展示的方式加以说明。工业设计师加入产品开发过程，可通过提高产品可用性、降低生产成本、开发更具吸引力的产品等为产品带来附加值。

工业设计也可专注于技术性概念、产品和流程。除了美学、可用性和人体工程学之外，它还包括工程设计、用途、市场布局和其他问题，如用户的心理、愿望和情感依恋。这些价值观以及与工业设计相生相伴的其他问题都因流派及职业设计师的不同而不同。

工业设计也成为建立企业形象的主要手段。小型企业往往把雇用工业设计师当作一种地位的象征，认为养一个设计师很了不起，没想到去用他。但是，大型企业则系统地使用设计师。他们不只是创造独特的单个产品，而是针对整个相关产品链条；他们不仅创造独特的产品，而且创造独特的企业形象。如果他是工匠、建筑师或工程师的后裔，那他还可以追寻祖先走街串巷出售秘方药品的血统。

Unit 2　Food Science and Chinese Food Culture

Warm-up（Passage A）

disharmony within the body	体内气血不和
health and longevity	健康长寿
herbal medicine	草药
diet therapy	食疗
pre-Qin dynasty	先秦朝代/时代
Yellow Emperor	黄帝
mutton	羊肉
greens	绿叶蔬菜
yin-yang dichotomy	阴阳辨证
white fungus	银耳

Translation（Passage A）

中国食品文化：饮食和健康

　　一直以来，中国人都相信饮食关系到健康，而疾病则源于体内气血不和。由此他们认为，维系气血调和、阴阳平衡才是健康长寿的关键。平衡一旦被打破，那就有必要通过干预措施进行纠偏，使人体机能恢复正常运转。中国人相信，这一措施有助于身体的自愈。时至今日，中国人依然使用传统疗法和草药来调和气血、平衡阴阳。

　　更重要的是，中国人懂得防患于未然，将食物用于预防疾病和调理身体。中国人还懂得寓医于食，相信合理膳食有助于强身健体和延年益寿。食疗理念构成了中华医学和药理实践中广受推崇的重要元素。

　　在黄帝诞辰2500年后的春秋时期，圣哲孔子在其编订的《诗经》中运用并拓展了这些思想。他收编的诗歌涉及了食材原料、饮食礼法、烹饪技法等。诗歌也通过列举有益健康的特定食物搭配探究了膳食平衡的原理。这些诗歌还详述了正向和负向、显性和隐性的相互作用原理，即中医所说的阴阳辨证关系。孔子认为，阴阳平衡对于维系宇宙和人体的内生秩序与和谐至关重要；同时，阴阳两性并非一成不变，而是一种对万物动态变化关系的描述，对天地发生演化现象的解释。孔子将黄帝视为上古时期（约公元前2100年）医学和食疗的鼻祖，并认为，源起于黄帝时期的许多概念，包括医药和健康，对后世子孙生活的方方面面都产生着深远的影响。

　　孔子认为，阴阳与"金、木、水、火、土"五行或者五相相辅相成。他认为，他们和"仁、义、礼、智、信"五常构成了宇宙律法，对世间万物乃至永恒的生命轮回施加了额外的影响。孔子等先哲认为参透五行意义重大，因为它们是一切天地道法和宇宙观的基石。它们构成了万物，包括营养健康和医学药理。

　　为何是五行呢？中国人喜欢将事物分类，5个一组最为常见。由于数字五是奇数，又属阳，因此人们赋予其吉祥之意。西方人的罗盘上有4个方向，即东、西、南、北；而中国人则讲"五方"，即"东、南、西、北、中"。谈到颜色时，中国人讲"五色"，即"青、赤、黄、白、黑"；祭祀先祖时，中国人摆"五畜"，即"牛、犬、羊、猪、鸡"；看病时，中国人谈"五液"，即"汗、涕、泪、涎、唾"；论及情绪，中国人讲"五情"，即"怒、喜、思、悲、恐"；论及人体器官，中国人分"五脏"和"五腑"，它们分别是"肝、心、脾、肺、肾"和"胆、小肠、胃、大肠、膀胱"；谈到书画，中国人讲"五清"，即"松、竹、兰、水、月"；提到典籍，中国人读"五经"，即《诗经》《尚书》《礼记》《周易》和《春秋》。

此外，还存在一系列与食品、饮食、营养及保健相关的五件套。其一是"五味"，即"酸、苦、甘、辛、咸"，而西方人则不局限于这五味，还囊括了香和鲜这两味，甚至更多。其二为中医里用于治病的五种药材，包括"草、木、虫、石、谷"。在中文里，"草药"一词包含了植物、动物和矿物。成五件套组合的还有"五谷"和"五肉"，前者为"稻、黍、稷、麦、豆"，而后者包含"鸡、羊、牛、马、猪"。类似五件套的分类概念还不止于此。

当然，并不是所有的东西都是一分为五的。西医将疾病归因于病菌——主要是细菌和病毒，而传统中医理念则认为疾病源于外因、内因、饮食和疲劳。导致疾病的外因分6个方面，它们是"风、寒、暑、湿、燥、火"；而内因则与"七情内伤"相关，它们是"喜、怒、忧、思、悲、恐、惊"。诚然，对中国人来说还有其他一些重要的五位一体式概念，但究其本质还是离不开五行。因此理解五行也构成了理解中医思想的基础。

五行构成了中国传统饮食和疗法的基本原理，它们相互联系，相互影响，与包括人体各部位在内的许多事物相对应。每个元素与其他元素相互作用，经由特定经络或路径贯穿全身。你可以设想有一颗五角星，其12点钟方向顶点对应火。接下来设想从这个顶点出发连到下一个顶点的环形路径，这样有助于看清哪个元素在与其他元素发生作用。这条路径是单向的，从一个顶点（一个顶点对应一个元素）通向下一个顶点，直到围绕五角星（的5个顶点）形成一个闭环。与其他元素的互动路径横贯这个闭环。再次设想自己一笔勾勒出一个五角星，其五条边对应了每个元素与其他元素（确切来说是另外两种元素）发生互动的路径。另一个极其重要的概念就是具有不同属性的两套互动路径：第一套路径中，一个元素总是生成另一个元素；而在第二套路径中，一个元素总是克制另一个元素。生成性路径沿圆形闭环运行，而克制性路径则贯穿闭环内部，呈五角星状。

生成性路径沿火—土—金—水—木行进（即火生土、土生金、金生水、水生木、木生火），循环往复；而克制性路径则沿火—金—木—土—水运转（火克金、金克木、木克土、土克水、水克火），循环往复。论及生成性路径，你可以这样记忆：木燃烧产生火，火燃成灰烬分解并生成土，土富含并产生金属，金属加热熔化为液体，水滋养植物生长。而论及克制性路径时，你可以这样理解：树木生长需破土而出；土吸水而限制其流动；水灭火而将其控制；火通过高温熔化金属；金属工具可用于砍伐树木。这便是五行相生相克的原理。

五行中的每个元素都与人体部位和经络相对应。因此，从宏观上看，这些联系不仅决定了作用的方向还决定了食物和草药的作用性质。比如，咸味的草药对应水元素，并包含海草等食物。这些都属于寒性食物，作用于肾脏和膀胱。中国人还认为，甜味的食物和草药具有滋补和营养的功效；辛味的食物和草药可以行气活血，常作用于肺和大肠；苦味有助于止咳和泻火，入心脏和小肠；酸涩的食物和草药可治多汗，入肝脏和胆囊。

按照英文字母表顺序依次研究会更容易理解这些元素。中国人认为，五行里的每种元素都有其相对应的季节、味道、情绪及脏器。我们从土开始依次介绍。土对应晚夏、甘甜、忧愁，以及胃、脾、口、肌肉等脏器；火对应夏季、苦涩、喜悦，以及心脏、舌头、血管、小肠等脏器；金对应秋季、辛辣、悲伤，以及肺、鼻子、皮肤、大肠等脏器；水对应冬季、咸味、恐惧，以及膀胱、骨头、耳朵、毛发、肾脏等脏器；木对应春季、酸涩、愤怒，以及肝脏、胆囊、肌腱、眼睛等脏器。

追根溯源，几乎每一道中国菜的问世或多或少都受到某位先哲的影响，或通过发明创新，或通过著述传播。大多数中国人都知晓这些菜式的历史和名人对其产生的影响。历经千年传统饮食习俗的熏陶，今天的中国人都养成了均衡膳食的意识。他们经常讨论人体内的"气"，通俗来说就是能量，但他们并不认为食物提供的是西方（营养学）意义上的能量，而是哲学意义上的气。

中国人理解的阳对应光明、干旱、炎热及男性，而阴则对应黑暗、潮湿、寒冷及女性，两者对立统一，相互作用，相互转化。在饮食方面，没有百分之百属阴或属阳的食物。所有的食物、健康状况，甚至器官和香味都兼具阴性和阳性。就食物而言，有的阴性占据主导，因此属阴；有的阳性占主导，因此属阳。中国人的三餐讲究阴阳搭配，即寒性食物和热性食物的组合。食物也可以是温性（属阳）或者凉性（属阴）的，当然也有一些归为平性的食物。有意思的是，许多中国人或许不能分辨食物是阴性、阳性抑或平性，但他们在每一餐中总能够将具有这些属性的食物搭配起来，并且他们似乎都知道哪种体质不适合哪类食物。

阴性或寒性所涉及的摄入方式和食物种类分别为吃、白色食物、清淡食物及沸煮食物。属阴的食物包括豆芽、卷心菜、胡萝卜、芹菜、粥、黄花菜、银杏、蜂蜜等。阳性或者热性所涉及的摄入方式和食物种类分别为喝、红色食物、油炸烧烤类食物及辛辣食物。属阳的食物包括竹笋、牛肉、黑胡椒、鸡肉、肉桂、鸡蛋、肥肉、大蒜、干姜等。平性、温性和凉性的食物较少，但在阴阳二分法体系中依然占据重要位置。平性食品包括大白菜、无花果、甘草、面条、花生、红枣、香菇和软米。凉性食物包括芦笋、豆腐、豆芽、柑橘皮、茄子和蜜橘。

然而，并非所有的食疗都是以阴阳为理论基础的。另一类概念叫作"补"或"滋补"。一般认为，所有的动物肉类都或多或少具有滋补的功效，尤其是将它们放在锅里加入草药蒸煮或慢煨之后。滋补食物（或补品）易于消化并且富含蛋白质和多种矿物质。这类食物有着强健和滋补身体的功效，有助于身体回归到气血调和、阴阳平衡的状态。

还有一个考量因素是那些看起来酷似滋补对象的食物。例如，因为胡桃长得像人脑，由此人们认为它具有补脑的功效。枣子，尤其是红枣，据称有补血功能。人参也属于这一类补品，是最高档次且最昂贵的药物。它的轮廓看着像一个人，是一种阳性补药，据说有大补元气的功效。意大利探险家马可·波罗认为人参是一种上好的补品。

还有一些稀有、贵重的舶来品据说也有着相同或类似的功效。它们包括海参、燕窝、鹿角、鱼翅、银耳、鲍鱼和其他稀有而昂贵的食材。中国人将它们视为大补之物——当然，这是哲学意义上的滋补。所有这些都有很强的心理暗示作用，也就是说，中国人热衷于食用它们是因为相信它们具有强大的功效。

中国传统理念指导人们如何强身健体、丰富膳食,并因地制宜地选用食材。中国传统的膳食观念并非建立于西方科学的基础之上,而是在一代又一代先人的实践观察中得以发扬光大。例如,神农在采集草药时会亲自试用并记录药效。中国人笃信,如果这些草药在神农身上奏效,那在他们身上也一定有效。

Warm-up(Passage B)

美食	culinary delights
烤乳猪	roast suckling pigs
舶来品	imported goods
本土化	naturalization
伊比利亚半岛	Iberian Peninsula
招牌菜	signature dishes
褐变效应	browning
蛋白质	protein
美食家	gourmet
乡愁	nostalgia

Translation(Passage B)

A Taste of Macau

For Lingnan folks, Qingming Jie(清明节) also serves as a herald of the unique flavor of a culinary delight.

Chen Deguang, a renowned chef who works in Macau, began, as usual, a journey home to worship ancestors. His first priority on his way back was to select a premium roast suckling pig. This, apart from a sentiment of nostalgia, represents a spirit of fastidiousness and persistence in pursuing best flavors. Behind the delicious suckling pig, however, lie many legends to be told and interpreted. As Chef Chen, the gourmet Yan Tao also takes a great interest in roast suckling pigs. His concern, though, lies in the reason why roast suckling pigs should differentiate into smooth skin and sandy skin at all. As a TV culinary producer, Chen Xiaoqing too is fascinated by roast suckling pigs, wondering whether the Guangzhou-style roast suckling pigs as we know them today were homegrown or imported from overseas, given that roast suckling pigs are featured in both Chinese and Western cuisines.

Chen Xiaoqing: "Roasting is certainly among the earliest cooking methods used by humans, which is explained by modern science as a chemical process known as the Maillard reaction. It is a browning process that gives roasted pigs distinctive flavor and leads to a significant change in taste, that is, a crisp taste sensation of the skin."

Yan Tao: "What we have here is a crispy-skinned roast, which has more or less affected the amount of meat juices retained during cooking. A smooth-skinned roast, however, seals in meat juices much more effectively."

Chen Xiaoqing: "Actually, the most obvious difference between the smooth-skinned and sandy-skinned (or crispy-skinned) roast piglets is whether you punch holes all over the skin before roasting them. Pockmarked in this manner, the skin will then allow grease to ooze out through pores more quickly. The smooth skin, which remains intact, however, helps trap water, proteins and fats really effectively."

Yan Tao: "In Chinese cuisine, the best quality roast pork has soft and crispy skin, the next best in order has crumbly and browned skin, and the most undesirable of all has hard and stiff skin. In other words, in ancient China, the most popular roast pork is the soft and crispy one, but the Guangzhou-style roast suckling pigs as we eat it today do not actually taste soft and crispy."

Today, many Guangzhou-style roast suckling pigs are vigorously touted for their allegedly authentic Macau flavor. How did it all begin?

Yan Tao: "Guangzhou is among the earliest port cities in China that opened to foreign trade. In the Qing Dynasty, only the port of Guangzhou was opened to trade with foreign merchants. So foreign cultures may exert their influence on Guangzhou."

Chen Xiaoqing: "So you may yet recover the authentic Guangzhou-style roast piglets by visiting Macau."

Macau, a city Chen Xiaoqing once called a "time freezer", has created a culinary landscape that brings together cultural elements ranging from traditional to contemporary and from Chinese to Western through its distinctive, all-inclusive cultural values. Its roast suckling pigs have long been a fascinating and much sought-after culinary landmark among gastronomes. But as you plunge yourself into this beautiful port city in seeking out special flavors and stories behind, you might well wonder why on earth do Macau suckling pigs become such an iconic centerpiece of various feasts and banquets?

Yan Tao: "Is roasting suckling pigs a local tradition or an imported product? Roast suckling pigs in Guangzhou are sold for their authentically Macau style. Now I am in Macau, and it occurs to me that roast suckling pigs here are truly different. So, is roast suckling pig native or exotic?"

Chen Xiaoqing: "The dietary habit of Iberians left its mark on the way pigs are roasted in Guangdong. This is the most palatable and succulent Chinese suckling pig I have ever had, really-palatable in the sense that it gives distinctive flavor as a result of the Maillard effect; succulent in the literal sense of being full of juice."

The Maillard reaction that Chen Xiaoqing is so fascinated with is nothing more than a natural phenomenon that has only recently come to be explained and generalized by scholars as a scientific law. This newly articulated scientific law, though, has long been skilfully applied by ingenious Cantonese Cuisine chefs to make delicious dishes. The roast suckling pig is just one example. In Wing Lei (永利轩), the Maillard reaction has been well harnessed by Chef Chen to create a long list of fine dishes. Tea smoked crispy chicken and many others are his widely acclaimed signature dishes.

Chen Xiaoqing: "Look at this, Maillard reaction everywhere, browning everywhere. Browning is a process in which certain sugars are converted into something which makes it easier for us to assimilate dopamine that produces in our central nervous system feelings of pleasure."

The French scientist Louis-Camille Maillard discovered the browning effect resulting from the chemical reaction between meat and sugars, which is now known in academia as the Maillard reaction. What scientists discovered serves only, time and again, as testimonies to the tale of the taste buds chefs and gourmets have long been co-authoring.

Chef Chen: "These are experiences acquired by all, based on innumerable trials and errors, over the years."

Behind the kitchen of Wing Lei, a Michelin star Cantonese restaurant, sits a culinary academy wherein delicacies such as roast suckling pig and culinary arts developed by generations of chefs are being taught and reinvented. The appeal of Macau consists in its inclusiveness and diversity. It is here that experiences collect into wisdom; it is here that the glistening pearls of wisdom (Macau), riding on the wave of the times, are being turned into culinary treasure.

Yan Tao: "One of the shackles that hinders us from making progress is the notion of equating the authentic to the traditional. It's not true. As far as I am concerned, the most authentic must be the most popular (among customers). So I would say it's ultimately down to a serendipitous rendezvous among the best foods of this planet."

Translation Workshop

Ⅰ. **Translate the following sentences and pay attention to abstract & concrete conversion**

1. 天地间竟有如此之多的食材适合人类摄取，或者更确切来说是娱悦人的味蕾，尤其是经由大自然都未曾预见的方式加工之后更是如此。这着实让人感到惊叹。

2. 我们即将看到，食品加工的主要目标在于从生长采摘到烹饪食用全程控制这些变化发生的速度，以最大限度延长食品的鲜美年华，也好让我等凡夫俗子尽情赞颂大自然的杰作。

3. 历史上，人类为了改善食物的口感和营养价值（如提高食物的消化吸收率）采用了各种烹饪技术。

4. 简言之，我的观点是这样的：对于基因组我们了解得越多，环境对基因的影响似乎就越大。

5. 纵观各种生命形式，细胞构造的细节或许各不相同（有些情况下——例如病毒——甚至可以说差异巨大），但是其持续参与的多数反应却如出一辙。

6. Wang Anshi: "A wise fiscal policy maker knows how to increase revenue for public spending without increasing taxes imposed on people."

Sima Guang: "Everything we ascribe value to—crops and livestock, properties and wealth—is a constant, and is held either in private hands or by the government."

7. This exceptional chemical diversity could be viewed as the "dark matter" of nutrition, as

most of these chemicals remain largely invisible to both epidemiological studies, as well as to the public at large.

8. Microorganisms reproduce themselves in many ways, but the most common way is by cell division. Basically, a cell grows to the point where it divides into two identical cells.

9. It was originally thought that there were four taste buds, for the taste equivalents of primary colors, these being salty, sweet, acidic, and bitter. However, it is now recognized that we also have receptors specifically for a taste sensation called "umami".

10. All of the so-called diseases of civilization, such as cancer, diabetes, and heart disease include a step involving oxidation of membrane lipids in cells of the body.

Ⅱ. Translate the following passage into English

Every city produces its own taste memory thanks to one of its traditional foods, and this is what people usually describe as "one city, one taste". So what does Macau really taste like as a small, densely populated city? Who would have thought that Macau should turn out to be so inextricably bound up with a food ingredient that seems so unrelated to and is so far away from it?

When I first came to Macau, I saw the characters "Ma Jiexiu" (or Bacalhau, in Portuguese, for cod) written everywhere and I thought it might be some calligrapher. But what is it? Actually, Ma Jiexiu is a kind of pickled fish, salted and dried. It is pickled in a highly concentrated sea salt solution, and then stiffened, dehydrated…It is not particularly different from the Chinese salted fish. However, it is not Portuguese people who first invented this curing technique but rather northern Europeans. When northern Europeans set out for Portugal to take a vacation, they brought with them some Ma Jiexiu, and from there it was exported to Macau, hence the distinct Macau-style Ma Jiexiu recipe.

More revered than time-honored brand names are Chinese maestro chefs. Chef Yang has been serving in his culinary career for over 60 years. It is well known to all those who have ever visited the Sullivan's Restaurant that he makes superb Ma Jiexiu fish balls (or Bacalhau fritters).

Chef Yang: "We use very simple ingredients really, very simple and few ingredients, nothing more than potatoes, Ma Jiexiu and eggs, in addition to some coriander added to flavor the dish, simple enough. But it's never simple to create so popular a dish with so simple a recipe. It's not a simple thing to do really. Why do we insist on kneading fish paste by hand? Because a sense of touch gives important texture cues as to its smoothness and elasticity."

Foreign ingredients like Ma Jiexiu, having undergone generations of adaptation and naturalization, have eventually found its way to Macau people's dining table as an integral part of the daily menu.

Ⅲ. Translate the following passage into Chinese

每年仲夏时分的端午节（也叫龙舟节），中国人都会以龙舟竞渡的方式纪念那些尝试拯救深受百姓爱戴的爱国诗人屈原的人们。屈原是战国时期（公元前475年—公元前221年）楚国著名的学者和政治家，曾在楚国朝廷任职。龙舟船体窄长，船头雕有一条龙，船尾放有一面鼓。鼓手擂着节奏紧凑、气势磅礴的鼓声激励20多名划手步调一致地倾力前进。据说，震耳欲聋的鼓声是为了吓跑任何试图伤害屈原的人。驻足观看龙舟赛的人们喝着防毒驱邪的雄黄酒，吃着精心制作的粽子。

　　传说，大约公元前278年，当屈原得知自己不再受到国君信任并即将被流放时，他心灰意冷，投江自尽。另一个说法感叹他身为政治家却也难逃成为宫廷斗争牺牲品的命运。不论哪种说法更确切，他的确在五月初五投汨罗江自尽。当地人试图用船只施救，但未能成功。为了将可能啃食屈原身体的掠食性鱼类引开，人们制作并向江里投喂了一包又一包的粽子。这些投入江里的粽子是用煮熟的糯米拌肉做成的，然后塞进竹片里，防止散开。

　　从此，对屈原的哀悼逐渐变成一年一度的节日。最早，人们将稻米放入竹筒中，用百合叶封口，并用彩色的丝线捆扎固定，防止蛟龙偷食。今天，粽子用竹叶包裹，做成了三角形，并用叶条和线绳将它们捆扎在一起。

　　这些贡品通常填入3种馅儿。第一种是肉，主要是猪肉，并配搭稻米和栗子。第二种是稻米和豆类，并添加些许经由碱液浸泡保存的苏木做驱邪之用。第三种是用稻米粉配搭石榴汁和蜂蜜。据说，后两种馅儿陈放越久食疗功效越佳。它们甚至被推荐用来治疗痢疾。

　　雄黄酒是端午节传统的重要组成部分。人们把它晒干后涂在孩子们的额头、鼻子甚至耳朵上做驱邪之用。雄黄酒液体可用来书写汉字"王"或"国王"，意为"王者"。出于同样的目的，它们也被画在额头上。菖蒲和艾蒿这两种古老植物的叶子被放在酒中浸泡，然后悬挂在家家户户的大门上，做驱邪之用。菖蒲外形似剑，而艾蒿似虎，两者显然都是大凶之物。据说，所有与酒相关的活动都能起到驱邪避凶的效果。

Unit 3 Textile Science and Fashion Culture

Warming-up（Passage A）

cotton yarn	棉纱，棉纱线
staple cotton	长绒棉，原棉
cotton gin	轧花机，轧棉机
staple fiber	纺纱用的人造短纤维
the Carolinas	南卡罗来纳州、北卡罗来纳州
cotton cultivation	棉花种植
seed pod	种荚
staple length	纤维长度
foreign matter	杂质

Translation（Passage A）

棉花种植、性能及用途

棉花是世界上使用最广泛的纤维。它的流行源于它相对容易生产并适用于各种纺织产品。然而，棉纱的价格在很大程度上依赖于劳动力成本。在工业化国家劳动力昂贵，因此棉纱的价格可能相对较高。

然而，直到最近，棉花还没有像羊毛和亚麻布那样广泛地使用。这是因为羊毛或亚麻更容易纺成纱，因为它们更长。此外，棉纤维必须从它们附着的种子中分离出来。如果用手工来做，这个过程是非常烦琐和耗时的。早期的机械只能用于长纤维棉，所以劳动力成本非常高。

锯式轧棉机的发明使短纤维的利用成为了可能，利用短纤维在美国的南卡罗来纳州、北卡罗来纳州和弗吉尼亚州盛行了起来。生产力的急剧提高，加上美国南部低廉的劳动力成本，使棉花在世界纺织市场中的份额不断扩大。纤维和纱线生产的日益机械化有助于保持棉织品的低成本，纺织机械的发展扩大了生产基地。

棉花种植需要温暖的气候、充足的降雨量或良好的灌溉。生长季节长达6~7个月。在此期间，种子发芽生长，在大约100天内开出白色的花朵。花产生种荚，在接下来的两个月里成熟。当种荚破裂时，棉花纤维就可以采摘了。

在纱线生产前，棉花被分等、分类和混纺，以确保均匀的纱线质量。棉花的分等是根据颜色、纤维长度、细度、有无异物等因素而定的。在美国，棉花根据短纤维长度、均匀性、强度、颜色、清洁度和弹性分为不同等级。这些标准与美国农业部提供的标准进行了比较。该标准提供6个中等以上等级和6个中等以下等级。最常见的等级是：

Strict good middling 次优级棉（二级）

Good middling 上级棉（三级）

Strict middling 次上级棉（四级）

Middling 中级棉（五级）

Strict low middling 次中级棉（六级）

Low middling 下级棉（七级）

Strict good ordinary 次下级棉（八级）

棉纤维长度为 0.3~5.5cm。在显微镜下，它看起来像一条沿其长度不规则扭曲的带状结构。这种捻度，又称卷绕结构，增加了纤维之间的摩擦，这是确保细纱强度所必需的。纤维的颜色从淡黄色到纯白色不等，可能非常有光泽。然而，大多数棉花的色泽都是黯淡的。

横切面显示纤维呈肾脏形状，其中央空心结构称为管腔。管腔在植物生长过程中为营养物质的输送提供了通道。纤维由围绕在主壁周围的外壳或角质层组成，主壁依次覆盖管腔周围的次壁。角质层是一种薄而硬的外壳，可以保护纤维在生长过程中不受擦伤和损害。在用作纺织纤维时，角质层增强了棉花的耐磨性。

相对较高的吸湿性和良好的排汗性能使棉花成为一种更舒适的纤维。由于纤维素中的羟基，棉花对水有很高的吸引力。当水进入纤维时，棉花会膨胀，其横截面变得更圆。对水分的高亲和性和遇湿膨胀的能力使棉花能吸收其自身质量 1/4 的水分。这意味着在炎热的天气里，来自身体的汗水会被棉织物吸收，沿着纱线输送到布料的外表面并蒸发到空气中，这样将有助于保持体温不升高。

不幸的是，棉花的亲水性使它容易受到水基污渍的影响。水溶性着色剂，如咖啡或葡萄汁中的着色剂，会随水渗入纤维；当水分蒸发时，着色剂被困在纤维中。也许棉织品的主要缺点是容易起皱，而且很难去除褶皱。棉纤维的硬度降低了纱线的抗皱能力，当纤维弯曲成一种新的结构时，将纤维素链连接在一起的氢键就会破裂，分子就会滑动，以减少纤维内部的压力。氢键在新的位置重新形成，因此当挤压力消除时，纤维仍停留在新的位置。正是氢键的断裂和重新形成有助于褶皱保持，所以棉织品必须熨烫。

棉花是一种中等强度的纤维，具有良好的耐磨性和良好的尺寸稳定性。它对家庭使用的酸、碱和有机溶剂都具有抵抗力。但由于它是一种天然材料，容易受到昆虫、霉菌和真菌的侵袭。最突出的是，如果让棉花保持潮湿，它就有发霉的倾向。

棉花能很好地抵御阳光和热量，尽管直接暴露在持续强烈的阳光下会导致其变黄并最终降解纤维。当棉织品在气体干燥器中干燥时，也可能发黄。这种颜色的变化是纤维素和氧气或氮氧化物在烘干机的热空气中发生化学反应的结果。棉花在自然晾干或用电干机烘干后，其白度会保持得更久。

最有趣的是棉纱在湿的时候比干的时候更结实。这种性能是纤维的宏观和微观结构特征导致的结果。当水被吸收时，纤维膨胀，其横截面变得更圆。通常如此大量的外来物质的吸收会引起高度的内应力，导致纤维的弱化。然而，在棉花中，水分的吸收导致内应力降低。因此，由于需要克服的内应力更小，膨胀的纤维变得更结实。与此同时，纱线内膨胀的纤维相互之间的压力变得更大，内部摩擦使纱线更结实。此外，吸收的水分作为一种内部润滑剂，赋予纤维更高的柔韧性，这就是棉布衣服受潮时更容易熨烫的原因。棉织品洗后容易缩水。

棉花也许比其他任何纤维都更能满足服装、家居、娱乐和工业用途的需要。棉织物结实、质轻、柔韧、容易干燥、易于洗涤。在服装方面，棉质服装穿着舒适、容易干燥、色彩明亮、不易褪色、容易护理。主要缺点是棉纱容易收缩，棉布容易起皱。收缩可以通过防缩整理来控制。耐压性能可以通过化学处理或将棉花与更抗皱的纤维（如涤纶）混纺来提高。

在家居装饰中，棉花用于耐用的、通用的面料中。尽管它们可能缺乏由其他纤维制成的材料的正式外观，但棉织品提供了一个舒适的家居环境。因为棉织品舒适、耐用、吸湿，几十年来一直是床上用品和毛巾的主要面料。聚酯/棉混纺面料为现代消费者提供了无须熨烫的床单和枕套，保持了清爽的感觉。

在休闲用途方面，传统上棉花被用来制作帐篷和露营装备、船帆、网球鞋和运动服。棉布特别适合做帐篷，因为帐篷织物必须能够"呼吸"，这样使用者就不会被自己的二氧化碳所窒息。此外，与外部空气的交换降低了帐篷内的湿度，使帐篷内不会变得闷热。棉织物的结构足够稀松，从而能够提供良好的透气性，保证了帐篷居住的舒适度。帐篷还要防水，当被雨水淋湿时，棉纱会膨胀，减少棉纱之间的空隙，从而可以抵抗水分的渗透。然而今天，在帐篷设备中，沉重的帆布装备正被轻质尼龙所取代。

棉线、细棉绳和粗棉绳在工业中被用来捆绑、固定和捆扎各种各样的东西，可作打包绳使用，也可作船上的缆绳使用。棉纱被用来加固驱动电机的传动带以及用来制作结实的工作服。

Warming-up（Passage B）

热衷	fall over oneself for
小兜肚	the small Chinese belly-cover
柏林国际电影节	Berlin International Film Festival
松糕鞋	"sponge cake" shoes
大卖	be the rage
时装化	adopt the fashionable elements
《花样年华》	In the Mood for Love
神韵	special charm
华服热	Chinese dress fashion
中式对襟袄	Chinese "button in the middle" style jacket

Translation（Passage B）

Keeping Pace with the World Fashion

It was from 1990s that many oversea famous brand costumes one after another aimed at Chinese consumer market and opened the monopolization stores in big cities such as Beijing, Shanghai, Shenzhen and Guangzhou. Domestic Chinese brand clothes and fashion models gradually attracted people's interests. Along with the first fashion magazine that used foreign copyrights coming into being in China in 1988, more and more newspapers, magazines, radio stations, television stations and networks entered the fashion promotion field. World latest fashion information could be introduced to China very quickly. The trend of garments in fashion, hairstyles and make-up styles from France, Italy, U. K and South Korea directly influence the trend in China. Life styles and dressing styles represented by "fashion" are accepted and went after by more and more Chinese.

In those years at the turn of century, fashion in China kept close pace with the world fashion. Following the international dressing fashion, dressing style tended to be more formal, especially white-collar women who paid particular attention to the charm of being a professional woman. They tried to wear formal and decent dresses. People no longer favored the so-called "original wildness", such as no edging for the straw hats or tearing thread off the trousers. The trend of exposing certain part of skin was restrained among people of some classes and in some occasions. Though mini-skirts were still popular, many young girls started to favor ankle-long long skirts to show the female elegance.

Of course, some adolescent young boys and girls who advocated the anti-tradition consciousness of the western society considered the weird as fashionable on purpose, for example, imitating the hairstyle of *The Last of the Mohicans* to shave head on two sides and leave the middle section and dye hair. Some wore "punk dress" — another kind of decadent style youth dress in western society after hippies. They glued the hair into animal horn shape using hair gel and embroidered skeleton pattern on black leather jackets; or intentionally tore or burned holes on the clothes. These were not dominant in China fashion scene. But a very interesting fact was that "opening a window" in an artistic way on clothes became popular at the turn of spring and summer in 1998. Holes could be dug in every part of the clothes and the edge of holes was dealt with carefully. As this style of clothes was different from the "transparent dress" made by translucent materials, it was called the "perspective dress". And then a kind of dress full of mesh appeared, which was synchronous with the "fishnet" dress in the Paris fashion stage.

In those several years, a "swimming suit trend" emerged in streets and lanes in China. Of course, the swimming suit here didn't mean the swimming suit for the water sport sold in the shop, but a kind of daily dress. It got this name because the suit was as short, small and sexy as the swimming suit. Imagine that a girl wears a tight upper dress that exposes the navel and with thin shoulder straps, a mini short skirt or short pants and a pair of slippers, one will easily think she is beside the beach or swimming pool but not in the streets of the city if not for the backpack she carries.

At the beginning of the 21st century, adult women including young ladies and university students fell over themselves for child style clothes and hairstyles as if they wanted to relive their childhood. They cut a kind of kid hairstyle, which was to curl the tip of hair on both temples, and put on pink or lemon yellow butterfly or flower hairpins. The upper clothes sometime were tight and small and sometimes loose and cute, which made them look like naughty kids. They wore kids style shoes with square openings and slanting shoelaces and carried satchels with patterns of bear head. Some students, like kids who refused to grow up, even hung rubber nipples or mobile phones in front of the chest.

In 2001, the small Chinese belly-cover was once very popular. In the awarding ceremony of Berlin International Film Festival, the movie star Zhang Ziyi attracted the attention of the fashion circle when she wore a specially made red belly cover, and draped a long piece of red silk around shoulder, which made her look like an ancient Chinese doll. Later, wearing a diamond shape belly-cover without any additional adornments, she appeared in the MTV awarding ceremony. So very soon, in all kinds of occasions and media formats, no matter stars or ordinary fashionable girls all began to wear all kinds of belly covers.

At the beginning of the 21st century, there was also a big change on the shoe vamp. In 2002, those cute "sponge cake" shoes were no longer popular while shoes with sharp turning up tips (like Charlie Chaplin style shoes) and decorated with shining adornments appeared. One year after, round tip style shoes that imitated the toe shoes were the rage in the market.

At the end of the 20th century, international fashion world began to favor oriental style. Oriental elegance, tranquility, simplicity and mystery became the global fashion elements. With the rising of China's position in the world, overseas Chinese started to feel proud to wear Chinese costumes, women in China's Mainland naturally put on Chinese jackets and many Chinese men consider Chinese cotton jackets as fashionable. Chinese dresses of nowadays are not like those classical traditional Chinese coats or jackets. Many female Chinese costumes adopted the fashionable elements. The costume arrangement looks rather interesting when girls put on print or flamboyant cotton cloth coats with edgings and stand collar, jeans and leather shoes in the latest fashion.

In 2000, Hong Kong movie *In the Mood for Love* was played at home and abroad. The actress in the movie changed cheongsams of different colors and styles (more than 20) under the dark lights. Audiences were amazed by the classical charm of the oriental beauty. The actress looked beautiful, elegant and sentimental with cheongsams. People for the first time found that Chinese traditional dresses had a kind of special charm. Due to the magic of the movie, the cheongsam once again was the rage.

Nobody would expect that APEC conference held in China — a very influential political activity, created another round of Chinese dress fashion. In autumn 2001 in Shanghai, the whole world was stirred when leaders from all countries who put on Chinese blue, red or green satin jackets appeared in the public. International media published the photos of the leaders wearing Chinese dresses and wrote articles with comments. The charm of Chinese "button in the middle" style jacket coupling with the huge effect created by Bush and Putin made a very successful advertisement for the Chinese costume. Some customers asked the shop assistant to give them a "Putin" style Chinese jacket. Another background behind this trend is the more and more important influence that China has on the world stage. The Chinese dress rage also signifies the constantly increasing confidence and cohesion of the Chinese nation.

What happened in the 20th century has proved that this century is till now the most fashionable century with high amount of clothes, accessories and cosmetics being sold. The development of the increasingly powerful media makes more and more people to come close, to appreciate clothes and to enjoy the beauty of the fashionable garments. Fashionable garments have become a kind of life style that people understand and love to invest.

Translation Workshop

I. Translate the following sentences and pay attention to transposition

1. 使用添加剂能稳定纱线的性能，抵御紫外线的辐射。
2. 设计师经常会被要求将畅销款式上的一些部分组合到类似款式的服装上，或结合在原版款式的衍生款式上。
3. 大部分设计师作品都被局限在由一些商店指定的类型中，因为公司的产品在这些商店里都有很好的销售业绩。
4. 改善棉纤维的光泽是丝光处理的目的之一。
5. 这个报告基于他3年的科学调查。
6. With slight repairs, this textile machine could be reused.
7. The delegates at the conference unanimously expressed their determination to support the further development of textile technology.
8. The composite material is not yet ready for commercial production.
9. For 20 years we were passive witnesses to the price deterioration of our raw material.
10. Only when we study their properties can we make better use of the materials.

II. Translate the following passage into English

Jeans also entered into China at the end of the 1970s. And since then, more and more people have started to wear jeans, expanding from fashionable young men to people of all classes and ages. In the 1990s, types of jeans developed including short skirts, short pants, waistcoats, jackets, hats, satchels, and backpacks. Colors were not limited to blue. New materials appeared such as water washing thin materials. At the beginning of the 1980s, bat clothes were very popular. This type of clothes look like bat wings when stretching the two sleeves. With various types of collars, a bat pullover's sleeves and clothes body integrate into a whole. There are no sewing threads on the sleeves. The lower hem of the pullover is tight. Later more types were developed such as the bat coats, bat overcoats and bat jackets etc. It is quite interesting that this clothes style re-appeared in 2004 spring and summer fashion trend as a kind of retro.

Till the middle of the 1980s, there were more and more clothes styles while the popularity circle became shorter and shorter. New styles and materials were kept being introduced to the market. As for upper outer garments, there were all kinds of T-shirts, jackets of mixing color, checkered shirts and cotton pullovers. Wearing suits and ties became social dresses for formal occasions, and accepted by most of the white collars. Under clothes included pailform trousers, elastic trousers, radish trousers, skirt trousers, 70% trousers, trousers skirts, pleated skirts, eight-piece skirts, western suits skirts, midis and sun skirts. The style changed constantly. By the time when the mini skirt that was born in the western world in the 1960s was once again popular in the 1980s, China has kept pace with the world fashion.

III. Translate the following passage into Chinese

没有理由认为人的身体是禁止谈论的话题。之所以害怕，似乎是因为身体携带着某些关联性涵义。毕竟身体已经被严严实实地包裹了几百年，直到近代才被揭开。这个过程一旦开始，就快速地发展。身体越来越暴露引起了震惊，而且这种现象仍然遭受很大的怀疑。

然而，必须承认，我们将很多自然方面的概念与人的身体对应起来。例如，我们说一座山的"脚"，一条河峡的"颈"，一棵"站立"的树。米开朗基罗（Michelangelo）对此有更深刻的阐述，"人如果不精通人的身体，尤其是身体的解剖，就永远不能理解建筑的含义"。

我们所有比例概念都与身体相关。运动使我们的视野拓宽了，也使我们肌肉反应更加灵敏。不管睡着还是走着，我们对节奏的情感与我们规律的心跳和呼吸的起伏密切相关。

服装只有穿在身体上时才有意义。当它们被悬挂在衣橱里时显得极其无助。它们似乎在无声地怒吼，残忍的裁缝逼迫它们处于悲伤孤独的境地。要想真正了解服装，必须先了解它们背后的原因，然后再了解它们，只有这样才是可行的。服装不仅仅是纺织工厂的产品，或博物馆展示的物品，它们是人工制品，人们在日常生活的各种活动中都用到它们——站立、坐着、跳舞、工作或临终。只有当我们思考它们与身体的关系如何，怎样适应身体的时候，它们真正的意义才变得明显。人的体型各种各样：瘦的、胖的；头大的、头小的。服装样式不能总是与身体框架一致，往往违背自然人体。如果身体不适合某种服装样式，那么应该修改服装，而不是身体。

Unit 4　Biotechnology and Wine-Liquor Culture

Warming-up（Passage A）

congener	酒类芳香物
sensory attributes/character	感官特征
cereal mash	麦芽汁；麦芽浆
gelatinize	淀粉糊化/胶化
kilning stage	窑化烘干（阶段）
Maillard reaction	美拉德反应
inorganic constituent	无机成分
secondary metabolite	次生代谢物；次级代谢产物
yeast strain	酵母菌株
Saccharomyces cerevisiae	酿酒酵母

Translation（Passage A）

原料对于威士忌感官特征的影响

原料所含的化合物赋予了威士忌不同的风味，而酿造工艺会进一步影响其风味特点。在威士忌行业中，影响香型、味道、口感和外观的化合物被称为酒类芳香物。威士忌生产中的每个步骤都会影响酒类芳香物的含量，从而影响其感官特征。图1概括了威士忌的主要生产阶段。生产威士忌酒，第一步是制作麦芽汁。尽管在酿造其他种类的威士忌时，可使用的谷物原料品种很多，但麦芽威士忌必须使用发芽大麦作为原料。生产威士忌的原料颇多，业内喜用的谷物类原料除了大麦之外，还包括玉米、黑麦和小麦（Miles and Richards，2009）。用来发芽的谷物在自然形态下是不会发酵的，因此必须将它们先转化为可发酵的基质。这包括分解谷物的结构以释放淀粉，然后用酶将淀粉转化为糖。

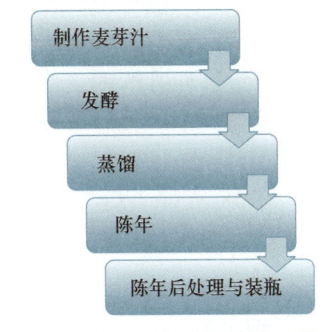

图1　威士忌的主要生产阶段

有两种方法可以实现这一目的。第一种是发麦，主要通过控制发芽过程和酶的生长来完成。发芽之后进行研磨，将热水注入研磨过的麦芽中使麦芽淀粉糊化，使其易于被酶分解。还有一种发麦和粉碎的方法是先煮熟谷物，然后加入少量麦芽或商业用酶使其分解。

在制作麦芽汁的过程中，许多因素都可能影响威士忌的风味。先是谷物的类型。例如，与小麦相比，使用玉米为原料酿造的酒口味重、油味浓。即使是同一谷物的不同品种也可能导致口感的细微差别。无论用什么方法来生产麦芽汁，都少不了热处理环节。如果谷物已发麦，那么热处理主要在窑化（烘干）阶段，而如果用煮熟谷物的方法，则需要足够的热量才能使谷物分解并使淀粉糊化。无论哪种热处理方式,温度的控制都很重要,因为那些塑造威士忌风味的化学反应都是通过热度来调节的。

最重要的热导反应类型之一是在氨基酸和糖之间发生的美拉德反应。不同的氨基酸和糖发生反应,会产生一系列不同的风味,尽管这些风味主要是由谷物烧焦或烤焦形成的。高温会使酶变性并分解为糖,导致出酒率降低。因此,要平衡好出酒率和风味之间的关系。在威士忌早期生产阶段,出酒率往往是生产商最感兴趣的。

发麦过程中的烘干步骤能进一步调节威士忌的口感。在干燥的早期阶段,可以将泥炭烟引入窑炉来熏制麦芽。烟雾中的风味活性化合物会附着在谷物的表面。这些化合物在威士忌生产过程中一直存在,给威士忌带来了独特的烟熏、药用芳香味。尽管很多国家现在正在尝试使用泥炭和其他材料熏制麦芽,但泥煤味麦芽通常被用于生产某些苏格兰和日本威士忌。最后,麦芽汁的生产需要添加水。不同的水其构成在有机和无机成分方面有所不同,这取决于水的来源和类型。水成分的不同可以影响发酵过程中酵母的生长和代谢,已有研究表明这对威士忌的风味会有影响,虽然细微,但仍可检测出来(Wilson,2010)。

随后对麦芽汁进行发酵。酵母将糖分转化为乙醇,产生酒精含量为8%~10%的发酵醪液("wash"或"beer",威士忌酿造相关术语,指发酵后待蒸馏的发酵酒醪)。在发酵过程中,酵母还产生一系列次级代谢产物,如其他醇类、酸类、酯类、醛类、酮类和含硫化合物。这些化合物大多具有高度的风味活性,对威士忌的感官特性有重要的影响。不同的酵母菌株代谢作用略微不同。因此,尽管酵母的选择一般是基于其优良的出酒性能,但的确会对酒的风味产生影响。尽管有时企业会用自己之前发酵用过的酵母,或者混合使用一些废酵母,但现在大多数威士忌企业都是使用商用酵母。酵母存在形式多样,有干酵母、压制酵母和奶油酵母。这些不同的酵母形式对发酵也会产生微妙的影响,从而影响风味。此外,发酵参数如发酵容器的容量、其构成材质、环境温度和发酵时间,也会影响酒类芳香物的形成。发酵过程中也可能存在非酵母菌种的微生物。其他微生物如乳酸菌,尽管量少,也会产生酒类芳香物,增加风味来源的复杂性。而污染类微生物,不但会导致出酒率下降,而且可能产生异味或怪味。

Warming-up (Passage B)

贵州茅台	Kweichow Moutai
酱香型白酒	sauce aroma *baijiu*
宫廷贡酒	a royal tribute
评酒会	liquor tasting and appraisal meetings
活性微生物	active/functional microorganisms
制曲	*daqu* making; *qu* production
固态发酵	solid-state fermentation
勾兑	blend; blending
基酒	basic distillate
风味物质	flavor compounds

Translation (Passage B)

Moutai — the National Liquor of China

I. Historical Background of Moutai

Kweichow Moutai, the first typical Chinese sauce aroma *baijiu* made from grains and *daqu* (also shortened as *qu*, a leavening agent that forms the starting point for liquor production), has a long history and a mysterious origin. Legend has it that the original inhabitants of Maotai Town on the banks of the *Chishui* or Red River (which marks the boundary between the Sichuan and Guizhou Provinces of Southwest China) were adept at making this liquor during the reign of Emperor Dayu of remote antiquity.

According to historical sources, Moutai was first developed in 135 BC during the Western Han Dynasty (206 BC–AD 25). At that time, Maotai Town and its neighboring areas produced a great deal of "wolfberry sauce aroma liquor", the predecessor of present-day Moutai. This liquor had been used as a royal tribute since Emperor Wu (156–87 BC) of the Han Dynasty (206 BC–AD 220) sampled it and acclaimed it as "sweet and delicious", according to historical records. All through the Song (960–1279), Yuan (1206–1368), Ming (1368–1644) and Qing (1616–1911) dynasties, it was offered to the emperors and kings as a major tribute. It is now regarded as the country's national liquor after the founding of the People's Republic of China. Thus, the history of Moutai has always been closely linked with the development of the Chinese People.

At the Panama Pacific International Exposition in 1915 held in San Francisco of America, it won a gold medal, achieving the same international status as the other two distilled liquor brands—Scottish Whisky and French Cognac, making it a pioneer to go international as a representative of Chinese national industry and commerce.

The state-owned Kweichow Moutai Distillery was founded in 1951 and since then it has made rapid progress. Moutai has won both national and international awards more than ten times in succession and was accredited to be No. 1 among the Top 4, Top 8, Top 13, and Top 17 long-established liquors in China in a series of liquor tasting and appraisal meetings. Moutai has gradually become the model of China's sauce aroma type liquor, and been recognized as the national liquor of China, the national gift from China and the diplomatic liquor for China.

From its origin as a primitive distillery at the ancient times to its development into a contemporary super-sized Chinese enterprise group, Kweichow Moutai Distillery's success can be attributed to its unique production processes, consistent high quality, distinctive attributive properties and brand culture, and to the unique ecological environment in which Moutai liquor is produced as well.

II. Eco-environment for Making Moutai

Moutai is produced at Kweichow Moutai Distillery Co. Ltd., Maotai Town, Renhuai County in the northwest of the Guizhou Plateau. The distillery, surrounded by mountains, is situated on the eastern bank of the Red River at an altitude of 450m. With long summers and short winters, the region enjoys an agreeable climate, high humidity and rare frost or snow weather. Temperatures of the region range from 3 to 40℃ with an annual average of 18℃. The relative humidity there is high, at about 78%, while its wind speed is about 1.2m/s on average through the year. All of these natural elements constitute the unique ecological environment for making Moutai.

The unique flavor of Moutai relies largely on the equally unique climate, water and other environmental conditions found in Maotai Town; as a result, it is impossible to distill Moutai elsewhere in the world. Speaking of the desirable natural conditions of Maotai Town, a diplomat once remarked after his visit to Kweichow Moutai Distillery, "It turns out to be even more difficult to make Moutai than to make atomic bombs as the later can be made all over the world while the former is confined to this region."

The successful production of Moutai results from a combination of three mysterious factors: firstly, the mysterious environment in the area of Maotai Town, which contains a vast community of active microorganisms essential for the production of the liquor; secondly, the unique red soil, climate and water supply from the Red River, which provide perfect conditions for distillation; and thirdly, the long-standing distillation processes practiced by the special group of original inhabitants in Maotai Town, which led to the development of the ideal production process for Moutai. It is the above mysterious factors that help make Moutai so mysterious and distinctive that its production cannot be imitated elsewhere, which also works a miracle in the global liquor industry.

III. Raw Materials for Making Moutai

The basic raw materials for making Moutai are *hongyingzi* (meaning "red-tasselled ears") glutinous sorghum. It is locally produced in Maotai Town and its neighboring areas, with the use of only natural organic fertilizers while no chemical fertilizers or pesticides. The locally-grown sorghum is perfectly suited to the production of Moutai: firstly, it has thick husks and small kernels, with a high proportion of germ and amylopectin starch; secondly, it can stand steaming and boiling, and thanks to its low rate of water absorption, is slow to gelatinize. This low rate of water absorption is another result of its high starch content of more than 60% and specifically, its amylopectin starch content of more than 88%.

The raw materials for *qu* production are all selected from the locally-grown wheat from Maotai Town or the surrounding area. The wheat is solid and evenly ripened, with a thin hull and plump kernel. It has no worm infestations or mould growth, and is high in purity and light yellow in color, with no browning at the end of the kernel. The wheat also has a starch content of over 60%.

The water used for distilling Moutai comes from the Red River and it is clean, colorless and transparent. Both its quality and purity level are high, and it is free from deposited solids and flavor taints. Its temperature is on the low side and its pH range fluctuates between 6.5 to 7.5.

IV. Production Processes of Moutai

The production of Moutai, mainly including fermentation and distillation, is carried out in approximately year-long cycles, and involves several typical Chinese liquor-making processes. These include stack fermentation, *qu* production and liquor distillation, and all require higher temperatures than those used for making other Chinese liquors. For example, the maximum recorded temperature for *qu* production is 67℃.

There are a total of four processes involved in making final products of Moutai: *qu* production, distillate production, blending, filling and packaging. The basic distillate, sorted by rounds, typicality and alcoholic strength, is sealed in big jars and stored in cellars for a long period prior to blending. The blended liquor is then filled in bottles and packaged for sale.

V. Flavor Compounds of Moutai

The *qu* and liquor production processes of Moutai make full use of the ecological advantages and the unique natural conditions and resources of the region. Such processes as *qu* production, stack fermentation and anaerobic fermentation all take place at high temperatures, which constantly promote the domestication of liquor-making microorganisms. Due to the variety of functional microorganisms present in the region and through heredity, mutation and evolution, extreme microbial communities have developed around the Moutai workshops that are resistant to high temperatures, acidity and alcoholicity.

During the Moutai production process, the metabolism of the extreme functional microorganisms gives rise to highly stable heat- and acid-resistant enzymes. All kinds of extreme microorganisms and enzymes, encouraged by the long production process and its repeated cycles, thus help to produce the rich flavor compounds of the liquor. These flavor compounds enter into the basic distillates by means of different processes and further assist in the formation of the unique taste and perfect quality of Moutai. The unique fermentation environment involved in the production of Moutai provides the liquor with its distinctive and unique flavor attributes, which also constitute its core competence to compete with other brands of *baijiu* in the market.

Translation Workshop

I. Translate the following sentences and pay attention to the translation of long sentences

1. A 型酒类芳香物,在各种乙醇(酒精)浓度下均易挥发,会流到蒸馏柱(蒸馏塔)的顶部。

2. 流入蒸馏器底部的热酒蒸气富含 A 型和 B 型(和乙醇挥发度差不多的)化合物,但只含有少量的 C 型化合物(比乙醇难挥发的),这些化合物将很快返回到分析器中。

3. 除非所有环节都使用符合饮用水质量标准的生产用水,否则以谷物为原料的酒厂需要仔细考虑供水来源问题。

4. 有许多科学论文探讨葡萄酒的风味特点,往往采用品评小组对葡萄酒感官特征进行描述的方法来实现。

5. 描述性分析这一术语,是一种用于描述感官体验的方法。这种方法可以实现对受试者食品感官指标(所谓的感官印象)的识别、量化和描述。

6. Sorghum is used as the main raw material for making Chinese *baijiu* whereas rice for making Chinese rice wine. As for *qu* production, there are varieties of raw materials, such as wheat and barley.

7. As the major raw materials for making Chinese *jiu*, or alcoholic beverages, are grains, whose main component is starch instead of sugar, the steps of making *jiu* then include saccharification of starch to fermentable sugars and fermentation of sugars further to alcohol.

8. Due to the function of *qu*, the unique Chinese saccharifying and fermenting agent, the production of Chinese *jiu* involves a unique process of simultaneous saccharification and fermentation, which is a far cry from the western ones.

9. Chinese liquor is mainly stored in pottery jars for ageing rather than in oak barrels as practiced in the West, which is probably due to the booming pottery industry in ancient China.

10. The aroma profiles of Chinese *baijiu* are quite different due to their varied production processes. According to the aroma properties, Chinese *baijiu* can be classified into strong aroma type, light aroma type, sauce aroma type, sweet honey aroma type, and other aroma types.

Ⅱ. Translate the following passage into Chinese

窑化烘干过程会产生新的化合物，而存在于青麦芽（指刚发过芽还没有烘干的发芽大麦）中的一些化合物则会被破坏。这些化学变化会影响最终蒸馏酒的风味品质。在烘干过程中，一些重要化学反应包括基于不饱和脂肪酸的酶氧化和化学氧化、游离氨基酸和还原糖的化合，以及风味前体物质的热降解，如发芽期间合成的S-甲基蛋氨酸的降解等。

形成风味化合物的化学过程很复杂，而且随着窑炉温度的提高，复杂性也会加剧。

蒸馏阶段既是一个风味形成的过程，也是一个分离的过程，具有极其重要的意义。从数量上看，主要的风味化合物（酒类芳香物）是在发酵过程中产生的。在感官方面，对风味影响较大的化合物往往只是微量存在。威士忌风味特点与化学成分之间的关系是什么？这些化学成分的源头在哪？对此我们还有很多工作要做。

Ⅲ. Translate the following passage into English

Jiu, or Chinese alcoholic beverages, play an important role in China's economy at modern times. As the largest liquor-producing country in the world, domestically-produced *jiu* occupies a lion's share in China's alcoholic beverage market. In 2014, the total sales income of Chinese *jiu* amounted to 541.8 billion yuan with a tax revenue of 125.1 billion yuan while the sales income of *baijiu* alone reached 525.9 billion yuan. Moreover, the output value of China's alcoholic industry accounts for 5% of that in the food industry. With about 0.439 million employees, China's alcoholic industry has also promoted the development of agriculture and industries concerned, contributing more than 110 billion yuan to China's GDP every year.

For the Chinese, *jiu* is not a daily necessity. However, in their social life, *jiu* plays a peculiar role which cannot be substituted by other forms of food. As summarized by Chinese ancestors, *jiu* can help to cure diseases, to keep health and to perform rituals or ceremonies.

Specifically, to say *jiu* can help cure diseases because it is related to medical treatment in the ancient times in China, as one structural component, that's "酉", of character *jiu* "酒" is part of the structural and semantic components of the traditional Chinese character for "医", namely "醫", meaning "medical treatment". As for keeping people healthy to live longer, there were records in the Han Dynasty (206 BC-AD 220), describing *jiu* as "the chief of all medicines and the favorite drink at parties and gatherings". In addition, *jiu* helps perform ceremonies as it is closely related to Chinese people's life, either for religious and sacrificial ceremonies in the ancient times or festivals and celebrations like weddings today. For example, Nverhong rice wine produced in Shaoxing of Zhejiang involves performing bridal ceremonies. People usually brew first-class Nverhong rice wine to celebrate the birth of their daughters and then the wine is buried underground or stored in a cellar for ageing until their daughters' wedding days when the wine is taken out and enjoyed by all guests.

Unit 5 Cosmetics and Oriental Aesthetics

Warming-up (Passage A)

powdered antimony	锑粉
perfumed hair oil	芳香发油
cold cream	冷霜
lead poisoning	铅中毒
foot powder	足光粉
soap with grit and flavor	香味磨砂肥皂
rather unpalatable	口味不佳，难以入口
do the job quite well	起到很好的清洁功效
tooth enamel	牙釉质
chemical formula	化学式
rather than	而不是
pure compound	纯净物
tooth decay	蛀牙
convert... to...	把……转化为……
sticky dextran	黏性葡聚糖
brushing and tossing	刷牙漱口
in turn	依次
corneal layer	角质层
slough off	脱落，脱皮
a moisture content of about 10%	水分含量约为10%
sebaceous gland	皮脂腺
oily secretion	油性分泌物
be permeable to	对……具有渗透作用
exposure to sun and wind	风吹日晒
protective film	保护膜
mineral oil	矿物油
petroleum jelly	凡士林；矿物油膏
a viscous liquid	一种黏稠的液体
a protective coating	保护性涂层
baby oil	婴儿油
fancy cream	高级乳霜
fatty odor	腥味
retard rancidity	延缓酸败
are responsible for	对……负责；起……作用

metal ions	金属离子
give off	散发
pleasant aroma	宜人的香气
important, but minor, ingredients	重要的微量成分
compound with large molecules	大分子化合物
in large quantities	大量的
vary with…	随着……而变化
concentrated solution	浓缩溶液
be sickeningly sweet	过于甜腻,让人作呕
odorous compound	有香化合物
ethyl alcohol	乙醇
methyl alcohol	甲醇
allergic reaction	过敏反应
an adhesive bandage	斑贴
hairy chemistry	毛发用化学
an anionic type	阴离子型
highly basic shampoo	强碱洗发水
strongly acidic shampoo	强酸洗发水
give the hair more body	让头发更有质感
literally	真正地;名副其实地
given volume	固定容量
advertising gimmick	广告策略;营销手段
add nothing to	对……没有任何意义
the back-to-nature movement	重返自然运动

Translation (Passage A)

化妆品之魅力化学

很久以前,原始人类使用天然材料进行清洁、美化和其他行为方式来改变容貌。有证据表明,7000年前,埃及人把锑(Sb)粉和孔雀石粉用作眼影。早在公元前3500年,埃及法老开始使用芳香发油。据说,公元二世纪,希腊医生克劳狄乌斯·加伦(Claudius Galen)发明了冷霜。十七世纪欧洲,衣着讲究的绅士们很少洗澡,为了掩盖体味通常大量使用化妆品。十八世纪,欧洲的女士们使用碳酸铅($PbCO_3$)来美白面部,结果许多人死于铅中毒。

人类使用化妆品的历史悠久而又有趣,但就其使用量和种类而言,过去的一切无法与现代工业社会相提并论。每年人们花费数十亿美元购买各种化妆品,从发胶到指甲油,从漱口水到足光粉。

本文将介绍各种化妆品,重点介绍那些你或家人可能使用最多的产品。

一、牙膏：香味磨砂肥皂

除肥皂之外（我们不谈肥皂，因为法律规定肥皂不属于化妆品类[①]），牙膏是最重要的化妆产品。牙膏的主要组分只不过是清洁剂和研磨剂。肥皂和碳酸氢钠可以很好地起到清洁功效，但因其口味不佳而难以入口。理想的研磨剂应具有适当的软硬度，既能清洁牙齿污垢，又不会损坏牙釉质。一些常用于牙膏中的研磨剂因过于粗糙而受到诟病。

任何药用等级的肥皂或清洁剂，用起来都可能令人满意。现今大多数牙膏都有薄荷味、色彩、香气和甜味，其成分包括：甜味剂，如山梨糖醇、甘油和糖精；香料，如薄荷油和薄荷；增稠剂，如纤维素胶和聚乙二醇（PEGs）；以及防腐剂，如苯甲酸钠。

牙膏有多种配方。化妆品的配方不是化学式，因为化妆品是混合物而不是纯净物，更恰当地可称之为配制表，即产品制备的原料清单和操作指南。

蛀牙主要是由细菌引起的。细菌将糖转化为黏性葡聚糖，形成牙菌斑，并产生乳酸（$CH_3CHOHCOOH$）等。酸会溶解牙釉质。刷牙和漱口可以去除牙菌斑，从而防止蛀牙。

许多现代牙膏中含有氟化亚锡（SnF_2），这种化合物被证明可以有效降低蛀牙率。

二、皮肤化学：膏霜和乳液

皮肤是一个复杂的器官，包裹着我们的身体。皮肤的外层称为表皮。表皮又分为两部分：外部是死细胞层（角质层），角质层下面是活细胞层。角质细胞脱落，活细胞不断进行替换。化妆品是应用在角质层的死细胞上的。

角质层主要由一种坚韧的纤维蛋白质——角蛋白组成。角蛋白的水分含量约为10%。水分含量低于10%时，皮肤干燥起屑；高于10%时，有害微生物易于滋生。皮肤通过皮脂（皮脂腺分泌的一种油脂）来防止水分丢失。皮肤有一个有趣的特性，即它不溶于水（否则我们会在淋浴时被溶解掉），不过，水和光对皮肤具有轻微的渗透作用。

风吹日晒可能会使皮肤干燥起鳞，频繁洗涤也会洗去皮肤上的天然油脂。我们可用各种乳霜、乳液治疗皮肤干燥。任何乳霜、乳液的基本成分都含有脂类或酯类，油性脂质可在皮肤上形成一层保护膜。凡士林和矿物油是两种具有代表性的原料成分，这两种成分有时在同一配方中使用。凡士林和矿物油是从石油中获得的烷烃混合物。凡士林是一种沸点高于矿物油的分馏物，呈半固体状态；而矿物油是一种黏稠的液体。乳霜、乳液中还含有其他成分，包括天然油脂和酯、香料、蜡、水和乳化剂（防止水油分离的物质）。用于皮肤的天然材料有羊毛脂（一种从羊毛中提取的脂类）和橄榄油。为增加产品的硬度，通常在乳霜、乳液中添加蜂蜡。

有些乳霜配方中会添加激素、蜂王浆和其他奇怪的成分，然而我们没有发现这些成分具有特殊的功效。就像增塑剂软化塑料一样，乳霜、乳液是通过提供保护性涂层和软化皮肤从而起到保护皮肤的作用。这种软化皮肤的物质被称为润肤剂。你完全可以使用矿物油膏（一种商标名为"凡士林"的产品）或优质白色矿物油（有时称为婴儿油）代替那些高级乳霜。

什么是皮肤保湿剂？这个术语没有明确的定义。所谓保湿剂，其成分通常是指凡士林、矿物油或类似物质。这些物质实际上起着保护膜的作用，从而防止水分流失，因此在一定程度上可以有助于保持皮肤柔软。

[①] 在我国，依据《化妆品监督管理条例》，香皂不属于化妆品，但宣称具有特殊化妆品功效的除外。

三、口红：蓖麻油和颜色

口红在成分上与护肤霜非常相似，由油和蜡制成。为了使口红形体保持结实，口红中蜡的使用比例比霜类产品中高。染料和颜料为口红提供颜色。口红中使用的油通常是蓖麻油。口红中常用的蜡有蜂蜡、巴西棕榈蜡和小烛树蜡。为了掩盖油脂难闻的腥味，口红中常常添加香料。口红中也添加一些抗氧化剂来延缓酸败。溴酸染料（如四溴荧光素，一种蓝红色化合物）被用来为现代大多数口红染色。这些化合物通常黏附在金属离子上形成有色络合物，称为色淀。

由于唇部几乎没有保护性油脂，容易干燥，因此常常发生嘴唇干裂。无论是否着色，口红都可以保护嘴唇，防止干燥。

四、香水、古龙水和须后水

没有人愿意自己的身体散发出难闻的气味，相反的，许多人喜欢自己的身体散发出水果或花朵般的宜人香气，但是为了避免香气刺激旁人的鼻子，可能会对香味进行适度调节。香水是最古老、使用最广泛的化妆品之一，然而，香水的化学成分却非常复杂。

最初，香水是从天然物质中提取的。如今，化学家已经确定了许多香水成分，并可以在实验室中合成。也许最好的香水仍然是由天然材料制成的，因为化学家迄今为止还无法确定香水中所有重要的微量成分。

一款好的香水可能含有一百种甚至更多的成分。通常，这些成分根据挥发性的差异被分为三类，即三种香调（notes）：前调（top note）、中调（middle note）和基调（end note）。最易挥发的部分被称为前调，由相对的小分子化合物组成。当香水刚涂抹时，前调成分负责产生气味。中调成分的挥发性居中。当大部分前调成分挥发后，中调成分负责产生持久的香气。基调成分的挥发性较低，它由大分子化合物组成。

具有花香或水果香气的化合物大量合成用于香水，其气味随稀释而变化。浓缩溶液（由大量化合物溶解在少量水或其他溶剂中形成的溶液）的气味可能令人不愉快，而相同化合物的稀释溶液（由少量化合物溶解在大量溶剂中形成的溶液）可能香气宜人。

许多花香或水果香气即使在稀释溶液中也会过于甜腻，让人作呕。为了调和这种气味，通常会添加麝香类物质。麝香和类似的化合物在高浓度时具有极其难闻的气味，但在极度稀释时其气味通常是宜人的。

香水中的有香化合物和固定剂通常占 10%～25%。其余是乙醇，用作溶剂。香水经过稀释制成古龙水，通常古龙水只含有 1% 或 2% 的香水精华，因此古龙水的浓度约为香水的十分之一。稀释时可以单独使用乙醇或者采用乙醇-水混合物。配制古龙水只需使用自己喜欢的香水并混合均匀即可。（请勿使用已被甲醇或其他有毒成分变性的乙醇。）

须后水与古龙水类似。须后水中通常会添加薄荷醇，以便在皮肤上产生凉爽的效果。

使用香水可以给许多产品带来宜人的气味。有些人对香水中的一种或多种成分有过敏反应。因此，在使用一款化妆品之前，应先对皮肤进行敏感性测试：取一滴化妆品，滴在手肘内侧，贴上斑贴，留置一晚。如果没有任何反应（皮肤发红或瘙痒），该产品应该相对安全，可以使用；如有任何反应，请勿使用。

五、毛发用化学：护发和养发

与皮肤一样，头发由角蛋白组成。洗头时，角蛋白会吸收水分，变得柔软，更具可伸展性。

现代洗发水使用合成表面活性剂作为清洁剂。成人用洗发水通常使用阴离子型表面活性剂，如十二烷基硫酸钠。婴儿和儿童用的洗发水通常使用的是一种两性离子型表面活性剂，对眼睛刺激性较小。

洗发水中唯一必要的成分是某种表面活性剂。那么，广告上都是怎么说的呢？你可以购买洗发水，有水果和草本味，富含蛋白质，酸碱平衡，专为油性和干性头发设计。让我们来看看广告中使用的一些噱头。

头发是带有酸性和碱性基团的蛋白质链。很显然，洗发水的酸碱度会影响头发。头发和皮肤呈弱酸性。强碱（高 pH）或强酸（低 pH）的洗发水会损伤头发。更重要的是，这些产品会刺激皮肤和眼睛。然而，大多数洗发水的 pH 在 5 到 8 之间，差异很小，不会对头发或头皮产生重大影响。洗发水刺激眼睛，通常是因为洗发水中其他成分引起的，而不是因为 pH 过高或过低。

因为头发是由蛋白质构成的，所以洗发水中的蛋白质确实可以让头发更有质感——或者广告上就是这么说的。一些白胶也含有蛋白质。洗发水中的蛋白质可以将分叉的发梢粘合在一起，并包覆在发丝上，使发丝变得更粗。如果这正是你想要的，那么蛋白质洗发水就适合你使用。

用于油性或干性头发的洗发水在一定容量下，表面活性剂的相对含量有所不同。用于油性头发的洗发水可能更加浓缩。然而，从一个品牌到另一个品牌，其配方似乎没有统一标准。针对油性或干性头发使用的洗发水似乎主要是一种营销手段。

那些香味、香气又怎么样呢？大量的证据表明，像牛奶、蜂蜜、草莓、草药、黄瓜、柠檬等"天然"成分对洗发水或其他化妆品的实用功效没有任何意义。那么为什么洗发水还使用这些成分呢？气味可以促销产品。对于那些追求回归自然的群体来说，这个特色具有一定的吸引力。然而，使用这些香气、香味有一种危险，因为蜜蜂、蚊子和其他昆虫也喜欢水果和花的气味，因此使用了这些有香产品去野餐或徒步旅行，可能会招来蜜蜂。

六、化妆品：经济与广告

多数化妆品都是由廉价成分配制而成的，然而经过广告的大肆宣传，许多化妆品售价高昂。物有所值吗？这个判断超出了化学范畴。如果一个产品可以让你容貌改善或让你心情愉悦，那么它的价值该是多少？只有你自己可以决定。

本文没有试图让你了解化妆品现有的全部知识。详细讨论这些有趣化学物质的诸多卷册都可以在图书馆里找到。然而，我们希望，你从本文获得的知识，再加上化妆品标签上提供的必要知识，能让你成为一个更加明智的消费者。你不必为化妆品中的一些额外成分支付过多的费用，因为这些成分对化妆品的功效几乎不起作用。

Warming-up（Passage B）

山寨欧美化妆品	to counterfeit European and American cosmetics
东方审美	oriental aesthetics
迎合	to cater for
原始人类	primitive people
化妆	make up
大量甲骨文、金文、竹简的记载	a large number of oracle bone scripts, bronze scripts and bamboo slips

脂、泽、粉、黛	rouge, balsam, powder (*fen*), and eyebrow color (*dai*)
铜镜	bronze mirror
《诗经》	*The Book of Songs*
汉代陶俑	the pottery figurines of the Han Dynasty
彩妆配方	makeup formulas
享有盛名	to enjoy a high reputation
缓步慢行的阶段	a slow development stage
追溯到	to be traced back to
红山文化女神像	the Goddess Statues of Hongshan Culture
红色的朱砂	red cinnabar
《新唐书·百官志》	*Records of Officials* in *The New Book of Tang*
文化碰撞	cultural contact
口红"达人"	a lipstick "master"
神灵的用品	articles special for deities
回归王座	to regain one's past glory
厚积薄发	to fully prepare for the rapid development
一见倾心	to be attracted at the first sight
《新唐书》	*The New Book of Tang*
彰显美德	to show their virtues
使用简便又便于携带	for the convenient use and carry
一妆多用	to be used multiply for one makeup
代称呼	surrogate name
西域	the Western Regions
想方设法	to try every means to do sth.
抛砖引玉	to throw out a brick to draw pieces of jade
在浩如烟海的传统文化中立足	to keep a foothold in the vast traditional culture

Translation (Passage B)

Three Thousand Years of Chinese Cosmetics

With the rise of traditional Chinese culture, domestic cosmetics, which once counterfeited European and American cosmetics, claiming the raw materials, packaging, and efficacy of their products were of the same quality as those of foreign brands but with lower prices, have turned to seek development of Chinese own products. With brands, packaging and raw materials positioned anew in line with traditional culture and oriental aesthetics, some of the domestic brands have become very popular among young consumers.

China has developed its own systems of makeup and makeup tools since ancient times. How should Chinese cosmetics be grafted into traditional culture to create brands that are loved by consumers and cater for the return of oriental aesthetics? Only by truly understanding the history of

Chinese makeup can this goal be achieved.

The Chinese nation has a long history and profound cultural heritage, and it is one of the earliest nations in the world to make and use cosmetics. Makeup originated in primitive society, when primitive people smeared varieties of pigments on their skin for survival and reproduction. Slave society saw a new era of makeup. During the Xia, Shang, and Zhou Dynasties of China, people were so busy making a living that they had little time and energy to make up, but priests would make up themselves to communicate with deities at the practice of sacrifice. Seen from a large number of oracle bone scripts, bronze scripts and bamboo slips, people at that time already used rouge, balsam, powder (*fen*), and eyebrow color (*dai*).

In recorded history, cosmetics appear together with beauties of different eras, and the descriptions of different makeup are also seen in literati's poems.

During the Xia and Shang Dynasties, people who make up were mainly in the upper class. During the Yin (Shang) Dynasty, the bronze mirror was invented, which greatly facilitated people's need to look at their own faces when making up and hence promoted the development of cosmetics. *The Book of Songs* records that when the husband went out to battle, the wife left her hair tumbled like grass, not because she was short of gaomu (膏沐 cosmetics), but because she didn't know for whom she powdered her face. We can see that there were mature cosmetics in the Zhou Dynasty. In the late Shang Dynasty, there was a makeup called *yanzhi* (燕支), also called *yanzhi* (胭脂 rouge).

With the development of social economy, people's aesthetic consciousness changed. From the Qin Dynasty to the Han Dynasty, makeup became more and more popular. Among the nobles and commoners, women paid much attention to their appearance, which can be seen from the unearthed pottery figurines of the Han Dynasty whose faces have obvious makeup. According to relevant historical records, women in the Han Dynasty liked to smear their cheeks with rouge and lead powder. In the Wei, Jin, Southern and Northern Dynasties, there appeared more styles of face makeup with types of cosmetics increasing.

In the heyday of the Tang Dynasty, makeup was even more popular. Women mostly used makeup of various colors to dress themselves, mainly on foreheads, cheeks, eyebrows, eyes and so on. In the Prosperous Tang Dynasty, "red makeup" was the most popular facial makeup then; after the Middle Tang Dynasty, "white makeup" was once popular, that is, white powder was smeared on faces, necks, and breasts to improve complexions; In addition, there was also another kind of makeup called "ocher face", that is, to smear the face, neck and other parts in reddish brown.

During the two Song Dynasties, makeup developed to a new height with the development of social economy, and complete makeup formulas can be found in historical documents. During the Southern Song Dynasty, Hangzhou powder enjoyed a high reputation among the people.

During the Ming and Qing Dynasties, makeup entered a slow development stage as facial makeup became simpler and lighter. During the period of the Republic of China, the aesthetics of people began to be westernized under the influence of European and American cultures and the

Hollywood movie stars. As a result, they chose to use foreign makeup products or their imitations that domestic cosmetics companies produced. And thus, the development of traditional makeup was paused.

I. Huadian

Huadian is also called *huazi*, *mianhua*, and *tiehua*. It is a kind of small flower ornament pasted on women's foreheads and faces. In ancient times, many materials were used to make *huadian* including gold foil, paper, fish scales, dragonfly wings, etc.

Huadian has different colors of red, green, yellow, etc., and beautiful and novel shapes of bird, fish and duckling besides plum blossom.

II. Lipstick—the king of makeup

In ancient times, lipstick was called *kouzhi* or *chunzhi* (fat used for lip makeup), and it has been loved by women since ancient times. In China, lipstick can be traced back to the Goddess Statue of Hongshan Culture, made more than 5000 years ago. People found red cinnabar on the lip of the statue, which was the earliest form of lipstick.

Nowadays, lipstick is a must-have makeup for all women, while in ancient times it was a luxury. The records of lipstick in the Tang Dynasty were the richest in all the historical materials from the Qin Dynasty to the Qing Dynasty. *Records of Officials* in *The New Book of Tang* has records of *kouzhi*, saying that *kouzhi* was offered to the dinitaries on the Laba Festival, one of the Chinese Traditional Festivals.

In addition, various makeups, with *kouzhi* as the main part, appeared in the Tang Dynasty, which were frequently seen in the poetry of literati. Under the influence of *Tubo* (Tibetan regime in ancient China) costumes and makeup, "weeping makeup" and "tears makeup" appeared at that time. This makeup, as the result of cultural contacts, however quickly disappeared due to the lack of beauty.

In modern times, *kouzhi* developed into lipstick. Eileen Chang, a modern Chinese writer, was a lipstick "master" of the Republic of China. She liked makeup, and some descriptions of cosmetics can be found in her writings.

In history, the more prosperous the dynasty was, the more the colors of lipsticks and the styles of makeup were, as can be seen in the literary works of the Tang Dynasty. After thousands of years of development, lipstick, which was once articles special for deities, has become the daily cosmetics of today. And its raw materials, shapes, colors, packaging, etc. have become complex and diverse with the changes in aesthetics and users. Today, the attributes of lipsticks have become more and more diversified during the brand building. East and West, modern and ancient, luxury and practical, these characteristics are intertwined to form a product that attracts consumers at their first sight.

Under the influence of COVID-19, the market of lipsticks performs sluggishly. However, with the effective control of the pandemic, lipstick will surely regain its past glory in the future. Prior to this should be an important period for lipsticks to fully prepare for the rapid development.

III. Foundation for both men and women

Fen (facial powder) is a kind of white powder used on face, neck, arms and so on. In China ancient times, the most common powders included rice powder (powder made by grinding natural rice), paste-like lead powder [*qianfen*, also known as *qianhua* (white lead)], lead powder with sandalwood red [also known as *tanfen* (sandalwood powder)] and pearl powder and so on. Facial powder was a basic makeup commonly used by the ancients as well as by the modern people.

Lead powder was preferred by ancients for its fine texture, smooth white color and easy preservation. And therefore, it gradually replaced rice powder. The production process of lead powder is much more complicated than that of rice powder. Without dehydration, the original lead powder was mostly paste-like. After the Han Dynasty, it was mostly dehydrated and made into powder or solid shape.

In addition to pure rice powder and lead powder, there appeared later powders made from complex raw materials, like "purple powder" "butterfly powder" "jade maiden peach flower powder" "jade hairpin powder" and "pearl powder", as well as powders famous for their origins, like "Hangzhou powder" "Fanyang powder" "Ding (Hebei) powder" "Gui powder" and so on. The most distinctive powder was the Southern Song makeup powder, which was made into blocks of different shapes, such as round, square, quadrilateral, octagonal and sunflower petals, and with various prints of plum blossoms, orchids, lotus flowers and so on.

White skin is a long-coveted complexion of beauty in China of all ages. In ancient times, women and men used facial powder when they could afford it. According to *the New Book of Tang*, when three sisters of Yang Guifei (Yang Yuhuan, Emperor Xuanzong's favorite concubine during his later years) were once called into the palace, they were vouchsafed as many as hundreds of thousands of silver coins for cosmetics.

Since ancient times, men have put on makeup. There were many celebrities in the historical and literary works of the Three Kingdoms, Wei Jin, Sui and Tang Dynasties, wearing hairpins and applying foundation and makeup to their faces. The ancient people put on makeup was, for one thing, to decorate their appearance, and for another, to show their virtues.

IV. *E'huang* (yellow foreheads) lost in the history

Yellow foreheads, also called crow yellow, was a kind of makeup by painting forehead yellow. It originated in the Southern and Northern Dynasties and prevailed in the Tang Dynasty. According to *Chinese Women's Makeup and Ornaments through all the Ages*, the emergence of this kind of make-up had a certain relationship with the popularity of Buddhism. During the Southern and Northern Dynasties, Buddhism entered its heyday in China. Inspired by gilded images of Buddha, women painted their foreheads yellow, which gradually became popular.

Until the Song Dynasty, *e'huang* was still popular. Peng Ruli, a poet, wrote in a song: "There was a beautifal girl named Xiniang, who adorned her temples and sideburns with pearl powder to give them a yellowish tint." This reflects the ancient women's love for *e'huang*.

V. *Dai* (a black pigment used by women in ancient times to paint their eyebrows)

Dai, also known as *shidai* (stone *dai*), is an ancient eyebrow pencil made from a kind of black mineral. Before painting the brows, *Shidai* needs to be first ground into powder in the inkstone, and then blended with water. Inkstones used to grind *shidai* have been found in a lot of Han tombs, indicating that this kind of cosmetics was already in use in the Han Dynasty.

Besides *shidai*, there are historical records of *luozidai* (livid eyebrow paint) and *qingquetoudai* (dark gray eyebrow paint). *Luozidai*, often seen in various films and television plays, was an eyebrow pencil in the Sui and Tang Dynasties. Made in Persia, *Luozidai* is a processed lump of *dai* in various shapes and one of the earliest cosmetics imported into China. Its production process and shape were similar to those of the ink ingots, while the usage of it was simpler than that of ink ingots, for no grinding was required before dipping in water to paint the eyebrow. *Qingquetoudai*, a dark gray material for painting eyebrow, was also a kind of imported makeup, which was introduced into the Central Plains from the Western Regions during the Southern and Northern Dynasties.

In the early 1920s, a series of changes took place in women's cosmetics in China as the Western culture spread to the east. The materials for eyebrow painting, especially the rod-shaped eyebrow pencils and chemically modulated black grease, have been used till this day for their convenient use and carry.

VI. Rouge used multiply for one makeup

Rouge, as a kind of red pigment, is the general name of ancient lipstick and blusher and can be used for multiple purposes. In historical documents, there are many spellings of rouge, such as *yanzhi* (焉支), *yanzhi* (烟支), *xianzhi* (鲜支), *yanzhi* (燕支), *yanzhi* (燕脂), *yanzhi* (阏氏) and so on.

There are many legends about the origin of rouge. One is that rouge comes from "*Yanzhi*" (阏氏), the name of the wives of the Xiongnu nobles (the Xiongnu were a tribal confederation of nomadic peoples who inhabited the eastern Eurasian Steppe from the 3rd century BC to the late 1st century AD). "*Yanzhi*" became the wives' surrogate name because it was often used to make up their faces. Another is that "rouge" is actually a kind of flower named "red and blue", whose petals contained red and yellow pigments. After the flowers bloom, they were picked off as a whole and repeatedly pestled in a stone bowl. And a bright red pigment could be obtained by washing away yellow juice. Zhang Qian (an outstanding diplomat in the Han Dynasty) brought the kind of flower back to the Central Plains during his diplomatic mission to the Western Regions.

In the early days, there were two kinds of rouge. One was made of silk wedding dipped in the extracted juice from red and blue flowers, called "silk wedding *yanzhi*", and the other was processed into small and thin flower pieces, called "golden flower *yanzhi*". The two kinds of rouge could both be dried in the shade to be applied after dipping in a small amount of water.

By the Southern and Northern Dynasties, ingredients such as ox marrow and pig pancreas were further supplemented into the red rouge to make a thicker and smoother grease of finer texture, which could moisturize the skin. And therefore, *yanzhi* (燕支) was also written as "*yanzhi*" (胭脂, rouge grease).

Until the Republic of China, rouge was still one of the main cosmetics used by Chinese women.

VII. *Koudan* (nail enamel/nail polish)

Koudan (impatiens flower) is a kind of flower, with its popular names as *qiancenghong* (thousand-tier-red flower) or fingernail grass. In ancient China, many people would plant *koudan* in their home, collect its petals, and mash and apply on nails. A few hours later or overnight, the nails were dyed pink and red.

Among many ancient make-ups, *Koudan* is the most natural and harmless one. Dyeing nails with it has become a fashion in China since the Tang Dynasty. In the Ming Dynasty, royal women would make lacquer from ingredients such as gum arabic, impatiens flowers, alum, egg white, gelatin and beeswax, with which to paint their nails red or black.

In addition to dyeing nails, the ancients also tried every means to protect their nails, and nail guards or nail protection were invented. For example, the golden nail guards, unearthed from the Han tomb in Laoheshen Village of Dapo Town in Yushu City of Jilin Province, were used to protect fingernails. They were a typical sign of both beauty and noble status.

VIII. Conclusion

These traditional cosmetics from *kouzhi* to *koudan* have gone through thousands of years of development, with many legends, allusions and poems related to them created. For domestic make-up, they are treasures handed down from ancestors. Of the myriad records of makeup in the historical and literary works of China, only a few are mentioned in this article. By summarizing them, we would like to throw out a brick to draw pieces of jade, arousing the interest of domestic cosmetics industries in and their thinking of the traditional culture. As for how cosmetic brands can keep a foothold in the vast traditional culture and arouse the interest of consumers, further research in practice needs to be carried out.

Translation Workshop

I. Translate the following sentences and pay attention to hypotaxis and parataxis

1. 无机颜料、有机颜料和金属色淀均用于强化和变化颜色。

2. 优质唇膏使用方便，能赋予唇部一层薄膜，油性适中，相对持久，颜色稳定，易于抹去。

3. 即使健康正常的皮肤也时常会发生变化，需要特殊的护理来使其恢复正常。

4. 保护皮肤，即保持皮肤光滑、柔软和清洁，消除因过多暴露在冷、热、阳光、风等外部因素下而造成的影响。

5. 消费者可以使用无色粉底，一旦涂抹在脸上，它能与任何肤色完美搭配。

6. With the awakening of Chinese aesthetics and the resurgence of cultural confidence, more and cosmetics brands are refining and innovating Chinese traditional culture, and applying it to the packaging design of domestic cosmetics. This has provided greater development opportunities for domestic cosmetics.

7. Pure plant and Chinese herbal medicine is one of the synonyms for domestic cosmetics,

whose brand advantage lies in the appealing healthiness and mildness of traditional Chinese herbs and their natural plant extracts. This aligns with the current consumers' mentality for seeking health and safety.

8. Vitamin C, also named as corbic acid, which has been widely used in whitening freckle cosmetics since the 1950s, is now the most popular whitening ingredients additives.

9. In the recent years, there has been an obvious rise of domestic Chinese cosmetics brands, to which Chinese-style packaging designs are widely applied, emphasizing the identity of domestic cosmetics brands, guiding consumers to discover brand heritage and cultural connotation, and successfully creating the image of Oriental aesthetics as a representative brand.

10. With advances in materials, highly functional makeup cosmetics have been developed, and they can make the skin surface look less rough and hide blemishes or freckles, not running due to sebum or other causes.

II. Translate the following passage into Chinese

今天，消费者都在寻求以科学为主导的护肤品，以期改善和防止皮肤老化，保护皮肤免受环境损害，并为各种皮肤问题提供治疗方案。他们想要的是天然、无刺激、不含防腐剂、绿色、经过全面测试的产品。对于生产商来说，这是一个艰巨的任务，他们不仅要保证产品的安全、稳定、一致和有效，同时还要满足消费者的需求。药妆的未来取决于创新。明确的产品定位、新的活性成分、高效的输送体系无疑为种类繁多、临床应用范围广泛的药妆产品提供了新思路。

尽管业界尽了最大的努力，消费者仍然对药妆产品持怀疑态度。他们对成分感到困惑，不信任产品宣传，因此怀疑这些产品是否真的物有所值。药妆产品的外包装标签比较模棱两可，缺乏主要活性成分的具体信息，这使得消费者在购买药妆产品时一头雾水。如果对药妆产品实施更严格的监管，那么这些担忧就可以迎刃而解。为了让医师认可药妆产品的合法化，药妆产品就要迎接更重大的挑战。许多皮肤科医师表示不相信药妆产品的效用，因为药妆产品的应用缺乏科学严谨性。针对这种观点，生产商只有通过客观的方法测试产品才能揭开谜团。令人鼓舞的是，一些新的药妆产品运用双盲对照实验证实产品的有效性。为了帮助医师收集有关药妆产品的可靠信息，美国皮肤病学会（AAD）成立了补充药物和替代药物团队，成员包括皮肤科医师和监管化妆品的政府部门。我们希望通过该团队为AAD成员提供有关药妆产品和其他替代品的安全性和有效性数据。

III. Translate the following passage into English

In the field of cosmetics, Chinese cosmetics brands are always marginalized compared with their western counterparts, an example of which is the dominance of foreign brands in domestic mid-to-high-end shopping malls. Local brands, with almost-zero brand visibility and consumption influence, basically withdraw from the primary and secondary mainstream sales channels and are hardly seen in the market.

Who will lead the beauty of Chinese women? Where are the dream factories that create the beauty for them? Until the financial crisis swept the world and China's economy survived the challenge, there is finally a silver lining for the future of Chinese cosmetics brands!

Also, as brands like L'Oréal, SHISEIDO, P&G and Unilever profited from China's market, their noble veils were ripped off. Chinese consumers gradually changed from worshiping foreign brands anymore and began to embrace diversified brands. This shift in their consumer psychology brought a huge market to Chinese cosmetics brands, which was confirmed by the market trends of many outstanding brands such as BAWANG, MARUBI, MIMOCLYS, MEIFUBAO, D·COLOR, TIMIÉR, etc.

With the growth of Chinese women's aesthetic cognition, cosmetics with new oriental styles will appear in a brand-new product form with the advent and dissemination of the concepts of makeup, beauty, and skin care that represent the oriental characters. This provides huge market opportunities for Chinese cosmetics brands.

There are both growth space and market opportunities for Chinese cosmetics! Surely appears a hopeful transformation in the Chinese cosmetics market! Soon comes the rise of Chinese cosmetics brands!

What preparations should Chinese cosmetics brands make for the oncoming transformation?

First, Chinese cosmetics brands should be strategically prepared to compete with the stronger ones.

Second, Chinese cosmetics brands must be prepared to "segment the market". The consumption characteristics of Chinese female consumers have undergone a huge transformation from "following suit" to "having diversified personal demands", which allows cosmetics companies to position themselves from more aspects. Each successfully differentiated positioning may forge a great brand.

The traditional pyramid brand pattern, with European and American brands in the first level, Japanese and Korean brands in the second level, and Chinese cosmetics brands in the third level, will inevitably be broken, and the Chinese brands shall not stay in the third level forever. With the ambition to be No. 1 and the determination to carve out space in higher-level markets, the Chinese cosmetics brands will surely be recognized by a large number of consumers with the help of strong marketing, and hence stand with foreign cosmetics brands as an equal.

Third, Chinese cosmetics brands must be prepared to develop "oriental products", which refer to the products that can cater for oriental consumers culturally and adopt new product forms or product concepts. To some extent, the acquisition of Volvo by Geely shows that foreign brands are not unchallengeable. As long as Chinese cosmetics brands can "carve out space in higher-level markets and go on parallel tracks with the stronger" in terms of strategies, "explore more development angles and make accurate brand positioning" in terms of tactics, and "seek innovation and creation boldly" in terms of products, they will be fully capable of facing the challenges from the opportunities of the new market.

Confident women are the most beautiful! Confident brands are the most dazzling!

As the saying goes, "if you do not seize opportunities given by God, you will be blamed by Him." Currently, facing opportunities brought by the times to rise to the top of the world market, Chinese cosmetics brands shall not be timid to seize them!

Face challenges bravely to forge Chinese advantages with the global ambition!

Glossary

Unit 1 Design Studies and Chinese Art

animation	动画
architectural design	建筑设计
Art Deco	新装饰主义
art gallery	画廊；美术馆
artifact	人工制品；造物
art nouveau	新艺术运动
Arts and Crafts Movement	工艺美术运动
Bauhaus	包豪斯
bespoke tailoring	量身定制服务
branding	品牌打造
brief	（设计）任务书
Chinese painting	国画
conceptual design	概念性设计
corporate design	企业设计
critical design	批判式设计
customization	定制
design competence	设计能力
design criticism	设计批评
design education	设计教育
design solutions	设计解决方案
design strategy	设计策略
design thinking	设计思维
drawing from nature	写生画
eco design	生态设计
emoticons	表情符号
environmental design	环境设计
ergonomics	人体工程学
exhibition design	会展设计
fashion design	时装设计
fine arts	美术
furniture design	家具设计
futuristic design	未来主义设计

garden design	园林设计
gender design	性别设计
gerontological design	老龄化设计
gestaltung	造型设计
good design	优良设计
grabertising	扶手广告
graphic design	平面设计
green design	绿色设计
human computer interaction（HCI）	人机互动
industrial design	工业设计
information design	信息设计
in-house designers	内部设计师
interaction design	交互设计
interface design	界面设计
interior design	室内设计
jewelry design	珠宝设计
knick-knack	小摆设
landscape design	景观设计
lighting design	照明设计
look and feel	外观与感觉
mechatronic design	机电一体化设计
media design	媒体设计
mood board	情绪板
non intentional design	无意识设计
olfactory design	嗅觉设计
packaging design	包装设计
participatory design	参与式设计
patina	做旧
plastic arts	造型艺术
poster design	海报设计
product design	产品设计
product family	产品系列
public design	公共设计
prototype	原型
rapid prototyping	快速成型
retro design	复古设计
scenario design	场景设计
screen design	屏幕设计
service design	服务设计

signature design	签名设计
sound design	声音设计
stage design	舞台设计
storyboard	故事板
streamline design	流线设计
target group	目标人群
template	模板
textile design	织物设计
texture	肌理
title design	字幕设计
typography	字体排印
universal design	通用设计
urban design	城市设计
usability	使用性
virtual reality	虚拟现实
visual communication	视觉传达
visual effects	视觉效果
visualization	可视化；形象化
web design	网页设计
wicked problem	诡异的问题
work of art	艺术作品

Unit 2 Food Science and Chinese Food Culture

altar	祭坛
balance	均衡
body pathways	经络
Book of Changes	《周易》
Book of Documents	《尚书》
Book of Rites	《礼记》
Book of Songs	《诗经》
browning	褐变
calamus	菖蒲
carbohydrate	碳水化合物
catalysis	催化作用
chef	厨师
Chinese cuisines	中餐
cholesterol	胆固醇
coagulation	凝固物
cod	鳕鱼

controlling	克
coriander	香菜
crispy-skinned	脆皮的
culinary arts	厨艺
cured	腌制的
dehydration	脱水作用
denaturation	变性作用
diet therapy	食疗
deoxyribonucleic acid（DNA）	脱氧核糖核酸
dopamine	多巴胺
dried fish	鱼干
duality	二元性
Duanwu Jie（Dragon Boat Festival）	端午节
enzyme	酶
eternal cycle of life	永恒的生命轮回
ethics	伦理
evaporation	蒸发作用
fat	脂肪
fermentation	发酵
fillings	馅料
fish balls	鱼圆
five aromas	五味
five body fluids	五液
five elements	五行
five emotions	五情
five hollow organs	五腑
five pures	五清
five sacrificial animals	五畜
five solid organs	五脏
five virtues	五常
flavor	风味
generating	生
ginseng	人参
glucose	葡萄糖
gourmet	美食家
harmony	调和
health	健康
herbal medicine	草药
homegrown	自家产的，本土的

hydrolysis	水解作用
imported	舶来的
ingredients	原料，食材
longevity	长寿
Ma jiexiu	马介休
macromolecule	大分子
Maillard reaction	美拉德反应
meridians	经络
nostalgia	乡愁
nutrition	营养
oxidation	氧化反应
pasteurization	巴氏杀菌法
pharmacological practices	药理实践
pickled	腌制的
preventive medicine	预防医学
probiotic	益生菌
protein	蛋白质
qi (vital energy)	气
Qingming Jie (Tomb-Sweeping Day)	清明节
redox	氧化还原反应
reduction	还原反应
restorative medicine	康复医学
roast suckling pigs	烤乳猪
salted	盐腌的
sandy-skinned	麻皮的
Shennong	神农
smooth-skinned	光皮的
Spring and Autumn Annals	《春秋》
starch	淀粉
sterilization	灭菌处理
stuffing	填料
taste	味道
time-honored brand names	老字号
toppings	浇头
trace mineral	微量元素
vitamins	维生素
western cuisines	西餐
yeast	酵母菌
Yellow Emperor	黄帝

yin and yang	阴阳
zongzi（sticky rice dumpling）	粽子

Unit 3　Textile Science and Fashion Culture

absorbent cotton	脱脂棉
accordion fabric	单面提花针织物
accreditation	认证
action wear	运动服
baby blue	淡蓝
bachelor's gown	学士袍
back fullness	后背宽松（服装设计）
camouflage pants	迷彩裤
campus wear	学生装
canvas sandals	帆布凉鞋
career fashion	职员工作服；白领职业装
darn	织补
daywear	日装
degrade	由深到浅的色调
denim jackets	牛仔布夹克
dewing	给湿；喷雾
diamond pattern	菱形图案
ease-of-care；easy care	免烫；随便穿
ecological textiles	生态纺织品
effective staple	（纤维）有效长度
embroidered motifs	刺绣花边
finished yarn	加工纱；成品丝
fitting model	试衣模特
flared skirt	喇叭裙
garment fair/exposition	服装展示会
gauge of cloth	经纬密度
gay color	欢快的色彩
glazed yarn	上光纱
golf wear	高尔夫装
gorgeous style	华丽风格
high thermal resistance	耐高温性
idealized drawing	示意图
in-work dress	上班装
individually-tailored yarn	特制丝；特殊专用丝
infant's wear	婴儿装

inner wear	内衣；内穿
jet loom	喷射织机
loafers shoes	懒汉鞋
long johns	长内衣裤
loom	织机
military uniform	军服
milkness of fibre	纤维乳白度
mini-plant	中试工厂；试生产用小型设备
naked sweater	紧身羊毛衫
occupational safety	职业安全
physical size	外形尺寸
piece counting	计件
piece dyeing	匹染
Pierre Cardin	皮尔·卡丹（巴黎高级女装设计师）
pigeon blood	鸽血红（暗红色）
pillow slip	枕套
pilot cloth	海员厚绒呢
plain clothes	便服；常服
recovered fibre	回用纤维；再生纤维
resilient fabric	弹性织物
scarf collar	方巾领
sea bag	水手旅行袋
seamless intimate	无缝内衣
self-figure	织花
self-ironing; self-smoothing	免烫；免烫整理
semi evening dress	简式晚礼服
seventies style	70年代风格
shade cloth	窗帘布
terylene	涤纶（聚酯纤维）
test run	试车；实验程序
textile glass	纺织玻璃纤维
textural design	织纹设计
three-piece suit	三件式套装
three quarter sleeves	七分袖
unisex look	中性风貌
uplift	胸罩
up-to-the-minute fashion	最新流行式样
vanity bag	梳妆包
variable hand	手感不一

vertical mill	全能厂；纺织染联合厂
visual impact	视觉效果
wash cloth; wash rag	毛巾
washing label	洗涤标签
yarn cake	丝饼
zories	人字拖鞋

Unit 4　Biotechnology and Wine-Liquor Culture

alcohol by volume（ABV）	酒精度（酒精含量的表示方法）
acidity	酸性
active/functional microorganisms	活性微生物
ageing/saturating	陈年；陈化；老陈
alcoholicity	酒精度
amylopectin starch	支链淀粉
anaerobic fermentation	厌氧发酵
acids	酸类
aldehydes	醛类
amino acid	氨基酸
baijiu	白酒
barley	大麦
basic distillates	基酒
blend	勾兑
beer/wash	发酵醪液；发酵酒醪
bottling	装瓶
cellar	酒窖
cereal malt	谷物麦芽
cereal mash	麦芽汁（浆）；谷物糖化
cognac	科涅克白兰地
condenser	冷凝器
congener	酒类芳香物
daqu/qu	大曲
denature	变性
deposited solids	沉淀物
distillate production	制酒
distillation	蒸馏
enzyme	酶
enzymic degradation	酶分解
enzymic oxidation	酶氧化
esters	酯类

extreme microorganisms	极端微生物
faints/feints	尾酒；末尾蒸馏出的劣质酒精
flavor attributes	风味特征
flavor compounds	风味物质/化合物
flavor taints	异味
fatty acid	脂肪酸
fermentation	发酵
fermentation parameter	发酵参数
fill and package	装瓶与包装；包装
germination	发芽
gelatinize	淀粉糊化/胶化
glutinous sorghum	糯高粱
heat- and acid-resistant	耐热耐酸的
heredity	遗传
impurities	杂质
inocula (inoculum 的复数)	菌种
inorganic constituent	无机成分
jar	酒缸；酒坛
jiu/alcoholic beverages	酒
light aroma type	清香型
liquor-making process	酿酒工艺
kernel	颗粒；果粒
ketones	酮类
kilning	窑化（烘干）
lactic acid bacteria	乳酸菌
maize	玉米
malting	发麦
mashing	磨碎；淀粉糖化
microorganism	微生物
metabolism	新陈代谢
microbial communities	微生物群落
mould growth	霉变；长霉
Moutai	茅台酒
mutation	变异
oak barrels	橡木桶
qu making/production	制曲
peat	泥煤
phenols	酚类物
rectifier/rectifying column	蒸馏塔；蒸馏柱

reducing sugar	还原糖
relative humidity	相对湿度
rice wine	黄酒
saccharification	糖化
saccharomyces cerevisiae	酿酒酵母
sauce aroma type	酱香型
seal and store	封存储藏
secondary metabolite	次级代谢产物；次生代谢物
s-methyl methionine	S-甲基蛋氨酸
sorghum	高粱
spent brewer's yeast (SBY)	废酵母；啤酒废酵母
spirit yield	出酒率；产酒率
stack fermentation	堆积发酵
strain	菌种
strong aroma type	浓香型
sulphur	硫
sweet honey aroma type	蜜香型
the Millard reaction	美拉德反应
whisky	威士忌酒
wolfberry sauce aroma liquor	枸酱酒
worm infestation	虫蛀
yeast growth	酵母生长
yeast strain	酵母菌株

Unit 5 Cosmetics and Oriental Aesthetics

abrasive	研磨剂
acidic	酸性基团
actives	活性成分
active ingredients	活性成分
aftershave	须后水
antioxidant	抗氧化剂
American Academy of Dermatology (AAD)	美国皮肤病学会
antidandruff shampoo	去屑洗发剂
antiperspirant	止汗剂
basic group	碱性基团
bathing bean	沐浴豆
bathing dew	沐浴露
beauty treatment powder	美容护肤粉
beeswax	蜂蜡

candelilla	小烛树蜡
carnauba	巴西棕榈蜡
cellulose gum	纤维素胶
cleansers	清洁剂
cologne	古龙水
cosmeceutical	药妆品
cream	膏霜；乳霜
detergent	清洁剂；表面活性剂
dilution	稀释
double-blind vehicle-controlled studies	双盲对照试验测试
dye	染料
emollient	润肤剂
emulsifier	乳化剂
end note	基调
epidermis	上皮；表皮；真皮
eyebrow blackener	眉黑剂
face brightener	高光
face drug	面药
face ornaments	面饰
face powder	散粉
face rouge	腮红
facial cleanser	洗面奶
food, drug, and cosmetic act	《食品、药品和化妆品法案》
fraction	分馏物
fragrant dew	香露
glycerol	甘油
grit	磨砂
hair moisturizer	润发产品，头发保湿霜
hand cream	护手霜
jade polishing powder	玉石抛光粉
keratin	角蛋白
lake	色淀
lead carbonate ($PbCO_3$)	碳酸铅（$PbCO_3$）
lotion	乳液
malachite	孔雀石
menthol	薄荷醇
microorganism	微生物
middle note	中调
moisturizer	保湿剂

mouth rouge	口红
mouthwash	漱口水
musk	麝香
note	香调
P&G	宝洁
paste rouge	胭脂膏
perfume	香水
pigments	颜料
plaque	牙菌斑
plasticizer	增塑剂
polyethylene glycols (PEGs)	聚乙二醇 (PEGs)
powdered antimony (Sb)	锑 (Sb) 粉
preservative	防腐剂
saccharin	糖精
sebum	皮脂
sodium benzoate	苯甲酸钠
sodium bicarbonate	碳酸氢钠
sodium dodecyl sulfate	十二烷基硫酸钠
solvent	溶剂；溶媒
sorbitol	山梨糖醇
stannous fluoride (SnF_2)	氟化亚锡 (SnF_2)
sweetener	甜味剂
synthesize	合成
tetrabromofluorescein	四溴荧光素
thickener	增稠剂
toothpaste	牙膏
top note	前调；头香
Unilever	联合利华
volatility	挥发性
work group on complementary and alternative medicine	补充药物和替代药物团队
BAWANG	霸王
white makeup	白妆
product concept	产品概念
product form	产品形态
D·COLOR	迪彩
ding (Hebei) powder	定粉
oriental product	东方型产品
e'huang (yellow foreheads)	额黄
Fanyang powder	范阳粉

Glossary

Gui powder	桂粉
foundation	粉底
Hangzhou powder	杭粉
red makeup	红妆
dai (a black pigment used by women in ancient times to paint their eyebrows)	画眉墨黛
huadian	花钿
nail guards; nail protection	护指套
Koudan; impatiens flower; nail enamel; nail polish	蔻丹
lipstick	口红
tears makeup	泪妆
luozidai (livid eyebrow paint)	螺子黛
MEIFUBAO	美肤宝
plum blossom	梅花
rice powder	米粉
MIMOCLYS	名门闺秀
European and American brands	欧美品牌
lead powder	铅粉
qianhua (white lead)	铅华
qingquetoudai (dark gray eyebrow paint)	青雀头黛
Japanese and Korean brands	日韩品牌
lead powder with sandalwood red	檀粉
TIMIÉR	婷美
hair cream	头膏
weeping makeup	啼妆
MARUBI	丸美
pigment	颜料
rouge	胭脂
clothing sachet	衣香囊
butterfly powder	迎蝶粉
jade maiden peach flower powder	玉女桃花粉
jade hairpin powder	玉簪粉
lead powder	朱粉
pearl powder	珠粉
ocher face	赭面
pearl powder	珍珠粉
Chinese cosmetics brand	中国化妆品品牌
purple powder	紫粉

References

Unit 1　Design Studies and Chinese Art

［1］NORMAN, DONALD A, VERGANTI, et al. Incremental and Radical Innovation：Design Research vs. Technology and Meaning Change［J］. Design Issues, 2014（4）：78-96.

［2］布鲁斯·布朗，等. 设计问题：创新模式与交互思维［M］. 孙志祥，辛向阳，译. 北京：清华大学出版社，2017.

［3］布鲁斯·布朗，等. 设计问题：本质与逻辑［M］. 孙志祥，辛向阳，译. 南京：江苏凤凰美术出版社，2021.

［4］布鲁斯·布朗，等. 设计问题：实践与研究［M］. 孙志祥，辛向阳，译. 南京：江苏凤凰美术出版社，2021.

［5］布鲁斯·布朗，等. 设计问题：服务与社会［M］. 孙志祥，辛向阳，谢竞贤，译. 南京：江苏凤凰美术出版社，2021.

［6］孙志祥，谢瑜. 设计学视阈下的学术翻译研究［M］. 苏州：苏州大学出版社，2022.

［7］孙志祥. 文本意识形态批评分析及其翻译研究［M］. 北京：中国社会科学出版社，2009.

［8］连淑能. 英汉对比研究［M］. 北京：高等教育出版社，1993.

［9］胡壮麟，等. 系统功能语言学概论（修订版）［M］. 北京：北京大学出版社，2005.

［10］王克非. 近代翻译对汉语的影响［J］. 外语教学与研究，2002（6）：458-463.

［11］彭雁. 艺术设计专业研究生英语选读［M］. 南京：江苏美术出版社，2013.

［12］迈克尔·厄尔霍夫，蒂姆·马歇尔. 设计辞典［M］. 张敏敏，等，译. 武汉：华中科技大学出版社，2016.

［13］艾红华. 艺术设计英语［M］. 上海：上海人民美术出版社，2016.

Unit 2　Food Science and Chinese Food Culture

［1］陈晓卿. 《濠江味传》（纪录片）解说词. 2018.

［2］冯庆华. 实用翻译教程［M］. 上海：上海外语教育出版社，5版. 2008.

［3］孙万彪，王恩铭. 高级翻译教程［M］. 上海：上海外语教育出版社，2020.

［4］陶全胜，等. 科技翻译教程［M］. 北京：清华大学出版社，2019.

［5］曾剑平. 汉英翻译的虚实转换［J］. 中国科技翻译，2006（1）：9-11.

［6］BARABÁSI A L, MENICHETTI G, LOSCALZO J. The unmapped chemical complexity of our diet［J］. Nature Food, 2020（1）：33-37.

［7］Kelly A. Molecules, Microbes, and Meals：The Surprising Science of Food［M］. New York：Oxford University Press, 2019.

［8］NEWMAN J M. Food Culture in China［M］. Westport, CT：Green wood Press, 2004.

［9］SHEWFELT R L, ORTA-RAMIREZ A, CLARKE A D. Introducing Food Science［M］. Boca Raton, FL：CPC Press, 2016.

［10］VACLAVIK V A, CHRISTIAN E W. Essentials of Food Science［M］. 4th ed. New York：Springer, 2014.

Unit 3　Textile Science and Fashion Culture

［1］HUA M. Chinese Clothing［M］. YU H, ZHANG L, translator. 北京：五洲传播出版社，2004.

［2］高秀明．服装英语［M］．上海：东华大学出版社，2018．
［3］郭平建，等．服装英语翻译概论［M］．北京：中国纺织出版社，2013．
［4］韩其顺，王学铭．英汉科技翻译教程［M］．上海：上海外语教育出版社，1990．
［5］华梅．中国服饰［M］．北京：五洲传播出版社，2004．
［6］黄故．纺织英语［M］．3版．北京：中国纺织出版社，2008．
［7］秦世福，盛宁明．英汉汉英纺织服装词典［M］．上海：东华大学出版社，2016．
［8］王卫平，潘丽蓉．英语科技文献的语言特点与翻译［M］．上海：上海交通大学出版社，2009．
［9］张干周，郭社森．科技英语翻译［M］．杭州：浙江大学出版社，2015．
［10］张宗美．科技汉英翻译技巧［M］．北京：宇航出版社，1992．

Unit 4　Biotechnology and Wine-Liquor Culture

［1］MONTELEONE E. Sensory methods for product development and their application in the alcoholic beverage industry［C］. In John Piggott（ed.）. Alcoholic Beverages：Sensory Evaluation and Consumer Research. Cambridge：Woodhead Publishing，2012.

［2］JACK F R. Whiskies：composition，sensory properties and sensory analysis［C］. In John Piggott （ed.）. Alcoholic Beverages：Sensory Evaluation and Consumer Research. Cambridge：Woodhead Publishing，2012.

［3］XU Y. Moutai（Maotai）：production and sensory properties［C］. In John Piggott（ed.）. Alcoholic Beverages：Sensory Evaluation and Consumer Research. Cambridge：Woodhead Publishing，2012.

［4］XU Y, et al. Traditional Chinese Biotechnology［J］. Advances in Biochemical Engineering/Biotechnology，2010（122）：189-233.

［5］陈兴睎，季克良．茅台酒的独特性概述［J］．酿酒科技，2006（2）：79-84．
［6］方梦之．应用翻译研究：原理、策略与技巧［M］．上海：上海外语教育出版社，2019．
［7］黄永光，黄旭，黄平．茅台酒酿酒极端环境与极端酿酒微生物［J］．酿酒科技，2006（12）：47-50．
［8］李长栓．非文学翻译理论与实践［M］．北京：中译出版社，2022．
［9］李长栓，施晓菁．理解与表达：汉英翻译案例讲评［M］．北京：外文出版社，2012．
［10］季克良，郭坤亮．剖读茅台酒的微量成分［J］．酿酒科技，2006（10）：98-100．
［11］苏金兰，徐柏田，林培．中国白酒香型发展的进展研究［J］．酿酒科技，2017（8）：102-111．

Unit 5　Cosmetics and Oriental Aesthetics

［1］PATRICIA K，FARRIS M D. Cosmeceaticals and Cosmetic Practice［M］. Oxford：John Wiley & Sons，Ltd，2014.

［2］JOHN W H，TERRY W M. Chemistry for Changing Times［M］. 4th ed. New York：Macmillan Publishing Company，1984.

［3］LI H L. Characteristics of China's Traditional Cosmetics［J］. China Detergent&Cosmetics，2018，3（01）：27-32.

［4］NATSUMI H. Handbook of Cosmetic Technologies［M］. Tokyo：Nikko Chemicals Co.，Ltd.，2016.

［5］ZHAO Y J. Analysis on Development of China's Cosmetics Industry from 2019 to 2020［J］. China Detergent & Cosmetics，2020，5（3）：54-58.

［6］FARRIS P K．药妆品与美容实践［M］．冯峥，陈阳，译．郑州：河南科学技术出版社，2020．
［7］郭丽．从春秋到民国——浅谈中国彩妆三千年［J］．中国化妆品，2020（7）：40-45．

［8］李运兴．英汉语篇翻译［M］．2版．北京：清华大学出版社，2003．
［9］连淑能．英汉对比研究［M］．北京：高等教育出版社，2010．
［10］刘宇红．化学化工专业英语［M］．北京：中国轻工业出版社，2000．
［11］颜林海．英汉互译教程［M］．北京：科学出版社，2015．